ENCOUNTERING EVIL

ENCOUNTERING EVIL

Live Options in Theodicy

A New Edition

Edited by Stephen T. Davis

Westminster John Knox Press
LOUISVILLE
LONDON · LEIDEN

Book design by Sharon Adams
Cover design by Mark Abrams

Published by Westminster John Knox Press
Louisville, Kentucky

This book is printed on acid-free paper that meets the American National Stan-dards Institute Z39.48 standard. ♾

PRINTED IN THE UNITED STATES OF AMERICA

01 02 03 04 05 06 07 08 09 10—10 9 8 7 6 5 4 3 2 1

Cataloging-in-Publication Data is on file at the Library of Congress, Washington D.C.

ISBN 0-664-22251-X

Contents

Introduction

This is the second edition of *Encountering Evil*. The book first appeared in 1981. Since that year, it has been widely read, commented upon, and discussed. Those of us who were involved in writing the book are gratified by the many instructors at universities, colleges, and theological seminaries across the country that have adopted it as a text for a course. We frequently encounter students and professors alike who testify to having profited from the book.

Doubtless the book is valuable for several reasons. One, of course, is its topic. No subject in philosophy or religion strikes closer to home than the problem of evil. In the normal course of life, people frequently find themselves asking questions like, "Why did this happen to me?" or "How can God allow such a thing as that?" Suffering is a topic of perennial interest. A second reason, in my opinion, for the book's value is that a great many intellectual options are covered in it. Indeed, virtually all the available Christian options on the theodicy problem are defended and/or criticized. The third and most frequently commented-on aspect of the book is its format, which, so far as I know, was unique in 1981. Many other books since then have adopted similar structures. Students have told me that the back-and-forth format makes the issues clear and causes the debate to come alive for them.

Why publish a new edition? Primarily because those scholars who were involved in writing the first edition have continued to think and learn and grow intellectually in the intervening years, and this includes our thinking about the problem of evil. A great deal has been written about the problem of evil since 1981, some of it of real value. While all of us continue to defend roughly the positions we espoused in 1981, we want to show where our thinking has changed and our arguments have sharpened on this critical intellectual and theological problem.

But what exactly is the problem of evil? Let me introduce it by pointing out that we live in a morally ambiguous world. Most of us experience moments of contentment, happiness, and even joy. But much unhappiness, discontent, and pain is present in the world as well: undeserved suffering, terrible poverty, excruciating pain, irrational acts of violence, and sudden, sinister twists of fate.

Here, for example, are five news items from the *Los Angeles Times* of March 16, 1980:

> A retired banker and his wife in Sheridan, Indiana, were charged with reckless homicide in the "slavery" death of a seventy-four-year-old man, one of three mentally retarded persons who worked for them and lived in a filthy trailer behind their home.

> Oil from the wrecked tanker Tanio spread along forty miles of Brittany coastline, polluting picturesque bays and tourist beaches. The French army was asked to send reinforcements to join the eleven hundred troops already helping villagers with the cleanup. About twenty-one thousand barrels of oil spilled into the sea when the Tanio broke in two during a storm.

> A two-bit bet in a Long Beach pool hall led to an argument that resulted in the slaying of one Long Beach man and the critical wounding of another. Police said the victims were playing pool with a third man, betting twenty-five cents a game, when the third man left in anger. He returned, armed, and shot both his opponents.

> The source of a mysterious outbreak of canine distemper in the Monrovia area, which has resulted in the death of nine raccoons in the last two weeks, has authorities puzzled and concerned for the safety of local domestic animals. Local pet owners are being advised to have their dogs immunized against the disease, which is almost always fatal.

> An aerial test of a laser beam "death ray" weapon will occur soon at White Sands missile range in New Mexico. A modified KC-135, an Air Force version of the Boeing 707, will fire a laser beam from an infrared light and attempt to destroy an air-to-air missile. The demonstration will introduce into a realistic battle situation a weapon that shoots packets of energy rather than explosive projectiles. Lasers seem certain to become the first of a new class of such weapons.

Most of us feel sorrow and revulsion when we hear such items. We share a feeling that our world would be better if they did not occur. So some perfectly sane and intelligent questions that can be asked are: Why do they happen? Why is our world so full of violence and suffering? Is there a reason?

This very "Why?" question forms the subject matter of this book: the problem of evil. One way to introduce the problem is to ask for whom is it a problem. The usual answer is that the problem of evil is a problem for *theism*. But what exactly is theism? Let me attempt to define the term. Although not intentionally polemical, the definition I offer is not neutral either. Doubtless many people will disagree with it, including some of the contributors to this book. Nevertheless, let me define "theism" as *the belief that the world was created by an omnipotent and perfectly good being.* Theism takes many forms. There are Christian theists, Jewish theists, Moslem theists, and many other theists. What holds them together, I believe, is their common commitment to the view of God stated above.

Five facets of theistic belief deserve comment at this juncture:

(1) *There is one God.*

Theism, as I define it here, is a form of monotheism.

(2) *God created the world.*

Theists claim that the world came into existence because of a decision on God's part and so is dependent on God. The world is a contingent thing.

(3) *God is omnipotent.*

This statement is controversial among theists. Let me suggest that God is omnipotent if and only if for any logically possible state of affairs such that the statement that "God brings about that state of affairs" is coherent, God can bring about that state of affairs.

(4) *God is personal.*

Theists say that God is a conscious being who has thoughts, intentions, desires, and will. In addition, unlike the God of the eighteenth-century Deists, God is concerned about and deeply interested in the lives of the creatures. Accordingly, God continues providentially to influence the world even after creation.

(5) *God is perfectly good.*

This statement, too, is controversial as to its precise meaning. Let me suggest it means that God never does what is morally wrong; all God's intentions and actions are morally right. In addition, theism claims that God is benevolent and loving toward the creatures; God never causes any sort of suffering unless overriding moral reasons exist for doing so (e.g., it will lead to a greater good if God does so). God works for the good of the creatures.

The problem of evil is *the* most serious intellectual difficulty for theism. The heart of the problem is the simple question: Why does God permit evil? Of course, this problem is practical as well as intellectual; the question deeply troubles all sorts of people. The problem of evil causes many sensitive theists to have doubts, perhaps even to question the truth of theism. For such a person, responding to the problem of evil is a spiritual as well as an intellectual necessity. But the question interests nontheists as well. Many such people say that the problem of evil is the main obstacle preventing them from embracing theism. Such people will also be deeply interested in responses to the problem of evil.

Although nontheists can be bothered by the question, *Why does God permit evil?*, the problem of evil is only a problem in the broad context of theistic religion. People who deny that God is perfectly good have less trouble answering the question: Evil exists because God's demonic side leads God to create evil. People who deny that God is omnipotent also find answering the question easier. Evil exists, they can say, because God does not have the power to prevent the existence of evil. Theists can take neither route. Accordingly, the question of evil is much harder for them to answer.

The problem is that if God is omnipotent (as defined above), God must be able to prevent evil (the state of affairs of no evil existing seems precisely the sort of state of affairs an omnipotent being can bring about). And if God is perfectly good, God must be willing to prevent evil. But if God is both able and willing to prevent evil, why does evil exist? Why do children die of inoperable cancer of the throat? Why do innocent people suffer in prison? Why do earthquakes and tornadoes and famines cause pain and death? Why do people lie, steal, and kill? Thus, in an oft-quoted passage, David Hume[1] asks about God: "Is he willing to prevent evil, but not able? Then he is impotent. Is he able, but not willing? Then he is malevolent. Is he both willing and able? Whence then is evil?"

But even this argument is still a bit vague. Precisely how is the problem of evil a problem? Precisely how does it constitute a threat to theism? Surely the problem must be more than just a set of questions that embarrass theists. People who use the problem of evil to criticize theism appear to take two main approaches. The first approach is *logical*: theists are said to be in some sort of logical difficulty because they hold all three of the following statements:

(3) *God is omnipotent,*

(5) *God is perfectly good,*

and (a new one)

(6) *Evil exists.*

But these three statements—so the critic claims—form an inconsistent set of statements. That is, they cannot all be true; the truth of any two of them implies the falsity of the third. Theism is thus a contradictory position because it involves acceptance of the following logically inconsistent statement:

(7) *God is omnipotent, and God is perfectly good, and evil exists.*

(which is merely the conjunction of [3], [5], and [6]). Theists simply contradict themselves.

The second approach is *epistemological*, holding not that the existence of evil is logically inconsistent with the existence of a perfectly good and omnipotent God but rather that it *constitutes powerful evidence against* the existence of such a God. That is, the existence of evil in the world constitutes very good reason to disbelieve or at least seriously doubt the existence of the God of theism.

Both approaches are serious *prima facie* threats to theism, but a second distinction should be made. Some critics of theism emphasize that the problem of evil is created for theists given the existence of any amount of evil in the world, however small. Other critics emphasize the problem of evil as being created by the actual amount of evil that exists in the world. What is said to constitute a threat to theism is not that evil exists but that too much evil exists. Still other critics emphasize *surd evil*—evil that is superfluous or morally unjustified. The problem of evil, they say, is created by the fact that at least some of the evil that exists in the world is surd evil.

A third distinction should also be made—between two sorts of evil, *moral evil* and *natural evil*. Roughly, moral evil is wrongdoing or suffering brought about by moral agents such as human beings. Moral evil is often called "sin"; it includes such things as pride, envy, lying, murder, selfishness, robbery, greed, etc. Roughly, natural evil (sometimes called *physical evil*) is pain and suffering brought about by such natural events as earthquakes, diseases, famines, floods, etc. (These terms are sometimes defined in a slightly different way, such that *moral evil* means sin [having exclusively to do with intentions, not consequences] and *physical evil* means suffering [whether caused by human or non-human agents]. However, our terminology in this book reflects the first way of making the distinction.)

The word "theodicy" appears in the subtitle of this book. Derived from the Greek words for God (*Theos*) and justice (*dike*), theodicy is the word traditionally used in theology for an argument that attempts to show that God is righteous or just despite the presence of evil in the world. Such an argument tries to show that God can be omnipotent and perfectly good despite evil. However, some of the "theodicies" contained in this book do not involve attempts to retain belief in divine omnipotence and perfect goodness (not all the contributors are theists, as I have defined the term). Furthermore, in the case of some contributors to the book, opinions differ whether they can legitimately call themselves "theists" (as I have defined the term). Some may fairly call themselves theists because they accept the belief that the world was created by an omnipotent and perfectly good moral being, even though they disagree with some of the comments I made subsequently about this belief.

Accordingly, I propose to use the word *theodicy* in a broader way. For our purposes, let us say that a theodicy is any response to the problem of evil from the perspective of Judeo-Christian religious belief, broadly construed. In this sense, all the contributors to this book are "theodicists" because all have religious beliefs within that tradition and all are deeply concerned about responding to evil from the perspective of those beliefs.

As with the first edition of *Encountering Evil* in 1981, this book was written by a group of philosophers and theologians who teach at the Claremont Colleges in Claremont, California. All of us have previously written on the problem, and it seemed worthwhile to pool our wisdom (from one perspective) or have a debate (from another) in a book in which our views on the problem of evil are presented and jointly criticized. Let me introduce the main contributors to the book. With one exception (to be noted below), the line-up is the same as in 1981.

Stephen T. Davis is Professor of Philosophy and Religious Studies at Claremont McKenna College. David Ray Griffin is Professor of Philosophy of Religion at the Claremont School of Theology and Co-Director of the Center for Process Studies. John Hick is Danforth Professor of Philosophy of Religion, emeritus, at Claremont Graduate University and Fellow of the Institute for Advanced Research in Arts and Social Sciences at the University of Birmingham, U.K. John K. Roth is the Russell K. Pitzer Professor of Philosophy at Claremont McKenna College. The one new addition since 1981 is D. Z. Phillips, Hick's successor in the Danforth Chair of the Philosophy of Religion at Claremont Graduate University and Rush Rhees Research Professor of Philosophy at the University of Wales, Swansea.

The design of the book is as follows. Each chapter consists of three sections. The first and longest section is the contributor's theodicy or (in some cases) antitheodicy. Each writing is the author's attempt to explain his latest thinking on the problem of evil; in the case of many if not all of us, criticisms of our previous writings have caused us to do at least some rethinking. The second section in each chapter consists of critical responses to the chapter's main essay, written by the other four main contributors. The third section in each chapter consists of the contributor's attempt to defend his theodicy or antitheodicy against the criticism presented.

Our method in writing the book was as follows: the main essays were written first and during the same period. They were then collected and distributed to the five contributors, at which point the critiques were written. The critiques, too, were then collected and distributed, at which point the final responses to the critiques were written. With the exception of the editor, no one saw anyone else's work at any point in the process until everyone did.

The result of this exchange, I believe, is fascinating and illuminating for a number of reasons besides the high caliber of the contributors. The first is the great variety of approaches represented here. The reader will find stylistic, methodological, and substantive differences among the authors, as well as disagreement on other fundamental issues in theology besides the problem of evil. Griffin, for example, is a Process thinker, i.e., one who approaches theology from the perspective of Alfred North Whitehead and Charles Hartshorne. Hick is a philosopher of religion and theologian who approaches religious issues from a global perspective, with the various religions and cultures of the world always in view. Roth is a liberal Protestant who writes from an existential perspective that has been heavily influenced by Jewish thinking and the Holocaust. Phillips is a Wittgensteinian philosopher of religion. And Stephen T. Davis is an analytic philosopher by training and a Reformed and evangelical Christian by persuasion.

The second reason I believe many will find this book fascinating and illuminating is the give-and-take found in the discussion sections. This volume is not an ordinary anthology containing just a collection of articles on some subject. Instead, each contributor subjects the other main essays to searching criticism and is forced to defend his own. Our hope is that the reader's understanding of the problem of evil will be significantly deepened and that, upon finishing the book, the reader will have had some assistance in deciding which approach to the problem of evil, if any, is most promising.

In this second edition, we are also fortunate to have helpful and perceptive postscripts from three excellent scholars. John B. Cobb Jr. is Ingraham Memorial Professor of Theology, emeritus, at the Claremont School of Theology. Marilyn McCord Adams is Pitkin Professor of Historical Theology at Yale Divinity School and Religious Studies at Yale University. Marilyn's presence in the book does not quite break the traditional Claremont-centered orientation of the contributors to *Encountering Evil*. During her years as Professor of Philosophy at UCLA, she frequently lectured at the Episcopal Theological School in Claremont. Finally, Frederick Sontag is Robert C. Denison Professor of Philosophy at Pomona College.

One interesting fact to emerge from recent discussions of the problem of evil is that the paradigm evil event to which virtually all theodicists now refer—including all the contributors to this book—is the Holocaust, i.e., the murder of six million Jews and millions of others by the Nazis during World War II. At one time the paradigm evil event referred to by theodicists was the infamous Lisbon earthquake of November 1, 1755. Followed by fires and even a flood of the Tagus, the disaster destroyed the city and killed tens of thousands of people. The Lisbon earthquake is an example of natural evil; the Holocaust exemplifies moral evil. Although both events are apt symbols of human suffering, that the one has replaced the other in our minds as *the* evil event is perhaps fitting. We who have just lived through the twentieth century—with its advances in technology, with the rise of mass organization and totalitarian political ideologies—are acutely conscious of the tremendous power human beings have to inflict suffering on each other.

Let me then pose this question for the authors and readers of this book: Are there any theodicies, represented here or elsewhere, that are credible when trying to account for the Holocaust?

1

A Theodicy of Protest

John K. Roth

Jesus gazed at them. "For men," he said, "it is impossible, but not for God: because everything is possible for God." (Mark 10:27 JB)

He is almighty, isn't He? He could use His might to save the victims, but He doesn't! So—on whose side is He? Could the killer kill without His blessing—without His complicity? (Elie Wiesel, *The Trial of God*)

And the LORD repented of the evil which he thought to do to his people. (Exodus 32:14, RSV)

We Are Consumed

In the first edition of *Encountering Evil*, this essay began by noting Albert Camus's estimate—it appeared when he published *The Rebel* in 1951—that seventy million human beings had been uprooted, enslaved, or killed in the twentieth century alone.[1] I went on to say that "God only knows" what the figure had become by the early 1980s, the time in which I was then writing. Whether God does really know such numbers is a good question to raise, especially in a book like this one, but human calculations now available about the recently ended twentieth century are more accurate and far more devastating than Camus's. Those calculations are related to two death-laden words that have been added to humankind's vocabulary.

One of those words—*democide*—was coined in the 1990s by the political scientist R. J. Rummel, a demographer of mass murder.[2] He defines *democide* as "the murder of any person or people by a government."[3] Rummel's research shows that democide's twentieth-century victims number more than 169 million, a figure that does not include war dead. Writing before he could include the atrocities in Rwanda, Bosnia, or Kosovo, Rummel estimates that "the human cost of war and democide" in the twentieth century exceeded 203 million persons.[4]

Fifty years before Rummel spoke of democide, Raphael Lemkin, a Jewish jurist from Poland, published a book called *Axis Rule in Occupied Europe*. It introduced another new word—*genocide*—to denote what Lemkin called, "an old practice in its modern development."[5] The "modern development" was the Holocaust, Nazi Germany's planned total destruction of the Jewish people and the actual murder of nearly six million of them, a death-dealing "final solution" whose perpetrators also murdered millions of other defenseless civilians. Rummel suggests that genocide, which he identifies as "the killing of people by a government because of their indelible group membership (race, ethnicity, religion, language)" is a subset of democide. Be that as it may, no discussion of democide or genocide is likely to go on for very long without reference to the Holocaust, which remains a watershed event in human history.

The twentieth century was one of unprecedented mass death. Will the twenty-first be different? As wars persist, scarcity continues to take its mammoth toll, and human misery—so graphically written on the faces of refugee children—rages unabated in a world with burgeoning population pressures and widening gaps between the rich and poor, people have few reasons to take comfort, especially if one cannot escape the conviction that such waste is wrong. If the twenty-first century is to be less deadly than the twentieth, human thought and action will have to change in remarkable ways to become less complacent and indifferent, more caring and compassionate. Senses of justice will have to become more acute, their appreciation for the interrelatedness and the preciousness of life much deeper. In the context of *Encountering Evil*, perhaps the same changes will have to be true of God, a concern that leads to this book's focus on theodicy.

In revising this essay, I have retained its original title—"A Theodicy of Protest"—and nearly all of its content. My perspective about the relationship between God and evil has not changed substantially, but it has deepened and intensified in ways that I can illustrate by referring briefly to three books that appeared in the 1990s.

First, I think of Marilyn McCord Adams's *Horrendous Evils and the Goodness of God*. The Holocaust, genocide, and democide must be considered as horrendous evils, or nothing could be. Considering that Adams criticizes reflection carried on at "too high a level of abstraction," and observing that her stated focus is on "the positive meaning of *individual* lives," I find it striking that her book scarcely mentions the Holocaust, let alone genocide and democide, and the millions upon millions of individual lives that have been consumed—mostly without a trace—in the midst of evils that are horrendous indeed.[6] Adams does cite Holocaust survivor Elie Wiesel and his memoir

Night, which describes his months in Auschwitz and Buchenwald. Consistent with her search for positive meaning, her brief discussion of the Holocaust underscores "moments of self-transcendence" in which human dignity could still be found.[7] In my view, her hopeful reading of Wiesel's narrative does little justice to what Wiesel aptly called the "Kingdom of Night." Adams recognizes that horrendous evils call God's goodness and power into question, but she also affirms that "horrendous evils can be defeated by the Goodness of God within the framework of the individual participant's life."[8] Unfortunately, Rummel's democide figures are all about individual lives—so many that he can scarcely believe the calculations himself—and those numbers stand in jarring conflict with Adams's optimistic claim. How are those evils to be "defeated"? That question remains a problem that neither Adams nor God is likely to solve.

As its title indicates, this essay's tone is protesting. I protest against philosophies and theologies that do not take the historical particularity of evil seriously enough, even when they claim that evils are horrendous. The Holocaust, genocide, and democide smash and destroy particular persons in ways that scar the world forever. The hunger and thirst for justice that people feel, the healing we seek, the hope we share are all *in spite of* the darkness and destruction that swirl around and through us. More comments will come later about that "in spite of," but two other books deserve attention first.

The Jewish theologian and Holocaust scholar David R. Blumenthal published *Facing the Abusing God: A Theology of Protest* in 1993. While affirming "the grace of human contact" and also "the reality of God's presence, God's power, and even God's love—insofar as we have experienced these," he also insisted that he would "accuse God of acting unjustly."[9] Refusing to overemphasize God's goodness, Blumenthal stated the following instead:

> We will try to accept God—the bad along with the good—*and* we will speak our lament. We will mourn the bad, and we will regret that things were, and are, not different than they are. This face-to-Face alone will enable us to maintain our integrity, even though it leaves an unreconciled gap between us and God. These steps alone will enable us to have faith in God in a post-Holocaust, abuse-sensitive world. Unity and reconciliation are no longer the goal; rather, we seek a dialogue that affirms our difference and our justness, together with our relatedness to God.

Blumenthal's protesting theology supports my theodicy of protest. Meanwhile, five years after Blumenthal's book appeared, another Jewish scholar, Zachary Braiterman, published *(God) After Auschwitz: Tradition and Change in Post-Holocaust Jewish Thought*, which includes significant interpretations of three post-Holocaust theologians: Richard Rubenstein, Eliezer Berkovits, and Emil Fackenheim. Braiterman suggests that their writings reflect what he calls *antitheodicy*, which means "refusing to justify, explain, or accept . . . the relationship that subsists between God (or some other form of ultimate reality), evil, and suffering."[10] Braiterman explains that *antitheodicy* became his term of choice after he read John Hick's response to my essay in the first edition of *Encountering Evil*.[11] Hick had observed that my view was not so much a theodicy as an antitheodicy. Hick was right—not least because my essay stated then, as it still does now, that my "theodicy of protest is antitheodicy."

In my present thinking, I consider *theodicy of protest* and *antitheodicy* as nearly synonymous. Religiously, I am a Protestant Christian. The idea of a theodicy of protest seemed natural to me, but increasingly I understand my position to be one that protests against theodicy itself, at least as theodicy's attempts to justify God's relationship to evil and suffering have usually been carried out. Thanks to Braiterman, I understand my own position better.

Usually *theodicy* refers to human vindications of God's justice in permitting the existence of evil and suffering. Most theodicies of the Protestant Christian variety belong in that tradition. The outlook developed here is related to it, too, but the breaks with classical Christian Protestantism are no less important than the lines of continuity. My approach underscores God's sovereignty. It allows for God's disappointment with human life gone wrong. It also holds out for the possibility of grace experienced through faith and for the hope of God's salvation. At the same time, and precisely because the accumulated devastation of history is so vast, this perspective echoes voices that are Jewish as well as Christian, some of them far older than those of Martin Luther or John Calvin. The Jewish voices belong to a dissenting spirit that quarrels with God over the use of power. That confrontation is rooted not so much in rejection of God but rather in recognition that such defiance is crucial in struggles against despair. Jewish insight, ancient and contemporary, calls for men and women—particularly Christians—to consider a theodicy of protest, which is a form of antitheodicy.

What does *evil* mean? That question itself is a crucial element in the problem of evil. The word often functions as a noun, suggesting that evil is an entity. In fact, evil is activity, sometimes inactivity, and thus is a manifestation of power. Displays of evil power are displays that waste. That is, evil happens whenever power ruins or squanders, or whenever it fails to forestall those results. Evil comes in many shapes and sizes. The kind of evil that concerns us here ignores and violates the sanctity of individual persons. Everyone inflicts that sort of pain, and yet some individuals and societies are far more perverse than others. The measure is taken by the degree to which one's actions waste human life.

Prior to death, and perhaps beyond, existence is in process. Because things move and change, waste may not be simply waste, nor evil simply evil. Capitalizing on that fact, some writers mute screams of pain by hearing them as instrumental. Destruction then becomes a means to what is new and better. Or, if not all havoc readily fits that scheme, ruins may still provide occasions for atonement, forgiveness, and magnificent attempts at redemption. To the extent that evil can be interpreted as instrumental, as somehow transcended by a better situation overall, power's waste is rendered less radical.

Eschatological hopes hinge on some version of an instrumental view of evil. They differ, however, in their optimism about evil's being overcome by good. Most Protestant theodicies affirm that this overcoming, at least from a divine perspective, will be complete. A protesting theodicy affirms that any overcoming of this kind, at least from a human perspective, should be less well regarded. The reason is clear: too much has been lost.

Theodicy consists of fallible options. That result is unavoidable because we are dealing with thoughts, emotions, and choices organized by finite human minds. It is equally true that such minds exist only in social contexts that decisively influence what they are. Therefore, that I speak of a theodicy of protest or, at times, of antitheodicy is not accidental. Before proceeding with a more detailed discussion of points only mentioned thus far, let me note some factors that produce this personal outcome.

My father was a Presbyterian pastor. I was raised in a home where God was alive, and that reality abides with me still. Early on I was introduced to theology and philosophy in my father's sermons, which emphasized human responsibility, social justice, and the sovereignty of God. Later encounters with Søren Kierkegaard would do much to deepen my understanding—and my questioning—of those ideas.

In the second half of the 1960s, while I was in my late twenties, the "death of God" was bandied about. Although I could not agree with the facile optimism that proclaimed God's demise as a joyous event signifying humanity's freedom and coming-of-age, I was profoundly moved by Richard Rubenstein's *After Auschwitz*. Rubenstein affirmed the death of a traditional God of history, but he neither rejected all views of God nor took the "death of God" as cause for celebration. His straightforward insights about the religious crisis lurking in the Holocaust sent me on a quest.[12] Could my own religious and philosophical experience muster a response that would work better for me? My journey is still underway.

Other currents touched me as well. The finite, limited Gods of William James, Alfred North Whitehead, and other "process theologians" offered some appeal. But as I wrote about American religious thought with my colleague Frederick Sontag, I became disenchanted with the sanguine assumptions about human nature and history that are required by those outlooks if trust in redemption is warranted.[13] Nonetheless, religious hopes remained in my bones, as they still do, and thus my convictions about human frailty and failure forced me to reconsider the power of God.

The context for that reconsideration was again provided by the consuming fire of Auschwitz, seen this time through the writings of Elie Wiesel.[14] Wiesel's authorship shows that life in a post-Holocaust world can be more troublesome with God than without God. And yet Wiesel does not let God go, any more than he will give up on humankind, although he has good reasons to do both. Instead he dissents, seeking to check despair not by acquitting or ignoring God but by putting God on trial.

The verdict reads "guilty," but that word is not the end. Wiesel's thought has a method, and the method is that of a protestant. Never failing for questions, he keeps asking, "What is the next step?" Reaching an apparent conclusion, he moves on. "And yet? And yet." . . . "In spite of this, something more must be noted." . . . "How is one to believe? How is one not to believe?" Those ways of thinking enable Wiesel not to discount the waste that indicts God, but to acknowledge God's power even as he argues against God for the sake of children, women, and men.

Wiesel's point is not to locate a divine scapegoat, nor does he think that any problems are solved by blaming God. On the contrary, his work demands human responsibility. And yet Wiesel understands that much also depends on God's reality or lack of it, on what God can and cannot do, will and will not do. Wiesel emphasizes that he opposes two things: indifference and absurdity. Religiously speaking, his aim is to map out boundaries of meaning in the wake of Auschwitz. To deny God outright could go too far. But to affirm God's total goodness, to apologize for God, to excuse or exonerate God . . . these steps go too far as well.

The epigraphs at the outset of this essay were chosen with care. Antitheodicy or a theodicy of protest puts God on trial, and in that process the issue of God's wasteful complicity in evil takes center stage. The God interrogated is the One for whom everything is possible, an awesome biblical announcement. According to the gospel narrative, when Jesus made that claim he did so where entry into the kingdom of God was at issue. One implication of that discussion is that God can bring about good ends that are completely beyond human energies. I agree, but not unequivocally. For those ends to occur in the fullest measure possible, human repentance will have to be matched by God's. Even then too much waste will be left over. Unlike most theodicies, this antitheodicy is not too good to be true.

How Long, Lord, Before You Relent?

History

Protestant theology usually holds that God cares about history. My theodicy of protest begins by probing that assumption, and it does so by agreeing with

Hegel: history is "the slaughter-bench at which the happiness of peoples, the wisdom of states, and the virtue of individuals have been sacrificed."[15] Granted, that appraisal does not contain all that should be said, but that fact itself produces more problems than it solves.

According to Genesis, God called the creation good. In some sense, everyone agrees. Corrupted though the world may be, our lives are not without optimism, which persists in the experience that life is worth living. If it were not, nobody would bother with theodicy. We do not inhabit a perfect world, but neither is this one the worst that might be. Therefore, questions about history's meaning and destiny loom large. One way to summarize those questions is to ask: if creation is good, and yet history is largely a slaughter-bench, how "cost-effective" are God's decisions?[16]

Theodicy must reckon with God-as-economist, and the question posed above deals with God's waste. When Jews and Christians say that history should be understood in terms of creation, they imply that God's purposes affect what comes to be. So consider a dilemma: either those purposes necessitate every jot and tittle of history, or they are compatible with alternatives that would reduce the slaughter-bench qualities of human life. All counts offer good grounds for protest.

In the former instance, for example, God's economy might be without waste, but the issue of whether God was bound to pursue only those particular purposes, with their exact and horrendous historical consequences, surely calls into question the freedom—divine and human—so central to the biblical records. On the other hand, if God is not so determined, God's purposes permit multiple routes to their achievement. Indeed the purposes themselves may have a flexible quality. Such largess, however, is not merely lavish. The slaughter-bench makes God's luxury wasteful. And one point more: No matter what horn of the dilemma is seized, any ways in which God could rationally justify God's economy as purely cost-effective in pursuing goodness that we can appreciate . . . well, those ways are beyond imagining. This result testifies that such a wasteful God cannot be totally benevolent. History itself is God's indictment.

Responsibility

Most people want a totally good God or none at all. In religious circles, then, putting God on trial has not been popular. For centuries, human beings have taken themselves to task in order to protect God's innocence, and not without reason. Even at the price of an unwarranted guilt-trip, the desire runs strong to separate good and evil neatly. Life is simpler that way. And so theology puts Father in the right and his children in the wrong. At least that tendency held until the idea of sin was replaced by an "I'm OK, You're OK" psychology. A protesting theodicy finds both of those views wanting. Nobody is OK. Otherwise the slaughter-bench would not be so drenched. And when one says "nobody," God is included as well as humanity. Whether considered in terms of violation of God's will, or simply in terms of goodness that is known and left undone, sin abounds in human life. But Camus is also correct: "man is not entirely to blame; it was not he who started history."[17]

It is irresponsible to assign responsibility inequitably. God must bear God's share, and this share is not small, unless God could never be described as One for whom all things are possible. God's responsibility is located in the fact that God is the One who ultimately sets the boundaries in which we live and move and have our being. True, since we are thrown into history at our birth, we appear in social settings made by human hands, but ultimately those hands cannot account for themselves. To the extent that they are born with the potential and the power to be dirty, credit for that fact belongs elsewhere. "Elsewhere" is God's address.

Do not take lightly what God's responsibility entails. It means: in the beginning . . . Auschwitz. The point is not that God predestined or caused such events directly. Some theodicies have taken that position, but the position taken here rejects such conclusions because it assumes the reality of human freedom. At the same time, that freedom—despite what some thinkers would like—does not remove God from the dock.

Freedom

Richard L. Rubenstein's penetrating study of the Holocaust, *The Cunning of History*, makes the following observation: "Until ethical theorists and theologians are prepared to face without sentimentality the kind of action it is possible freely to perpetrate under conditions of utter respectability in an advanced, contemporary society, none of their assertions about the existence of moral norms will have much credibility."[18] The inference I draw from Rubenstein's assertion is this: human freedom has been used as God's defense; in fact, it is crucial in God's offense.

Using freedom as a defense for God is a well-known strategy. Moving from the idea that freedom is a good, the argument has usually been that God gave freedom to human life in innocence. The gift, to be sure, did include a destructive capacity. God knew that fact and perhaps even that liberty would be abused. Still, the apology continues, God's gift is justified. Only with the freedom we were given can men and women truly be human children of God. Moreover, where sin infests us, God's own freedom is gracious enough to offer forgiveness and love that can release us to try again and also rectify every wrong. On all counts, apparently, God's benevolence is validated even as humanity's is not.

Already the cost-effectiveness of God's creative acts has been challenged. In that challenge a critique of the gift of freedom was implied. To make the critique explicit, the nature of human freedom must be focused. In a word, our freedom is both too much and too little. It is far more an occasion for waste than a defense of God's total goodness can reconcile.

On one hand, freedom constitutes an insufficient defense for God because of its paucity. Two areas of life make this fact evident. First, as René Descartes emphasized long ago, human ignorance wreaks havoc everywhere. In his optimism about human reason, however, Descartes underplayed his hand: too often our freedom is helpless to dispel ignorance in time to save countless victims from their tragic fate. Cancer, for example, kills millions every year. If we could, we would use our freedom to stop its waste, but a shroud of unknowing is more than the powers of our freedom can presently penetrate. Granted, that situation may give opportunity for us to use freedom nobly in a struggle to obtain knowledge or in a battle with pain and death. Meanwhile the mound of corpses rises.

Evidence of the paucity of freedom is not restricted to our struggles against natural forces that can kill. It also exists in the social structures that bind our lives. Rubenstein's example of the Holocaust offers a telling case. The Holocaust was no sport of history. When the fury of Auschwitz was unleashed, the powers at work there were so deeply entrenched that none of humanity's countervailing energy, individual or collective, could halt them before millions perished. Only vast military force and massive killing brought Nazi Germany to its knees and the Holocaust to an end.

To think of millions, however, may not make the point sharp enough. Consider, therefore, a story. Sophie Zawistowska was a Polish survivor of Auschwitz. As William Styron tells her story, his novel, *Sophie's Choice*, becomes a commentary on the powerlessness of individual freedom as it faces overwhelming forces of social domination. For a time, Sophie had been a privileged prisoner, assigned to secretarial duties in the house of Rudolf Höss, the commandant of Auschwitz. Urged to use her position to assist the underground resistance movement, Sophie tried to steal a radio from Höss's house.

Sophie knew where one could be found, a small portable that belonged to Höss's daughter, Emmi. She passed the girl's room every day on her way upstairs to the office where Höss did his work. Once she tried for the radio, but Emmi caught her, and Sophie was nearly undone. Her sense of failure ran deep, only less so than the realization that she would never regain her courage to steal the radio again. Sophie learned "how, among its other attributes, absolute evil paralyzes absolutely."[19]

She knew the frailty of freedom not simply because of the incident with the radio, but because of the setting that surrounded it. And nothing was more

important in that setting than her children, Jan and Eva. Jan was alive somewhere in the children's camp at Auschwitz. Höss had promised that Sophie
could see him, and her attempted theft took place with the knowledge that she
would jeopardize her chance to embrace the boy whose life gave hers a reason
for going on. Sophie was not without courage—far from that—but once was
enough. She could not put the radio ahead of her need for Jan.

Who could blame Sophie, especially when Eva is remembered? Eva is gone,
gassed. And Sophie's freedom, or the lack of it, showed how pathetic a "free-
will defense" for God can be. Eva's life was lost because human freedom
handed Sophie what the Holocaust scholar Lawrence Langer has aptly called
a "choiceless choice."[20] As she disembarked from the stifling train that brought
her and the children from Warsaw to Auschwitz, a selection took place. An SS
official—Styron calls him Dr. Jemand von Niemand—decided to make freedom real, dreadfully so, by forcing Sophie's choice. Instead of losing both Jan
and Eva to the gas, which was the fate of almost all young children there,
Sophie could pick one of hers to live. *"Ich kann nicht wählen!'* she screamed."[21]
"I cannot choose" . . . and then so as not to lose them both, Sophie let Eva go.
Sophie's choice stayed with her. She experienced liberation in 1945, but only
fully in 1947 when she gave up her own life, also by choice.

Styron's narrative is only a story, but truth resides in it because paralysis and
untimely death are results of freedom that is allowed, like Sophie's and that of
millions of actual Holocaust victims, to be too little. Of course there was heroism in Auschwitz, and ultimately the death camps died. The price, however, was
horrendous, and even to suggest that there could be no adequate display of
human virtue—or no sufficient glory in heaven—without such testing odds . . .
well, that proposition mocks the victims far more than it honors them. Sophie's
choice, emblematic of so many real choices, accuses God and rightly so.

The matter does not end there, however, because the freedom God gives
us is also too much and too soon. That fact follows as a corollary from what
has gone before. So often the waste of human life is of our own making. Cancer often illustrates that we are free to abuse our bodies until things go too far,
and the Holocaust shows that human beings can and will do anything to each
other. We have more power and more freedom than is good for us. Perhaps in
some past Eden all the factors of freedom were in healthy equilibrium. In present history, however, that dream is a myth at best.

Freedom's defense for God looks more and more like a ploy by the devil's
advocate. That defense cannot avoid saying that only if freedom has the potential to be what it has become can there be a chance for the highest goods. But
can the end justify the means? That is the question. A protesting theodicy is
skeptical because it will not forget futile cries. No good that it can envision,

on earth or beyond, is worth the freedom—enfeebled and empowered—that wastes so much life.

Excuses

Perhaps God's only excuse is that God does not exist. Not so, suggest some contemporary voices. God, they say, has been mistakenly viewed as all-powerful. In fact, God's creative activity reveals limitations in God's existence, and thus the claim that God is totally benevolent can be preserved. In effect, then, this God's excuse is that God always does the best God can. Originally, God brought order out of chaos and fashioned a world of beauty and richness. Within that setting God lured humanity into existence, endowed with freedom to choose. But if God's authority can minimize the confusion that we produce with our liberty, it is also true that God cannot both intervene directly and still retain the integrity of free human creatures. God's breath, as it were, is held while we act . . . and then the best God can do is to pick up the pieces so that survivors can try again.

Such a view would be fine if the pieces were not so many and so bloody. Such a God may indeed be excused, not least because such a God is hardly worth bothering about. This God is simply too ineffectual to forestall waste decisively, unless of course one holds that God has some heretofore unwitnessed potential for eschatological power. On what ground, however, could such a claim be based? Most versions of Jewish and Christian faith would locate that ground in historical events: the exodus or the resurrection, for example. But to speak of a God who leads people out of bondage or who raises persons from death is surely not to speak of a God who, by history's ongoing testimony, is always doing the best God can. God's saving acts in the world are too few and far between.

Christians claim that God raised Jesus from the dead. If God did so, then God plausibly had the might to thwart the Holocaust long before it ended. Coupled with the view that resurrection is not merely the release of an immortal spirit from a lifeless physical body, but rather the re-creation of a person for whom all life has ceased, that premise is one that governs this Protestant antitheodicy. In doing so, God's actions are harder to excuse. But that fact, in turn, leaves us to ask: Why should anybody bother with a God like this one, who seems so infrequently to do the best that is within God's power?

Despair

Things are not going very well. A protesting theodicy does not say that God's love controls the universe, nor does it hold that claims which find this world to be the best one possible make good sense. Thus, this antitheodicy must reckon with despair.

To despair is to lose or give up hope. For our purposes, two dimensions of that experience are of special significance. First, this theodicy of protest despairs over the hope that history is evolving toward a kingdom of God on earth. That claim does not deny the existence of progress, which one writer defines as "a condition that is better by far than what it replaces after accounting for any side effects."[22] What it affirms, however, is that all progress is cunning, and so one can agree when Rubenstein states, "the Holocaust bears witness to *the advance of civilization*."[23] Far from assuming that things will get better and better if only we work well enough together, this outlook supposes that human life is always under siege. All gains are precarious, periodic, and problematic. Life is one damned problem after another. Many of them are killing.

And yet the human prospect is not hopeless, nor is it without reasons for joy and thanksgiving. In fact, that prospect can be enhanced to the degree that the widespread experience of despair is turned on itself to yield a spirit of dissent. The logic of this reversal makes a straightforward appeal, namely, that once we realize how strong the good reasons for despair really are, then short of abdicating to waste, little is left to do but to turn and fight. Such responses have no utopian illusions. They stand instead with this conviction: Unjustifiable waste is everlasting, but it deserves no more victories.

Second, our theodicy of protest despairs over the hope that there will be any future good "so great as to render acceptable, in retrospect, the whole human experience, with all its wickedness and suffering as well as all its sanctity and happiness."[24] Nor will it be much convinced by the prospect of a "Divine resourcefulness" that guarantees—somehow, somewhere but probably well beyond this world—a life for each individual that is "a great good to him/her on the whole, a life in which horrendous evil is not only balanced off but endowed with positive meanings, meanings at least some of which will be recognized and appropriated by the participant him/herself."[25] Put another way: No matter what happens, God is going to be much less than perfectly justified.

But wait, someone may say, even if it is true that we cannot now fathom how God could possibly salvage this mess in a way that justifies God, surely that task can be fulfilled. Indeed the very claim that with God all things are possible would seem to demand such an option. People can believe in that optimistic outcome if they wish, but dissenters demur and the reason is simply history itself. The irretrievable waste of the past robs God of a convincing alibi. Only if God fraudulently obliterates truth by wiping out the memory of victims can a disruptive, protesting, and unreconcilable "Why?" be stilled forever. So long as that question can sound, the whole human experience stands as less than acceptable and the "positive meaning" of horrendous evils will remain scarce, if it can be found at all.

And yet the human prospect is not hopeless, nor is it without reasons for joy and thanksgiving. Life can be less unacceptable. We know that to be true because from time to time people perform works of love. Those realities, linked with despair that finds love not enough, may lead us to affirm life by refusing to give despair the final say. In those experiences, one may discover that the issue of whether God is without any justification depends on what God does with the future, God's and ours.

May Your Blessings Be with Us

Power

Dissenting moods are at the foundation of my approach to theodicy. But those moods also seek to turn dissent into a religious response that can make more sense out of life, not less, without abandoning honesty in facing life's harshest facts. To fill out that response, particularly with regard to its views about what God might be like, requires first a further assessment of power.

This theodicy of protest affirms the existence of an omnipotent God.[26] That is, God is bound only by God's will. Ultimately, nothing except it determines what he shall do or become. All possibilities are within God's reach, and so God could have created very differently. Likewise, God's relation to our world could take many forms, even now. The one God establishes may have its reasons, but it is contingent nonetheless.

Why make these affirmations? My answer resides in choices made from experience. In a word, I find that the world cannot account for itself. It demands a creator. My understanding of what that creator might be comes to me through the tradition carried forward in Jewish and Christian scripture. Much, but not all, of that tradition continues to ring true in my life, and thus I work to reconcile those aspects with notes of dissonance. The struggle, more than the result, unfolds here.

If God is sovereign, bound only by God's will, then apparently God chooses to be the creator and master of this universe. Although God could intervene dramatically at any point in present history, God elects to let freedom work out its own course as it lives in individuals and communities. Thus, God's "plan" for history is virtually no plan at all. It can release the worst as well as the best that is in us, and therefore the presence of this God may feel like the absence of all gods.

God could predetermine the future, but God declines so as to make freedom real. But if the future is in the making, the past is not, at least not enough.

Committed to what has taken place, God can respond to those outcomes, but God's own omnipotence is also binding. God cannot take back the wasted past completely. Therefore, no good that God can do will totally fill the void.

Everything hinges on the proposition that God possesses—but fails to use well enough—the power to intervene decisively at any moment to make history's course less wasteful. Thus, in spite and because of God's sovereignty, this God is everlastingly guilty, and the degrees run from gross negligence to murder. Perhaps we should feel sorry for a God so soiled. Not so, says Berish, one of the characters in Elie Wiesel's play, *The Trial of God*: "If I am given the choice of feeling sorry for Him or for human beings, I choose the latter anytime. He is big enough, strong enough to take care of Himself; man is not."[27]

God's guilt could be reduced to the extent that God lacks power. But to the extent that God lacks power, God may also be ineffectual. Short of no God at all, what people have to ask religiously, therefore, is whether we should settle for an innocent but ineffectual God or whether we should run the risks of relating to a God who is really master of the universe but much less than perfectly good by any standards that we can comprehend. Are there any good reasons that such risks should be accepted?

Suffering

History refutes more than it confirms God's providential care. And yet some moments, personal and collective, hint of something more. Promise lives, for example, in the messianic hopes of Judaism and Christianity. Although interpretations of those hopes are pluralistic and often at odds, a core in both affirms that God can and will intervene to heal and restore, if only in part. Persons who hunger and thirst after righteousness cannot be filled by those claims alone, but to share in their hope is better than nothing. However, to do so without abandoning the world's victims, confrontations with suffering are required.

A Jewish confrontation with suffering occurs in the continued delay of the Messiah's arrival. Whether that arrival is equated with the collective transformation of Jewish and human spirit, achieved by men and women themselves, or whether it is regarded as God's intervention in the midst of human recalcitrance, the waste keeps piling up. The messianic promise is not easy to accept. It may, in fact, be impossible to believe except as one embraces it as an expression of defiance over what has been permitted. Suffering brought on by such acts of commitment may be redemptive, but if so, those same experiences testify that most suffering is not.

At least once, most Christians say, the Messiah came in Jesus of Nazareth.

His life, death, and resurrection may make all the difference in the world for those who accept him, but such promise also enjoins face-to-face encounters with suffering. One of those encounters is prompted by a question: Was God really serious about making all things new in Christ when Calvary—including the anti-Semitism it unleashed—could lead to the crematoria of Auschwitz?

If God suffered in Christ—as a blood sacrifice to appease God's own wrath over human sin, as a sign of grace to show that nothing can separate the world from God's love, as atonement for God's own injustice toward men, women, and children, for whatever reason—good sense remains in question. God suffers with humanity, according to Christian claims. But the mass of agony does not have to be, and if God is only a suffering God, then we do indeed need a God to help us. The very idea of a suffering God provokes one to insist: What is going on here? God's promises call for protests. And yet the same realities that make one dissent against the promises can also be the facts that impel us to struggle toward them—unless, of course, we are willing to let suffering rage with impunity or to resign ourselves to death as the end-in-itself. To see how that tension might be real, consider God's servant Job.

Trust

"Though he slay me, yet will I trust in him" (Job 13:15, KJV). Job's ancient declaration is crucial for a theodicy of protest. Indeed his entire story is at the heart of the matter. Some interpretations highlight Job's "repentance" for daring to question God, stressing how he seemed to receive back his fortune as well. But if one concentrates on the statement quoted above, the situation is different and also more honest.

At this point Job argues. *Yes, things are wrong, but the wrong is not my doing, nor is it obviously owing to the other victims,* whose loss has plunged Job into a defiant grief. Or, at the very least, a serious disproportion exists between crime and punishment that cannot and must not be accepted. And yet Job's argument is no rejection of God. Rather it trusts that God will vindicate him.

Job's trust is bold, even extreme. It entails God's confession that God has treated Job unfairly—abusively and brutally—for according to the story it was only by God's choice that Job was all but destroyed on the pretense of testing his faithfulness. Job was faithful all right, almost with a vengeance. But did he win or lose? God thundered back with his nonanswer, challenging Job with a "Who-do-you-think-you-are?"

Then came Job's repentance. Elie Wiesel suggests, however, that Job's humility was no simple resignation. Wiesel reads it instead as resistance and rebellion masked in hasty abdication. Ultimately God cannot be defeated, which is both our hope and our despair, but in confessing—when God, with greater reason to do so, did not—Job "continued to interrogate God."[28] A protesting theodicy takes heart from that reading, not least because it implies that Job did not give up. Whatever the form of his protest and so long as it lasted, he could still be saying, "Though he slay me, yet will I trust in him."

Hope

Carl Jung's *Answer to Job* states that "God is not only to be loved, but also to be feared."[29] These days talk about fearing God is religiously unfashionable. God's love is more in vogue, and religious observance tends to drown out all sense of awe and judgment in gluts of celebration. A theodicy of protest both acknowledges and yearns for the love of God. The acknowledgment comes because life is a created gift, one that is basically good and able to become even better. To that assumption a theodicy of protest adds risk-filled acceptance of the biblical promises that life more abundant is still to come. The yearning moves from that same base but is rooted even more in the apprehension that there is too little love to be seen. Men and women do not love as well as they can, but neither does God, and therefore Wiesel is right again: "To have hope in God is to have hope against God."[30]

Such a God has no simple nature. This God is tugged and pulled by multiple desires, but God is not at their mercy. They are controlled by God's own acts of will. This God is no bumbler. God knows what God is doing, and that reality is the problem. Our protests do God no harm. Indeed, God's license gives us a mandate to say what we feel, and we must . . . so long as we speak for the sake of human well-being. When dissent is raised in that spirit, its rebellious care may grip God's heart.

Still, the fact remains: the net result of God's choices is that the world is more wild and wasteful than any good reason that we can imagine would require it to be. Thus, to be for such a God requires some sense of being against God as well. To defend the good as we know it best—especially to carry out God's own commandments that we should serve those in need, heal the sick, feed the hungry, forestall violence—we must do battle against forces that are loose in the world because God permits them.

Job, says Elie Wiesel, "did not suffer in vain; thanks to him, we know that it is given to man to transform divine injustice into human justice and compassion."[31] Neither individually nor collectively can human beings fulfill that task completely. The odds set by God are too high. Nonetheless, one can still be for God by being against God, and the way that we do so best is by giving life in care and compassion for others. Then there is reason for hope on earth and perhaps beyond.

Answers

Most theodicies have a fatal flaw: they legitimate evil. They do so by saying too much or too little as they answer questions posed by waste. The first tendency is illustrated in theories that would make all suffering deserved. The second is found in attempts to ensure happy endings by appealing to God's unfathomable wisdom and goodness, even though we have not the vaguest notion of how such endings could possibly be. In basic ways, then, this theodicy of protest is *antitheodicy*, with no desire to legitimate waste. Such antitheodicy must be wary of answers or of the lack of them, including its own.

To acknowledge evil's existence is not to legitimate it. This antitheodicy does so without blinking, and that quality is one of its greatest assets. A possible trap, on the other hand, may lie in its insistence that God is guilty and even without apology for apparent refusal to change God's worldly ways in the foreseeable future. Without caution, that outlook could become a form of scapegoating, one that places a premium on blaming God, leaving the impression as it does so that human beings cannot really do very much.

We face great odds. Still, there is much that we can do. Indeed we shall have to act or too little action will take place on humanity's behalf. The world—too much no doubt—is in our hands. For if God listens and answers, it is usually in silence. God operates as judge or ally less by intervention that metes out justice in total equity and more by letting events fall as they may to reveal the corrupt absurdity, as well as the grandeur, of what we do together. The future is more open than it ought to be. We have all that we can do and then some, and if we fail to act well, the waste will only increase.

"My God, my God, why have you deserted me?" (Matt. 27:46, JB).[32] Jesus' question is contemporary. It evokes others: Can we learn not to blame God as a way of covering over our responsibilities? Can we learn to be boldly honest with God and with ourselves as a means to deepen compassion? A theodicy of protest must keep raising those questions for itself. It must also keep struggling to answer them affirmatively. Coupled with those emphases, its vision of an omnipotent God, whose nature is a self-controlled mixture that gives us freedom and that may yet reduce evil's waste, is an option that can set human souls on fire for good.

Lord, You Have Been
Our Refuge Age after Age

As William James summed up *The Varieties of Religious Experience*, he observed that "no two of us have identical difficulties, nor should we be expected to work out identical solutions." A few sentences later, he went on to say, "the divine can mean no single quality, it must mean a group of qualities, by being champions of which in alternation, different men may all find worthy missions."[33] Such wisdom informs all sound theodicies. Human religious needs are diverse. No single response can encompass them all or nourish every spirit. Thus, every good theodicy will be an antitheodicy in more ways than one. It will be suspicious of every claim that seeks to justify God. It will also disclaim the full adequacy of its own outlook.

Imperfect as it is, the antitheodicy explored here does originate in felt needs. Two are fundamental: a sense that human affairs are far worse than any good reason can justify or than our powers alone can alter; and, second, a yearning that refuses to settle for despair that the first feeling generates. A God encountered in Jewish and Christian experience makes possible an option that keeps hope from dying, without making the dreary facts unreal. But this God offers little tranquility because God defers rescue. God allows us, and thereby participates in, our own undoing.

Life is outrageous. Hardly anyone will deny that conclusion outright. Tragedy, pain, injustice, premature death—all of these and more waste us away. No explanation seems quite able to still our anger, hostility, and sadness. A theodicy of protest believes not only that such emotions are profoundly real, but also that they are in many cases justified. Any religious perspective that fails to give them expression diminishes the human spirit. Whether unintentionally or by design, the Christian emphasis on God's love has had a repressive effect in this regard. It strains to make everything fit the care of a Father or nowadays a Mother who is love itself. For some persons that strain is too much. For others, an open admission of that fact may bring healthy release. Although the faith of us Christians would not be rendered easier, it would be quickened by quarreling with the claim that "God is love," even as we refuse to let it go (1 John 4:8).

Annie Dillard's poetic book, *Holy the Firm*, is a meditation prompted by the crash of a small airplane. Miraculously no one was killed, but Julie, a seven-year-old flying with her father, has had her face burnt beyond recognition.

A small church stood in the Puget Sound country where Annie Dillard lived while she wrote her book. She believed that its minister, a Congregationalist, knew God. "Once," she writes, "in the middle of the long pastoral prayer of intercession for the whole world—for the gift of wisdom to its leaders, for hope and mercy to the grieving and pained, succor to the oppressed, and God's grace to all—in the middle of this he stopped, and burst out, 'Lord, we bring you these same petitions every week.' After a shocked pause, he continued reading the prayer." For his protest, Annie Dillard adds, "I like him very much."[34] Practicing her own version of antitheodicy, Dillard also dissents against much that she hears in "religious" places. In a later book, *For the Time Being*, she writes, "Many times in Christian churches I have heard the pastor say to God, 'All your actions show your wisdom and love.' Each time, I reach in vain for the courage to rise and shout, 'That's a lie!'—just to put things on a solid footing. . . . Again, Paul writes to the Christians in Rome: 'In all things God works for the good of those who love him.' When was that? I missed it."[35]

These vignettes suggest that a theodicy of protest has a place in Christian life. Indeed such a theodicy should take that life back to some of its most important origins. For instance, the subheadings in this essay are phrases from Psalm 90.[36] Like many others, that psalm is full of lamentations and awesome questions. It can even be read to include dissenting cries over what God has done and left undone. And yet all of these moods are also lifted up not as rejections of faith and hope, but because God is encountered as One whose good promises can be more real than they have been. Such outlooks are not restricted to the Psalms. We have seen them in Job. Anyone who studies the life of Moses or Abraham, Jeremiah or Ezekiel, will find them there as well.

Christians may think, mistakenly, that these Jewish expressions have been superseded by the New Testament, which apparently plays down such themes if they are present at all. A second reading, however, reveals notes that may not stand out at first glance. Jesus brings signs of what good can be. He urges people to give their lives for others, and at least some people try. But the world does not yield, then or now, and Jesus himself ends up crucified, God-forsaken. So goes one part of the Christian story, balanced by another that stresses resurrection and victory to come in spite of losses now. Promises, glimpses, failure, and waste—taken together, as they must be, those realities make the New Testament a source of protesting faith as well. If that is the case, then Christian churches can enhance the disclosure of those feelings by reaffirming Jewish voices that set them out forthrightly. By doing so, Christian preaching may offer less cheap grace and inspire more the fear of God that provokes righteous rebellion. In a similar spirit, prayer, like that of the preacher Annie Dillard likes, will aim less at peace of mind and more at seeking God's strange ways in the disruption of our plans.

The American philosopher William James distinguished between outlooks that are healthy-minded and sick-souled. The former find that, at worst, evil is instrumental; disagreement drives the latter. Shadowed by the Holocaust, genocide, and democide, ours is a time for sick souls. If some people can look evil in the eye and still be healthy-minded . . . well, that possibility may be a sign of hope in itself. But healthy minds are not for everybody. The antitheodicy outlined here is one for sick souls who know that their sickness cannot—must not—be cured, and who likewise refuse to acquiesce because to do so would accomplish nothing.

Long ago a Jewish family was expelled from Spain. Plagued at every turn, they could find no refuge, except that sleep turned into death for them, one by one. At last only the father was left, and he spoke to God:

> "Master of the Universe, I know what You want—I understand what You are doing. You want despair to overwhelm me. You want me to cease believing in You, to cease praying to You, to cease invoking Your name to glorify and sanctify it. Well, I tell You: No, no—a thousand times no! You shall not succeed! In spite of me and in spite of You, I shall shout the Kaddish, which is a song of faith, for You and against You. This song You shall not still, God of Israel!"[37]

That Jewish story summarizes well one strand of a protesting theodicy. An ageless dialogue sounds out another. God's creation is at stake. It is far from perfect, and thus who speaks first? Humankind? God? Both together? . . .

> "Could you have done better?"
>   "Yes, I think so."
>   "You could have done better? Then what are you waiting for? You don't have a minute to waste, go ahead, start working!"[38]

A theodicy of protest is for those who need it. Like the victims of waste in our own day, who knows how many they may be?

CRITIQUE BY STEPHEN T. DAVIS

Roth's eloquent and evocative essay expresses an attitude all sensitive theists should feel—horror, deep sadness, and even outrage at the excesses of evil in human history. Despite massive differences between his God and mine and consequently between his theodicy and mine, I can strongly identify with much in Roth's essay. For example, I agree that God is ultimately responsible for what has happened in the world; that this could have been a much better world than it has thus far turned out to be; that no theodicy has all the final answers; that whether or not God is justified in creating this sort of world depends on what God does with the future; and that we need to trust in God despite the theological and spiritual problem created by the presence of evil in the world. I also applaud the note of moral imperative in Roth's theodicy. I too think we need to "turn and fight" against evil.

The essential difference between Roth's theodicy and mine is that his response to the problem of evil involves giving up something I regard as religiously essential, central to scripture and Christian tradition, and personally precious: the notion that God is perfectly morally good. Roth explains the presence of excessive waste in human history by positing, so to speak, a demonic side to God that allows or causes it. I suspect I can do little to deflect Roth from this path, which is, I believe, something of a gut-level, emotive (I do not intend these words in any pejorative sense) reaction to the suffering he sees in the world, especially the outrages of the Holocaust.

Nevertheless, I will offer three criticisms of Roth's theodicy. They concern, respectively, omnipotence, hope, and solidarity.

(1) We must first notice that Roth needs a strong view of divine omnipotence in order to ensure that God is (unlike a finite God) indictable for evil, i.e., so that God cannot be excused on the grounds of being too weak to prevent evil. Thus Roth says that God is "bound only by his will" and that with God "everything is possible." God is, Roth believes, powerful enough to have prevented the Holocaust and indeed to intervene against any wasteful event in history. As Roth admits, his entire program in theodicy hinges on this strong view of God's power. Thus, the essential puzzle I have with Roth's argument is that he apparently goes on to weaken God's omnipotence in order to rule out the possibility that God can retain perfect goodness by redeeming all evil. The notion that God can redeem all evil, Roth says, is "beyond imagining"; no good "that can be envisioned," however great, can do so; "we have not the vaguest notion" how history could reach a totally happy ending.

But surely this approach goes back on the strong view of omnipotence sketched above. (Roth hints at this at one point: He says he agrees, "but not unequivocally," with the notion that God can bring about good ends that are completely beyond human energies.) Surely everyone will admit that some of the evil that we see in the world is redeemable. But if God is omnipotent—i.e., is limited only by the divine will—why can't we say *both* that God's will is wholly good *and* that God can and therefore will one day redeem all evil? If Roth is correct when he says that "all possibilities are within God's reach," then at the very least he owes us an explanation why redeeming all evil is not possible and thus won't be achieved by God (and thus requires abandoning the notion of divine perfect goodness).

Of course Roth is within his intellectual rights if his response is a personal one, that is, if he says simply that the best judgment he can make in the light of all the evidence is that more waste has taken place than can ever be redeemed. I agree with Roth that some evil is "irretrievable" in the sense that the past is set and irrevocable. Nothing that God or anyone else can now do can alter, for example, the fact that six million people died. But it does not follow from this that an omnipotent being cannot successfully "retrieve" all evil in the sense that this being will one day achieve such great goods that all past evils will pale into insignificance, even for the victims and sufferers. I believe three factors—Roth's strong view of omnipotence, his willingness to appeal to scripture, and his emphasis on hope—should lead him to recognize this.

The point, in sum, is that Roth says he cannot understand how God could possibly redeem and render acceptable all the waste that has occurred (and I must admit that I cannot understand it either). Roth denies that any kind of eschaton will suffice to do so, and then he adds "at least from a human perspective." But I want to reply that that is just the point: in the eschaton we will no longer see things merely from that perspective. At that moment, as Paul affirms, "I will know fully, even as I have been fully known" (1 Cor. 13:12). The point is that an omnipotent being is not bound by the inability to understand that Roth and I share. I do not claim to understand how God can render the Holocaust acceptable, any more than I claim to understand how God raised Jesus from the dead. But my lack of wit does not limit God. Perhaps God will some day do the one, just as I believe with Roth that God once did the other.

(2) Religious hope runs like a drumbeat throughout Roth's essay. Clearly hope is crucial to his obviously deep and sincere religious beliefs. He mentions grace, joy, salvation, and thanksgiving. Of course, as seen above, Roth does not hope for a total redemption of all evil, but he does think there is ground both for present joy and thanksgiving, and for hope of "life more abundant" in the future. God's good promises can be real, he says; Judaism and Christianity both affirm that "God can and will intervene to heal and restore." What exactly does Roth hope for? In precisely what sense will God "heal and restore"? Perhaps Roth hopes, just as Hick and I do, for a good eschaton in which all will be well. He will only insist that no matter how good the eschaton is, it will never justify the evils that have occurred as history moved toward it.

But my question is this: If God truly has a demonic side, what ground is there for hope? Surely a partially evil God may well decide perversely to give us "life *less* abundant." I think Roth sees the problem; I take it this is why he calls trusting in God a risk. But surely with Roth's God, the risk is too great. If God is partially demonic, the risk that God will be in a testy mood when the eschaton dawns is too much to take. Indeed, if God is partly evil, despair—which Roth argues eloquently against—may well be the rational choice. I will trust such a God no more than I would trust a momentarily calmed manic-depressive who is holding a gun. If God is, as Roth says, a grossly negligent murderer, I will no more worship God than I will worship a Caligula or a Stalin. I will only worship and trust a being who I believe is wholly good.

(3) One of Roth's objections to the notion of a happy eschaton in which all is made right is that such schemes "legitimate evil." And to borrow a Rothian turn of phrase, I say both "Yes" and "No" to that. If a happy ending is designed to show that all the suffering that people experienced on their way to the eschaton was not really evil after all, Roth is correct. That scheme legitimates evil

and is accordingly at fault. But if the happy ending is designed to overcome all the evil and suffering, make it pale into insignificance in the light of the experience of an infinite and everlasting good, Roth is wrong. Evil will not have been legitimated, only defeated, redeemed, and overcome.

But I now think I grasp something about Roth's theodicy that I missed in 1981. I think his deepest reason for rejecting eschatological schemes that redeem all evil is not that he thinks it cannot be done. If I can be forgiven a personal reference about a colleague who has been one of my closest friends for some thirty years, I think Roth already does, at least partly, believe that it is within God's power to do it. He may even partly believe that God will do it. But I now see that he thinks the deepest problem is this: to embrace such schemes is to fail to have solidarity with the victims and sufferers. It is to allow their screams of pain to be muted. To retain this solidarity is one of Roth strongest *desiderata* in theodicy. And that desire, in my view, is to be accorded nothing but the honor and respect it deserves.

But real solidarity with the victims and sufferers is telling them the truth. And the truth is that the Christian message of hope through the love of God as expressed preeminently in Christ is good news for all people, even those who suffered and died unjustly, maybe *especially* for them. Part of that truth is that "the sufferings of this present time are not worth comparing with the glory about to be revealed to us" (Rom. 8:18).

CRITIQUE BY D. Z. PHILLIPS

To think that the opening essay in the collection, John Roth's "A Theodicy of Protest," is, in fact, an antitheodicy is tempting. At one point, Roth uses this term to describe his essay. To give in to this temptation, however, is to miss the importance of four tensions in his paper that leave fundamental questions unresolved.

The first tension is found in the character of Roth's objections to theodicies. Roth rightly criticizes the instrumentalism in them that makes human suffering the means to achieving a greater good. We are told to take this greater good on trust, since we have no conception of its result. Roth is horrified at any attempt to mute the screams of the innocent, or to modify the destruction of people, by treating them as means to such an end. Should we have any truck with such eschatological optimism? I do not think Roth does, but what is the nature of his objections?

At first, he objects to the cost-effectiveness of God's plan. It simply does not work. The waste in human suffering shows that God has gone too far. At other times, however, Roth seems to be criticizing the very conception of such a plan, and the inadequacy of the means-end relation as a central feature of moral action. No matter how splendid a prospect, it cannot be pursued by any and every means. Decency says, "Not that way." The means have to be as decent as the ends, and for that reason Roth concludes that no future good can possibly justify what human beings have suffered. His argument is not that the justification fails, but that even contemplating it is indecent. The problem is that Roth does not seem to appreciate the difference between his criticisms: the difference between criticizing the effectiveness of a plan and criticizing the very conception of a plan.

The first tension is bound up with the second: Roth's conception of God's power. He claims that God is bounded by nothing but his will. Roth's God is thus a God of sheer power. This view cannot be sustained. God's power is a power of a certain kind. If we say that God is *more* powerful than the Devil, what measure are we using?

God's will is bounded by God's nature. Were it not so, one ought to be able to say that God could commit murder, but simply chooses not to, which I hope we agree is nonsense. Roth does not consider the possibility that God's only sovereignty is the sovereignty of love. As Kierkegaard never tires of saying, love cannot conquer by force. Sometimes it simply suffers, led like a lamb dumb to the slaughter. To Roth's credit, he wants to give full weight to these facts, but his conception of God's power will not allow him to do so.

The above conclusion is relevant to the third tension in Roth's paper: his conception of creation. On the one hand, he thinks of God as the master of the universe. On the other hand, he sees that the gift of human life with its dark and destructive aspects is the gift of something imperfect. On the one hand, Roth says that God knows this imperfection from the outset. On the other hand, he says that God is disappointed with how human life has turned out. Tension exists between the "knowledge" and the "disappointment." A deeper view is to say that both divine love and sorrow are present in the gift of life: love in the freedom of the gift, but sorrow in the realization of what it entails. So I cannot say, with Roth, that everything hinges on the proposition that God fails to use well enough the power he possesses to act decisively in history. As I understand it, for Christians, God acts decisively on Calvary in showing what love is: something that can be crucified.

This knowledge makes us address the fourth tension in Roth's paper: his claim that, with God, all things are possible. In *Purity of Heart*, Kierkegaard speaks of our desire to turn "the possible" into "the necessary." But with God, that's what all things are: possible, graces from God's hand. The natural world and other human beings are graces we do not deserve; they are unearned gifts. And when the world victimizes the innocent, we see, often with horror, that this outcome, too, is possible—a realization that is central to compassion for such victims. As we know, on countless occasions we can do something about evils that violate grace in human life, but unavoidable evil and suffering still occur. A compassion which understands that fact can sometimes create a fellowship that does not purchase the sufferer. There is no suggestion of the vulgarity which pretends that the suffering is *for* anything, a means to God's ends. But on some occasions such compassion is not forthcoming, when love and innocence simply suffer.

The four tensions I have mentioned come together in Simone Weil's conception of creation as divine withdrawal in allowing something other than perfection to exist. To reveal such a God in the world, God enters it as a beggar, a helpless child, and dies the death of a common criminal with spittle on his face. This approach is a far cry from "the master of the universe." It is a love that intercedes for us through the terribleness of the sacrifice. That terribleness, that sacrifice is what is exalted, raised on high. Wittgenstein said that only love believes in the resurrection. For Roth, the resurrection is an act of power. Even if I understood that, it would not take love to believe it.

CRITIQUE BY DAVID RAY GRIFFIN

I appreciate much about Roth's essay, especially his moral passion and his rejection of any theodicy suggesting that the evils of our world will, in the long run, be seen to have been insignificant. The genocides of recent times will, as he says, "scar the world forever."

I also appreciate the support Roth provides for points made in my essay. In the first place, he brings out clearly the implications of the traditional doctrine of omnipotence, which I sometimes call "extreme voluntarism" because it says that everything depends solely on the divine will. Saying that "God is bound only by God's will," Roth adds that "nothing except it determines what he shall do or become." This doctrine means that "God could have created very differently," producing a world without, for example, cancer, earthquakes, and holocausts. Likewise, "God's relation to our world could take many forms." Human beings, who have "more power, more freedom, than is good for us," could have had less. God could even have wholly predetermined the future. Or, having chosen to give us freedom, "God could intervene dramatically at any point in present history." Hence, "the mass of agony does not have to be."

Roth also illustrates the prediction of Hermogenes, cited in my essay, that this view of divine power threatens belief in the perfect goodness of our creator. In response to the idea that "God is love," Roth argues instead that God's love and compassion must be incomplete, that God's will must be less than perfect, so that, regardless of what kind of eschaton is eventually produced, God will be "everlastingly guilty."

Roth supports, finally, my view that this conclusion holds true even if one posits that God has given human beings genuine freedom. Agreeing with Hick and Davis that there are no uncreated metaphysical principles, so that God sets literally all "the boundaries in which we live and move and have our being," he sees that the existence of human freedom "does not remove [this] God from the dock."

Roth's own conclusion is that God must be a mixture of good and evil. On this basis, he concludes that we should "be for God by being against God," his hope being that our protests on behalf of humanity "may grip God's heart," thereby converting God to more perfect goodness. Although I agree that, given the traditional doctrine of divine omnipotence, Roth's conclusion about the divine character is realistic, his overall position seems to have several serious problems.

First, I see no basis for hope that a partly evil deity could be led to repent. The moral defect in God is presumably eternal, and many philosophers, from Aristotle to Hartshorne, have held that the eternal and the necessary are identical. In the first edition of this book, Roth replied to this point by saying: "If God's power is bound only by his own unnecessitated will . . . , then God can change his ways." However, the traditional doctrine that God's will is not necessitated by anything outside of God did not entail that God's basic character or will could change. For example, Luther, an extreme voluntarist if ever there was one, said that "[God's] will is eternal and changeless, because His nature is so" (quoted in my *God, Power, and Evil*, p. 103). It seems a rather desperate hope that, assuming that God has had a mean streak for not only the past 15 billion years but from all eternity, our protests in the next century or so will bring about a change. Even if we were to assume that, by analogy with human beings, God could in principle undergo a moral conversion, the basis for expecting such an occurrence would be missing. Moral conversions in human beings usually involve coming to adopt a larger perspective on things, but God by definition already has an all-inclusive perspective.

A second problem is that Roth's position seems to contradict the very nature of religion. Vital religion, as I understand it, is driven by the desire to be in harmony with what is taken to be the Holy Reality. The extraordinary moral concern in cultures decisively affected by Judaism, Christianity, and Islam is due to the fact that the Holy One worshipped by devotees of these religions has been perceived to be perfectly just and righteous. It is true that many of the doctrines of the theologians of these traditions have implications that make God's goodness questionable. But ordinary believers have almost always held God's holiness to include goodness without qualification. When the problem of evil has challenged this belief, theologians and ordinary believers have taken comfort in the assurance that in some way, perhaps totally mysterious to our finite minds, God is nevertheless totally good.

But Roth now urges us to adopt a position in which we would consciously be working for justice in partial opposition to God. We are to "turn divine injustice into human justice." This attitude may be psychologically possible in the short run, at least for people whose basic perceptions and purposes were originally molded by the drive to be in harmony with a Holy One of perfect goodness. But if my understanding of religion is correct, the attitude Roth advocates is psychologically impossible in the long run. Although he believes that his antitheodicy's "vision of an omnipotent God" who may yet be convinced to work more wholeheartedly to overcome evil is a vision that "can set human souls on fire for good," I suspect that, given the dynamics of the *imitatio dei*, the belief that the supreme power of the universe is not perfectly good would eventually undercut our own concern for moral goodness. Although Roth is strongly opposed to any position that legitimates evil, his position could have this effect by saying that deity itself, the Holy One with whom we want to be in harmony, fosters evil unnecessarily.

In response to my earlier articulation of this criticism, Roth replied that he is advocating only partial harmony because "harmony with God ought to be problematic after Auschwitz." I doubt, however, that the dynamics of the *imitatio dei* are so subject to our wills. For example, although moralists from at least the time of Thomas Huxley's *Evolution and Ethics* have urged people not to imitate the cosmic process as portrayed by Darwinism, such imitation has become increasingly rampant.

Roth's view that God is less than perfectly good follows from his retention of the traditional doctrine of omnipotence, as he points out: "Everything hinges on the proposition that God possesses—but fails to use well enough—the power to intervene decisively at any moment to make history's course less wasteful." From my point of view, of course, Roth is shaking his fist at a God who is merely a product of human imagination. Whereas Roth quarrels with God over the use of power, I think he should quarrel with those theologians who attributed to God the kind of power that makes God seem indictable for the world's evils. Why does Roth not, with process theologians, reject this attribution?

One of Roth's answers is that if "God raised Jesus from the dead," then "God had the might to thwart the Holocaust." When I in the first edition questioned this claim, suggesting that the power needed to evoke new life is different in kind from the power that would be needed to prevent such evils, Roth replied that "God could have changed the minds of Nazi leaders." That is true: God *might* have done so. But if the Nazi leaders had genuine freedom, then whether God *actually* did so would have been partly up to them. Roth's indict-ment of God for not changing their minds hinges on his assumption that God could have overruled their freedom. The question remains why he does not, with process theologians, reject this assumption.

One of his answers is that hope for redemption on process theology's premises would require "sanguine assumptions about human nature and his-tory." However, in a work in progress (*The Divine Cry of Our Time*), I argue that a God of persuasive power can provide the basis for hope for salvation not only in the sense of sanctification in a life beyond death but also, while fully recognizing with Hegel and Roth that history thus far has been a "slaughter-bench," in the sense of a time when human civilization will be controlled by divine rather than demonic values.

Another reason Roth rejects the God of process theism is that he finds this deity "ineffectual" and therefore "hardly worth bothering about." But I believe that this God is now calling us to a form of global order through which our present trajectory toward omnicide could be overcome, namely by a global democracy. If so, this God's call would certainly be worth bother-ing about. Whether this God will be effectual in bringing about this new form of civilization will depend on whether we respond to this call. Whether we do so will depend partly on whether we believe that such a God is issuing such a call.

This discussion brings me to my main objection to Roth's position. Blam-ing God could, as Roth himself recognizes, detract attention from our respon-sibility for overcoming the sources of evil. Although Roth says that the protests he advocates "do God no harm," they may, by reinforcing the idea that the world's evils could be overcome unilaterally by God, harm God's chances of persuading enough of us to respond to the present divine call. I would hope Roth would no longer expend his time and energy protesting against a God that has never existed except in human imaginations, instead lending his pas-sionate voice to echoing the divine call to create the kind of global order through which the divine commands of which Roth speaks—to "heal the sick, feed the hungry, forestall violence"—could be universally implemented.

CRITIQUE BY JOHN HICK

I have a double reaction to Roth's paper. On the one hand he eloquently and passionately expresses the almost overwhelming despair that we all feel in face of the horrors and agonies to which so many people are subjected in our world, and at least as much in the twentieth as in any previous century. This sense of despair also includes within it, for me at least, a sense of (perhaps irrational) guilt at having been, on the whole, so undeservedly fortunate in life, in contrast to so many others. The same probably applies to Roth also. But I respect his chosen role as spokesperson for the millions who have been oppressed and ground down, or savagely slaughtered, by "man's inhumanity to man" or by the unfeeling forces of nature.

The other side of my reaction to Roth's chapter arises from a different intuition about the meaning and worth and potentialities of human existence. Roth rejects (as I also do) the idea of a finite God who would prevent these evils if he could, but lacks the power to do so. Roth is closer—though in a different style altogether—to Davis in emphasizing our human freedom and responsibility. His complaint against God is that God does not intervene to overrule this freedom and responsibility when humans are freely oppressing and slaughtering one another. He is aware that if God were to overrule our freedom whenever we do such things, even to the extent of such gigantic evils as the Holocaust, we would no longer be free and responsible beings. Roth sees this but believes that "We have more power, more freedom, than is good for us. . . . No good that [he] can envision, on earth or beyond, is worth the freedom . . . that wastes so much life."

This approach seems to me too small and too short a view, made possible I suspect by a rejection of the conviction of all the great world faiths that our present life is only a very small part of our total existence. The passage just quoted provides a glancing reference to the possibility of a future life, but Roth nowhere tries to give any serious consideration to this possibility. In my view, this omission is his disabling blind spot. I would agree that if this life, so creative for some but so destructive for many others, is all, then despair at the human situation as a whole is appropriate. Indeed if an all-powerful God has deliberately created a situation in which this present life, with all its horrors, is the totality of human existence, we should hate and revile that God's callous disregard for his/her helpless creatures. If we dismiss the eschatological dimension of the world's religions, Roth's protest against God, instead of being a bold defiance, would be a feebly inadequate response. He goes either too far or not far enough.

To press the point, if Roth really believes that the situation is as bad as he depicts it, then the God he still seems to believe in is the Devil! For even if we manage to moderate the world's evils in the future by our own efforts, as Roth hopes, that will do nothing for the thousands of millions who have already lived and died, and so nothing to justify belief in the goodness of the Creator. As Roth says, "unjustifiable waste [of human life] is everlasting." Nevertheless, despite all this, Roth somehow clings to a faith in the reality of a good as well as all-powerful Deity. But this clinging is either intellectually indefensible, or it implies much more than Roth is willing to face. For without some conception of how this may be—in other words, without a theodicy of some kind, however sketchy and tentative—his position is irrational and, in its clinging to a residual Christian faith, purely sentimental.

If Roth were to give serious attention to the eschatological dimension of the religions, he would see options other than the unattractive idea of heavenly compensation for the ills of earth. The alternative is the ultimate fulfillment of human potential through a long and often painful process of moral and spiritual growth in a universe that is, in Bonhoeffer's phrase, "*etsi deus non daretur*" ("as if there were no God"). Not every situation in which we humans find ourselves is creative; on the contrary, very many are purely destructive. But from this stance we can conclude that the total process, with all its unplanned contingencies and all the crushing setbacks that occur so unequally within the human community, will in the end be seen as the path by which all have finally arrived, in Christian language, at a complete and totally joyous fulfillment as "children of God" in the "kingdom of God." Nor does this eschatological dimension necessarily involve the traditional Christian picture of heaven or hell immediately after death. Many people hold alternative ideas of this ultimate outcome.

This critique is not the place to pursue these alternative options.[39] My argument is simply that if Roth were more tough-minded in following through with the implications of what he says, he would either boldly reject belief in the goodness of an all-powerful God or explore further the difference made by the eschatological dimension of religious faith. He may find this further dimension either improbable or utterly incapable of bringing a sufficient eternal good out of the temporal process. If so, he ought to abandon belief in the goodness of God.

These words are hard, but they are honestly addressed, and they do not come out of a less painful awareness than Roth's of the grim reality of the Holocaust and of the other horrors of human history. But those people among us who have not ourselves personally suffered those horrors, but nevertheless engage in the theodicy (including antitheodicy) debates, have a duty to exercise our reason as well as our emotions. I am suggesting that we then have to recognize that the only ground for a continued belief in the goodness of an all-powerful God lies in the hope that God is bringing a limitless good out of the use and misuse of our powers and our freedom. The logical alternative is not a Christian theodicy of protest, but atheism.

REJOINDER

No statement, theological or otherwise, should be made that would not be credible in the presence of burning children. (Irving Greenberg,

"Cloud of Smoke, Pillar of Fire: Judaism, Christianity, and Modernity after the Holocaust"[40)]

God is light and in him there is no darkness at all. (1 John 1:5)

"Perhaps some day I shall know how to laugh again."[41] When those words were published in 1944, a Jewish carpenter named Jankiel Wiernik was unsure. Deported by the Nazis from Warsaw to Treblinka on August 23, 1942, Wiernik would escape in a death-camp revolt. But prior to that time, he went through experiences that made him say, "My life is embittered. Phantoms of death haunt me, specters of children, little children, nothing but children. I sacrificed all those nearest and dearest to me. I myself took them to the execution site. I built their death chambers for them."[42]

Jankiel Wiernik is on my mind as I reflect on the insightful replies that Stephen Davis, David Griffin, John Hick, and D. Z. Phillips have made to "A Theodicy of Protest." So is Irving Greenberg's statement about burning children. So is the New Testament. I also recall William James's conviction that people have different spiritual needs.

Is my view intellectually defensible? No criticisms of my Christian theodicy of protest are more challenging than Hick's. He respects and shares much of my protesting response to evil, which, he rightly observes, is intensified by the unjustified and undeserved disparity between the especially fortunate ones in this life—I count myself among them—and so many others. Irrational, sentimental, inclined to turn God into "the Devil," perhaps even atheism in disguise—Hick brings all of those charges against my outlook unless I correct what he takes to be my "disabling blind spot." In his judgment, that blind spot involves my giving insufficient attention to "the possibility of a future life" beyond death and to "the eschatalogical dimension of the world's religions." Put another way, Hick wants me to provide the very thing I resist: "a theodicy of some kind, however sketchy and tentative."

I think that my essay places more emphasis on eschatology and life beyond death—at least by implication—than Hick discerns. Some summary points may help: (1) I am a practicing Christian. (2) Believing in the possibility of a future life beyond death, I affirm the resurrection, which I also take as a sign of God's omnipotence. (3) A future life beyond death is crucial, because without it, history's slaughter-bench debris accumulates without redemption. (4) I affirm that God is good, but not perfectly good, and that both God and humanity could be better. (5) Given history's course, the quality of God's goodness depends largely on eschatalogical factors—that is, on God's relationship to human life beyond death. (6) Protest against God, which is part but only part of my religious and philosophical stance, declares faith in God and God's goodness.

Would those "sketchy and tentative" ingredients begin to meet Hick's theodicy requirement? Probably not, for theodicy calls for a full justification of God's relation to evil and an account that involves, in Hick's words, God's bringing "limitless good out of the use and misuse of our powers and our freedom." Neither condition, I suspect, can be met. So my Christian theodicy of protest is antitheodicy. The amount, degree, and intensity of evil are too great to justify fully God's creation of the world we inhabit. In addition, even an omnipotent God cannot undo the past completely. While God can bring immense good out of evil, that good is not limitless—even if God denies or falsifies history by erasing memory. As long as memory persists—God's and humanity's—shadows of injustice, suffering, unjustifiable waste, and the unanswerable questions they raise will haunt reality.

It does not follow, however, that my antitheodicy's God is "the Devil." I start from the conviction that life is preciously good and that it is God's gift. Yes, this life is flawed from the outset, and we do not know completely why. Nevertheless, its actual and potential goodness are unmistakable and awesome. So is life's source. Furthermore, because I am a Christian, I have the eschatalogical hope that death and evil do not have the last word. Hence, my view does not incline toward atheism. To the contrary, this outlook defends God's reality, accountability, and caring in spite of evil's waste. This belief, moreover, is neither intellectually indefensible nor sentimental.

My version of Christian faith is intellectually defensible, not because it can be "proved" or because it is the only sensible way to approach life, but because it is grounded in scrutinized experience. That experience includes heartfelt yearnings for justice and love, which I take to be more important, not less so, when the world thwarts them. Thus, my faith is not "residual," as Hick alleges, but primary. It informs my philosophical concerns, for example, and my commitment to Holocaust studies.

True, my version of Christianity quarrels deeply with that tradition, not to reject it but to find an honest way to affirm it. Thus, I find unpersuasive Hick's alternative that existence is a total process leading to "complete and totally joyous fulfillment." My sense of intellectual defensibility finds evil's stain too deep for such completeness and total joy. When I say that death and evil do not have the last word, I mean, among other things, that our personal identity lives and is not abolished by death, and that goodness—justice, healing, caring, love, and joy—prevail. Given history's reality, however, I doubt that goodness should or can prevail without remainder. I hold that view to avoid sentimentality that would claim, for instance, that everything works for good, that everything is part of a divinely coherent plan that makes evil's waste acceptable. If God has a "plan," it is wanting, but that fact does not mean that life cannot be more fulfilling or goodness more complete than it has been before. Everything depends on what human persons and God accomplish—together and alone, now and in life to come.

Cannot all evil be redeemed? Davis, who shares with me a belief in God's omnipotence, raises this question to criticize the consistency of my emphasis that "for God all things are possible" (Matt. 19:26). If God is limited only by God's will, then why can it not be true that God "will one day achieve such great goods that all past evils will pale into insignificance, even for the victims and sufferers"? Davis admits that the past cannot be retrieved. Jankiel Wiernik's experience cannot be undone, but could not an omnipotent God render Wiernik's pain insignificant in comparison to greater goods that lie beyond it? Indeed, would not solidarity with victims such as Wiernik—or perhaps even the burning children recalled by Irving Greenberg—entail "telling them the truth" that their sufferings, in the words of St. Paul, "are not worth comparing to the glory about to be revealed to us" (Rom. 8:18)?

No doubt God could render Wiernik's suffering insignificant. God may have done so already, but the issue is how and, specifically, whether God can do so with complete moral integrity. God could forget Jankiel Wiernik. Or, beyond death, God might erase Wiernik's memory, or even persuade him with overwhelming good. But if God does so, should the outcome be accepted without question and unequivocally praised? Or would integrity require reiteration that God's omnipotence is bound by God's own will, the very will that permitted Treblinka and underwrote a not-so-new testament from the tortured hand of a surviving Jewish carpenter?

As for "telling them the truth," the suggestion—with due respect to Davis and St. Paul—that the torment of burning children and their parents is "not worth comparing to the glory about to be revealed to us" may get high marks as religious hyperbole, but it scarcely seems like solidarity with the victims. A protesting antitheodicy would find it incredible, if not obscene, to utter such words in the presence of the Holocaust's burning children.

Should Jankiel Wiernik discover that *anything* pales his past into insignificance, I hope that he laughs . . . madly.

How should God's nature be understood? Each respondent criticizes my basic understanding of God and, in particular, my claim that "God is bound only by God's will." Phillips, for example, insists that my claim entails "a God of sheer power" and thus overlooks that "God's will is bounded by God's nature." To that point, Phillips adds that "God's only sovereignty is the sovereignty of love."

Discussion about God's relation to evil raises more questions than it answers because human views about God's nature are so many and varied. The Hebrew Bible's narrative about the revelation of the divine name to Moses (see Exod. 3:13–14) illustrates important dimensions of that reality. As the story goes, crystal clarity did not characterize the answer God told Moses to give the Israelites when they asked to know God's name. That puzzling name could be understood as "I Am Who I Am" or "I Will Be What I Will Be." The dynamic, restless, surprising, and conceptually elusive God described in scripture, which I take seriously, suggests that God's nature remains less than fully determined. What happens in God's creation affects God, and perhaps does so in ways that are fundamental to God's nature, but *ultimately*, and that qualifying word is important, it is God's will—I Will Be What I Will Be—that determines who God is.

Power has much to do with God's nature, but my view does not entail that "sheer power" is the beginning and end of the matter. Love, for instance, can be God's sovereignty, and we should hope that it is. But love is not God's only sovereignty, as Phillips has it, because will goes "all the way down" in God's nature—at least it does in the perspective that I am exploring here. If will does go that way, then God's nature remains in the making.

How long has God had a "moral defect"? Griffin raises this issue, and the defect in question—God's penchant for needless waste—impugns God's total goodness. Griffin assumes that the answer to his question would have to be "presumably forever," and then he surmises that such a divine defect might also be necessary and therefore beyond redemption altogether. Although Griffin's speculations may be right, I reject them. If God's power is bound only by God's own unnecessitated will, as I believe, then God's ways can change. Moreover, if the biblical narratives can be trusted at all, God's activities do form changed ways from time to time.

Conviction that God acted in events such as the exodus and Easter stands in stark contrast to what would otherwise be inferred about the nature and destiny of human life: for instance, that Jankiel Wiernik witnessed Jews exterminated and the matter ends there as far as their personal lives are concerned. Ironically, then, Christianity's "good news" is one factor that makes God's moral defect stand out, unless one is persuaded when Griffin questions my view that God had the might to thwart the Holocaust if—but not only if—God raised Jesus from the dead.

Griffin criticizes that view on the grounds that "the power needed to evoke new life is different in kind from the power that would be needed to prevent such evils." This distinction's force escapes me. The resurrection, as I understand it, is not simply identical with "evoking new life," whatever that phrase might mean in this context. In the resurrection a life that really ended in death begins again in transformed continuity with the personal identity that went before. Resurrection, as Phillips rightly credits me with affirming, is an act of power that is also an act of love, indeed an act that shows love to be much more than "something that can be crucified," to cite Phillips's weak claim. Instead,

I think that the resurrection shows love's potential power to transform all existence far more than has been the case to date.

What makes religion vital? According to Griffin, the vitality of religion entails "the desire to be in harmony with what is taken to be the Holy Reality." That desire is fundamental. At the same time, harmony with God ought to be problematic after Auschwitz, and Griffin's updated response helps to show why religion's vitality depends not only on the desire that he has identified but also on what is done with that desire when it cannot be easily satisfied.

Griffin is correct: Vital religious life depends on God's goodness. Another of his concerns—"belief that the supreme power of the universe is not perfectly good would eventually undercut our own concern for moral goodness"—cannot be regarded lightly either. Thus, a theodicy of protest starts with God's goodness and persists in emphasizing that goodness until the end. To be for-God-against-God only makes sense in light of the good that God has done and still might do in the future. Specifically, that stance only makes sense in light of this good news: God "loves righteousness and justice" and "love never ends" (Ps. 33:5 and 1 Cor. 13:8).

Elie Wiesel says that a Jew "defines himself more by what troubles him than by what reassures him."[43] Jewish or not, morally concerned and vitally religious persons can be defined in the same way. Griffin worries that time and energy spent protesting against God would be better spent "echoing the divine call." His assessment of my outlook overemphasizes blame, but a protesting antitheodicy emphasizes responsibility—God's and humanity's. The purpose of this emphasis is not to dwell on blame but lucidly to take stock of our situation in the world. Here the tradition of process theology is simply different from the one that informs a protesting antitheodicy. Through its distinctive form of protest, the latter underscores the divine call. Religious vitality depends on more than one way of encountering the divine. None lacks risks and problems, but a religious perspective that allows room for quarrelsome protest against God can, in fact, be an asset and not a hindrance to moral commitments that Griffin and I endorse.

Still, for what do I hope? This question comes from Davis. Behind the query stands another: In a theodicy of protest, does any ground for hope exist at all? My reply turns to December, the time—where I live—of shortest light and longest night. December's winter days are also the season of Hanukkah, the Feast of Lights, which commemorates the rededication of a Temple and tells us that energy to keep lamps burning can be replenished. In cold darkness the Christian calendar marks Advent, a time of expectant waiting, and then Christmas, which celebrates a promise made good, at least in part.

We shall pass through December, but not completely. Advent remains because God's promises, good though they are, still keep us waiting. Acceptance of those promises, especially when they are perceived as coming from a God whose goodness is less than whole, is as risky as childbirth in a Bethlehem stable. Is the risk too great? Responses to that question depend on the content of hope and on the odds against it.

In the words of the Christian creed from Nicaea, I "look for the resurrection of the dead, and the life of the world to come." Thus, I hope that Jankiel Wiernik will laugh again—joyously, honestly, without his past paled into insignificance, and without derangement. As for life right now, I hope that waste, such as that which stole Wiernik's laughter, can be checked. In this world I expect no ultimate beating of swords into plowshares, but absence of strenuous effort in that direction will be—more than a sin—a move toward punishment itself, for indifference to our own existence may finish us all. If that realization does not foster protesting hope against despair, we are in deep trouble.

Healing and restoration are badly needed. They will not, however, set everything right. Existence is permanently scarred. Still, life can be better. If the risks and odds are vast, as surely they must be for anyone who will look and see, then my hope entails the conviction that those very odds must themselves become reasons that provoke us to do battle against them. Davis says he will only trust a God who is wholly good. He seems to have located such a God, and I am glad for the trust that he can have. Nevertheless, I cannot share Davis's conviction, because he intends it to include a theodicy that, for example, makes the Holocaust acceptable. My protesting dissent makes hope theologically risky. But risky hope need not die, and it does not.

Does a theodicy of protest make worship impossible? The criticism implied here is that any God less than wholly good deserves no worship. But does authentic worship really depend so much on God's purity and innocence? Like Davis, I do not wish to honor a Caligula or a Stalin. Such notions are abhorrent. From this argument, however, does not follow that I can sing a doxology—"Praise God from whom all blessings flow"—only if I believe that expressions of thanksgiving and awe-filled love are sufficient worship responses.

Worship cannot have vitality without praise and thanksgiving. But honesty is no less important to its life. In worship one professes and celebrates God's goodness to the extent that such goodness is experienced and thereby anticipated. Other things have been experienced, too, and they rightly produce lamentation and rage, heartbreak and melancholy. *God, why did you create this world? Why do you let injustice and suffering so often have their ways? Why did you form men and women in your image?* Those questions belong in post-Holocaust sanctuaries. Responses to them do as well: love, freedom, soul-making—those motifs have a place—but the "Whys?" remain. All good worship ends by sending people forth to relieve suffering, to create joy, and to make friends out of enemies. Thus, by showing that our task is to turn divine injustice into human justice and compassion, by giving voice to commitment for-God-against-God, a theodicy of protest is itself a fitting act of worship after Auschwitz.

What have I learned from these exchanges? First and foremost, none of the views expressed in these pages, including my own, satisfy me completely. Yet all of them express something that appeals to me, something I would like to share.

I admire Davis's confidence, and if I cannot possess it, that outcome is no cause for celebration. All can be well in the end, says Hick. That message is winsome. I need to hear such claims from time to time even if I do not embrace them fully. Griffin's yearning for goodness, his hunger and thirst for righteousness, are unmistakable. I thank him for his fervor, even as I find him saying too much and too little. Sharing much of my skepticism about theodicy, Phillips presses me to think deeper and better about God's love, even as he advances the inadequate view that "God's only sovereignty is the sovereignty of love." My protest, a fragmentary effort to wrestle with God and human life, has its place, too.

A problem remains. How, if at all, can these pieces fit together? One possibility is shown, more than said, by this book. Its words have taken the writers on more than one journey. All of us—I hope—have been stretched, changed by being prodded. Where theodicy, or antitheodicy, is concerned, perhaps that outcome is the point: Do not sit tight, but instead question and move.

In his memoir, *Night*, Elie Wiesel recounts a boyhood conversation with his eccentric teacher, Moché the Beadle.

> "Man raises himself toward God by the questions he asks Him," he was fond of repeating. "That is the true dialogue. Man questions God and God answers. But we don't understand His answers. We can't understand them. Because they come from the depths of the soul, and they stay there until death. You will find the true answers, Eliezer, only within yourself!"
>
> "And why do you pray, Moché?" I asked him.
>
> "I pray to the God within me that He will give me the strength to ask Him the right questions."[44]

Jankiel Wiernik remains on my mind. So do burning children. So does the message that "God is light and in him there is no darkness at all." Questions remain as well. I pray they are the right ones.

2

An Irenaean Theodicy

John Hick

Can a world in which sadistic cruelty often has its way, in which selfish love-lessness is so rife, in which there are debilitating diseases, crippling accidents, bodily and mental decay, insanity, and all manner of natural disasters be regarded as the expression of infinite creative goodness? Certainly all this could never by itself lead anyone to believe in the existence of a limitlessly powerful God. And yet even in such a world, innumerable men and women have believed and do believe in the reality of an infinite creative goodness, which they call God. The theodicy project starts at this point—with an already operating belief in God, embodied in human living—and attempts to show that this belief is not rendered irrational by the fact of evil. It attempts to explain how the universe, assumed to be created and ultimately ruled by a lim-itlessly good and limitlessly powerful Being, is as it is, including all the pain, suffering, wickedness, and folly that we find around us and within us. The theodicy project is thus an exercise in metaphysical thinking, in the sense that it consists in the formation and criticism of large-scale hypotheses concerning the nature and process of the universe.

Since a theodicy both starts from and tests belief in the reality of God, it naturally takes different forms in relation to different concepts of God. In this paper I shall be discussing the project of a specifically Christian theodicy; I shall not be attempting the further and even more difficult work of compara-tive theodicy, leading in turn to the question of a global theodicy.

The two main demands upon a theodicy hypothesis are that it be (1) inter-nally coherent, and (2) consistent with the data both of the religious tradition on which it is based, and of the world, in respect both of the latter's general char-acter as revealed by scientific enquiry and of the specific facts of moral and nat-ural evil. These two criteria demand, respectively, possibility and plausibility.

Traditionally, Christian theology has centered upon the concept of God as both limitlessly powerful and limitlessly good and loving; this concept of deity gives rise to the problem of evil as a threat to theistic faith. The threat was definitively expressed in Stendhal's bombshell, "The only excuse for God is that he does not exist!" The theodicy project is the attempt to offer a different view of the universe that is both possible and plausible and which does not ignite Stendhal's bombshell.

Christian thought has always included a certain range of variety, and in the area of theodicy it offers two broad types of approach. The Augustinian approach, representing until fairly recently the majority report of the Christian mind, hinges upon the idea of the fall as the origin of moral evil, which has in turn brought about the almost universal carnage of nature. The Irenaean approach, representing in the past a minority report, hinges upon the creation of humankind through the evolutionary process as an immature creature living in a challenging and therefore person-making world. I shall indicate very briefly why I do not find the first type of theodicy satisfactory, and then spend the remainder of this paper exploring the second type.

In recent years the free-will defense has dominated the philosophical discussion of the problem of evil. Alvin Plantinga and a number of other Christian philosophers have made a major effort to show that it is logically *possible* that a limitlessly powerful and limitlessly good God is responsible for the existence of this world and that all evil may ultimately result from misuses of creaturely freedom. But, they add, it may nevertheless be better for God to have created free than unfree beings; and it is logically possible that any and all free beings whom God might create would, as a matter of contingent fact, misuse their freedom by falling into sin. In that case it would be logically *impossible* for God to have created a world containing free beings and yet not containing sin and the suffering that sin brings with it. Thus it is logically possible, despite the fact of evil, that the existing universe is the work of a limitlessly good creator.

These writers are in effect arguing that the traditional Augustinian type of theodicy, based upon the fall from grace of free finite creatures—first angels and then human beings—and a consequent going wrong of the physical world, is not logically impossible. I am in fact doubtful whether their argument is sound, and I will return to the question later. But even if the Augustinian approach is sound, I suggest that their argument wins only a Pyrrhic victory, since the logical possibility that it would establish is one that, for very many people today, is fatally lacking in plausibility. Most educated inhabitants of the modern world regard the biblical story of Adam and Eve, and their temptation by the devil, as myth rather than as history; they believe further that far from having been created finitely perfect and then falling, humanity evolved out of lower forms of life, emerging in a morally, spiritually, and culturally primitive state. Further, they reject as incredible the idea that earthquake and flood, disease, decay, and death are consequences either of the human fall or of a prior fall of angelic beings who are now exerting an evil influence upon the earth. They see all this as part of a prescientific worldview, along with such stories as the world having been created in six days and of the sun standing still for twenty-four hours at Joshua's command. One cannot, strictly speaking, disprove any of these ancient biblical myths and sagas, or refute their elaboration in the medieval Christian picture of the universe. But people for whom the resulting theodicy, even if logically possible, is radically implausible, must look elsewhere for light on the problem of evil.

I believe that we find the light that we need in the main alternative strand of Christian thinking, which goes back to important constructive suggestions by the early Hellenistic Fathers of the church, particularly St. Irenaeus (120–202 A.D.). Irenaeus himself did not develop a theodicy, but he did— together with other Greek-speaking Christian writers of that period, such as Clement of Alexandria—build a framework of thought within which a theodicy becomes possible that does not depend upon the idea of the fall, and which is consonant with modern knowledge concerning the origins of the human race. This theodicy cannot, as such, be attributed to Irenaeus. We should rather speak of a type of theodicy, presented in varying ways by different subsequent thinkers (the greatest of whom has been Friedrich Schleiermacher), of which Irenaeus can properly be regarded as the patron saint.

The central theme out of which this Irenaean type of theodicy has arisen is the two-stage conception of the creation of humankind, first in the "image" and then in the "likeness" of God. Re-expressing this concept in modern terms, the first stage was the gradual production of *homo sapiens*, through the long evolutionary process, as intelligent ethical and religious animals. The human being is one of the varied forms of earthly life and continuous as such with the whole realm of animal existence. But a human is uniquely intelligent, having evolved a large and immensely complex brain. Further, humans are ethical— that is, gregarious as well as intelligent animals, able to realize and respond to the complex demands of social life. They are also religious animals, with an innate tendency to experience the world in terms of the presence and activity of supernatural beings and powers. This portrayal, then, is early *homo sapiens*, the intelligent social animal capable of awareness of the divine. But early *homo sapiens* does not include the Adam and Eve of Augustinian theology, living in perfect harmony with self, with nature, and with God. On the contrary, the life of early *homo sapiens* must have been a constant struggle against a hostile environment, necessitating the capacity for savage violence against their fellow human beings, particularly outside their own immediate group. This being's concepts of the divine were primitive and often bloodthirsty. Existence "in the image of God" was thus a *potentiality* for knowledge of and relationship with one's Maker, rather than such knowledge and relationship as a fully realized state. In other words, people were created as spiritually and morally immature creatures, at the beginning of a long process of further growth and development, which constitutes the second stage of God's creative work.

In this second stage, of which we are a part, intelligent, ethical, and religious animals are being brought through their own free responses into what Irenaeus called the divine "likeness." Irenaeus's own terminology *(eikon, homoiosis; imago, similitudo)* has no particular merit, based as it is on a misunderstanding of the Hebrew parallelism in Genesis 1:26, but his conception of a two-stage creation of humanity, with perfection lying in the future rather than in the past, is of fundamental importance.

The notion of the Fall was not basic to this picture, although it later became basic to the great drama of salvation depicted by St. Augustine and accepted within Western Christendom, including the churches stemming from the Reformation, until well into the nineteenth century. Irenaeus himself could not, however, in the historical knowledge of his time, question the fact of the Fall, though he treated it as a relatively minor lapse—a youthful error—rather than as the infinite crime and cosmic disaster that has ruined the whole creation. But today we can acknowledge that no evidence at all exists of a period in the distant past when humankind was in the ideal state of a fully realized "child of God." We can accept that, so far as actual events in time are concerned, a fall from an original righteousness and grace never occurred. If we want to continue to use the term "fall," because of its hallowed place in the Christian tradition, we must use it to refer to the immense gap between what we actually are and what in the divine intention we are eventually to become. But we must not blur our awareness that the ideal state is not something already enjoyed and lost, but is a future and as-yet-unrealized goal. The reality is not a perfect creation that has gone tragically wrong, but a still continuing creative process whose completion lies in the eschaton.

Let us now try to formulate a contemporary version of the Irenaean type of theodicy, based on this suggestion of the initial creation of humankind, not as finitely perfect, but as an immature creature at the beginning of a long process of further growth and development. We may begin by asking why humanity should have been created as an imperfect and developing creature rather than as the perfect being whom God is intending to create. The answer, I think, consists in two considerations that converge in their practical implications, one concerned with our relationship to God and the other with our relationship to other human beings. As to the first, we could have the picture of God creating finite beings, whether angels or humans, directly in the divine presence, so that in being conscious of that which is other than oneself the creature is automatically conscious of God, the limitless reality and power, goodness and love, knowledge and wisdom, towering above oneself. In such a situation the disproportion between Creator and creatures would be so great that the latter would have no freedom in relation to God; they would indeed not exist as independent autonomous persons. For what freedom could finite beings have in an immediate consciousness of the presence of the one who has created them, who knows them through and through, who is limitlessly powerful as well as limitlessly loving and good, and who claims their total obedience? In order to be a person, exercising some measure of genuine freedom, the creature must be brought into existence, not in the immediate divine presence, but at a "distance" from God. This "distance" cannot of course be spatial, for God is omnipresent. The distance must be epistemic, a distance in the cognitive dimension. And the Irenaean hypothesis is that this "distance" consists, in the case of humans, in their existence within and as part of a world that functions as an autonomous system and from within which God is not overwhelmingly evident. The world exists, in Bonhoeffer's phrase, *etsi deus non daretur*, as if there were no God. Or rather, the world is religiously ambiguous, capable of being seen either as a purely natural phenomenon or as God's creation and experienced as mediating his presence. In such a world one can exist as a person over against the Creator. One has space to exist as a finite being, a space created by this epistemic distance from God and protected by one's basic cognitive freedom, one's freedom to open or close oneself to the dawning awareness of God that is experienced naturally by a religious animal. This Irenaean picture corresponds, I suggest, to our actual human situation. Emerging within the evolutionary process as part of the continuum of animal life, in a universe that functions in accordance with its own laws and whose workings can be investigated and described without reference to a creator, the human being has a genuine, even awesome, freedom in relation to one's Maker. We are free to acknowledge and worship God, and free—particularly since the emergence of individuality and the beginnings of critical consciousness during the first millennium B.C.—to doubt the reality of God.

Within such a situation the possibility enters of human beings coming freely to know and love their Maker. Indeed, if the end-state that God is seeking to bring about is one in which finite persons have come in their own freedom to know and love him, this condition requires their initial creation in a state which is not that of already knowing and loving him (or her). To create beings already in a state of having come into that state by their own free choices is logically impossible. The other consideration, which converges with this in pointing to something like the human situation as we experience it, concerns our human moral nature. We can approach it by asking why humans should not have been created at this epistemic distance from God, and yet at the same time as morally perfect beings. That persons could have been created morally perfect and yet free, so that they would always in fact choose rightly, has been argued by such critics of the free-will defense as Antony Flew and J. L. Mackie, and argued against by Alvin Plantinga and other upholders of that theodicy. On the specific issue defined in the debate between them, it appears to me that the criticism of the free-will defense stands, that a perfectly good being, although formally free to sin, would in fact never do so. If we imagine such beings in a morally frictionless environment, involving no stresses or temptation, then we must assume that they would exemplify the ethical equivalent of Newton's first law of motion, which states that a moving body will continue in uniform motion until interfered with by some outside force. By analogy, perfectly good beings would continue in the same moral course forever, with nothing in the environment to throw them off it. And even if we suppose morally perfect beings to exist in an imperfect world, in which they are subject to temptations, it still follows that, in virtue of their moral perfection, they will always overcome those temptations—as in the case, according to orthodox Christian belief, of Jesus Crist. It is, to be sure, logically possible, as Plantinga and others argue, that a free being, simply as such, may at any time contingently decide to sin. However, a responsible free being does not act randomly, but on the basis of a moral nature, and a free being whose nature is wholly and unqualifiedly good will accordingly never in fact sin.

But if God could, without logical contradiction, have created humans as wholly good, free beings, why did God not do so? Why was humanity not initially created in possession of all the virtues, instead of having to acquire them through the long, hard struggle of life as we know it? The answer, I suggest, appeals to the principle that virtues that have been formed within the agent as a hard-won deposit of right decisions in situations of challenge and temptation are intrinsically more valuable than ready-made virtues created within her without any effort on her own part. This principle expresses a basic value judgment that cannot be established by argument but which one can only present, in the hope that it will be as morally plausible, and indeed compelling, to others as to oneself. It is, to repeat, the judgment that a moral goodness that exists as the agent's initial given nature, without ever having been chosen in the face of temptations to the contrary, is intrinsically less valuable than a moral goodness that has been built up over time through the agent's own responsible choices in the face of alternative possibilities.

If, then, God's purpose was to create finite persons embodying the most valuable kind of moral goodness, he (or she) would have to create them, not as already perfect beings but rather as imperfect creatures, who can then attain to the more valuable kind of goodness through their own free choices. In the course of their personal and social history new responses would prompt new insights, opening up new moral possibilities and providing a milieu in which the most valuable kind of moral nature can be developed.

We have thus far, then, the hypothesis that humanity is created at an epistemic distance from God in order to come freely to know and love their Maker; and that they are at the same time created as morally immature and imperfect beings in order to attain through freedom the most valuable quality of goodness. The end sought, according to this hypothesis, is the full realization of human potential in a spiritual and moral perfection within the divine kingdom. The question we have to ask is whether humans as we know them, and the world as we know it, fit the hypothesis.

Clearly we cannot expect to be able to deduce our actual world in its concrete character, and our actual human nature as part of it, from the general concept of spiritually and morally immature creatures developing ethically in an appropriate environment. No doubt an immense range of worlds is possible, any one of which, if actualized, would exemplify this concept. All that we can hope to do is to show that our actual world is one of these. And when we look at our human situation as part of the evolving life on this planet we can, I think, see that it fits this specification. As animal organisms, integral to the whole ecology of life, we are programmed for survival. In pursuit of survival, primitives not only killed other animals for food but fought other humans when their vital interests conflicted. The life of prehistoric persons must often have been a constant struggle to stay alive, prolonging an existence that was, in Hobbes's phrase, "poor, nasty, brutish and short." And in his basic animal self-regardingness, humankind was and is morally imperfect. In making this statement I am assuming that the essence of moral evil is selfishness, the sacrificing of others to one's own interests. It consists, in Kantian terminology, in treating others, not as ends in themselves, but as means to one's own ends, as the survival instinct demands. Yet we are also capable of love, of selfgiving in a common cause, of a conscience that responds to others in their needs and dangers. And with the development of civilization we see the growth of moral insight, the glimpsing and gradual assimilation of higher ideals, and tension between our animality and our ethical values. But that the human being has a lower as well as a higher nature, that one is an animal as well as a potential child of God, and that one's moral goodness is won through a struggle with innate selfishness, are inevitable given our continuity with the other forms of animal life. Further, the human animal is not responsible for having come into existence as an animal. The ultimate responsibility for humankind's existence, as a morally imperfect creature, can only rest with the Creator. We do not, in our degree of freedom and responsibility, choose our origin, but rather our destiny.

In brief outline, then, this line of thought is the Irenaean theodicy's answer to the question of the origin of moral evil: the general fact of humankind's basic self-regarding animality is an aspect of our creation as part of the realm of organic life, and this basic self-regardingness has been expressed over the centuries both in sins of individual selfishness and in the much more massive sins of corporate selfishness, institutionalized in slavery, exploitation, and all the many and complex forms of social injustice.

But nevertheless our sinful nature in an often harsh world is the matrix within which God is gradually creating children out of human animals. For as men and women freely respond to the claim of God upon their lives, transmuting their animal nature into that of children of God, the creation of humanity is taking place. In its concrete character this response consists in every form of moral goodness, from unselfish love in individual personal relationships to the dedicated and selfless striving to end exploitation and to create justice within and between societies.

But one cannot discuss moral evil without at the same time discussing the nonmoral evil of pain and suffering. (I propose to mean by "pain" physical pain, including the pains of hunger and thirst; and by "suffering" the mental and emotional pain of loneliness, anxiety, remorse, lack of love, fear, grief, envy, etc.) For what constitutes moral evil as evil is the fact that it causes pain and suffering. Conceiving of an instance of moral evil, or sin, that is not productive of pain or suffering to anyone at any time is impossible. But in addition to moral evil, another source of pain and suffering is present in the structure of the physical world, producing storms, earthquakes, and floods and afflicting the human body with diseases—cholera, epilepsy, cancer, malaria, arthritis, rickets, meningitis, AIDS, etc.—as well as with broken bones and other outcomes of physical accident. A great deal of both pain and suffering is humanly caused, not only by the inhumanity of man to man but also by the stresses of our individual and corporate lifestyles, causing many disorders—not only lung cancer and cirrhosis of the liver but many cases of heart disease, stomach and other ulcers, strokes, etc. But nevertheless, in the natural world itself, permanent causes of human pain and suffering remain. We have to ask why an unlimitedly good and unlimitedly powerful God should have created so dangerous a world, both in its purely natural hazards of earthquake and flood, for example, and in the liability of the human body to so many ills, both psychosomatic and purely somatic.

The answer offered by the Irenaean type of theodicy follows from and is indeed integrally bound up with its account of the origin of moral evil. We have the hypothesis of humankind being brought into being within the evolutionary process as a spiritually and morally immature creature, and then growing and developing through the exercise of freedom in this religiously ambiguous world. We can now ask what sort of a world would constitute an appropriate environment for this second stage of creation? The development of human personality—moral, spiritual, and intellectual—is a product of challenge and response that could not occur in a static situation demanding no exertion and no choices. So far as intellectual development is concerned, this well-established principle underlies the whole modern educational process, from preschool nurseries designed to provide a rich and stimulating environment to all forms of higher education designed to challenge the intellect. At a basic level the essential part played by the learner's own active response to environment was strikingly demonstrated by the Held and Heim experiment with kittens.[1] Of two littermate kittens in the same artificial environment, one was free to exercise its own freedom and intelligence in exploring the environment, while the other was suspended in a kind of gondola that moved whenever and wherever the free kitten moved. Thus, the second kitten had a similar succession of visual experiences as the first, but did not exert itself or make any choices in obtaining them. And whereas the first kitten learned in the normal way to conduct itself safely within its environment, the second did not. With no interaction with a challenging environment its capacities did not develop. I think we can safely say that the intellectual development of humanity has been due to interaction with an objective environment functioning in accordance with its own laws, an environment that we have to explore actively and cooperate with actively in order to escape its perils and exploit its benefits. In a world devoid both of dangers to be avoided and rewards to be won, we may assume that virtually no development of the human intellect and imagination would have taken place, and hence no development of the sciences, the arts, human civilization, or culture.

The presence of an objective world—within which we have to learn to live on penalty of pain or death—is also basic to the development of our moral nature. For because the world is one in which men and women can suffer harm—by violence, disease, accident, starvation, etc.—our actions affecting one another have moral significance. A morally wrong act is, basically, one that harms some part of the human community, while a morally right action is, on the contrary, one that prevents or neutralizes harm or that preserves or increases human well-being.

We can imagine a paradise in which no one can ever come to any harm. Instead of having its own fixed structure, the world would be plastic to human wishes. Or perhaps the world would have a fixed structure, and hence the possibility of damage and pain, but a structure that is whenever necessary suspended or adjusted by special divine action to avoid human pain. Thus, for example, in such a miraculously pain-free world, one who falls accidentally off a high building would presumably float unharmed to the ground; bullets would become insubstantial when fired at a human body; poisons would cease to poison; water to drown, and so on. We can at least begin to imagine such a world. A good deal of the older discussion of the problem of evil—for example, in Part XI of Hume's *Dialogues Concerning Natural Religion*—assumed that it must be the intention of a limitlessly good and powerful Creator to make a pain-free environment for human creatures, so that the very existence of pain is evidence against the existence of God. But such an assumption overlooks the fact that a world in which there can be no pain or suffering would also be one without moral choices and hence no possibility of moral growth and development. For in a situation in which no one can ever suffer injury or be liable to pain or suffering, no distinction would exist between right and wrong action. No action would be morally wrong, because no action could ever have harmful consequences; likewise, no action would be morally right in contrast to wrong. Whatever the values of such a world, its structure would not serve the purpose of allowing its inhabitants to develop from self-regarding animality to self-giving love.

Thus, the hypothesis of a divine purpose in which finite persons are created at an epistemic distance from God, in order that they may gradually become children of God through their own moral and spiritual choices, requires that their environment, instead of being a pain-free and stress-free paradise, be broadly the kind of world of which we find ourselves to be a part, a world that provokes the theological problem of evil. Such a world requires an environment that offers challenges to be met, problems to be solved, and dangers to be faced, and which accordingly involves real possibilities of hardship, disaster, failure, defeat, and misery as well as of delight and happiness, success, triumph, and achievement. By grappling with the real problems of a real environment—in which a person is one form of life among many, and which is not designed to minister exclusively to our well-being—people can develop in intelligence and in such qualities as courage and determination. In relationships with one another, in the context of this struggle to survive and flourish, humans can develop the higher values of mutual love and care, self-sacrifice for others, and commitment to a common good.

However, this condition will not apply to the rest of the animal kingdom, whose members are not undergoing moral and spiritual development. From our human point of view the teeming multitude of life-forms, each nourishing and nourished by others in a continuous recycling of life, constitutes the vast evolutionary process within which humanity has emerged; the fact that we are part of this ever-changing natural order is an aspect of our epistemic distance from God that we noted earlier. But if we ask why so many animals are carnivorous rather than vegetarian, killing and eating other species, no evident answer is available. We can note that the lower animals live almost entirely in the immediate present, unaware of their mortality, and without anxiety for the future or painful memories of the past—except, it would seem, for some individuals that have been in varying degrees adopted and domesticated by humans. But caution is in order. As the psychologists Eugene d'Aquili and Andrew Newberg say, "While it is difficult to determine with any certainty the emotions of animals, it seems that they must have some type of value response that tells them what to avoid and what to be drawn to. Whether these responses imply the emotions of fear and love as humans know them is, however, difficult to discern. . . . Suffice it to say that all animals must at least be able to derive an operational value from their experiences even if there is no emotional response similar in form to that of human beings."[2] Anthropomorphizing is easy here, and yet on the other hand it seems safer to risk erring on that side rather than the other; in any case the question mark about emotion does not lessen the immediately felt physical pain that takes place all the time. One can only say that pain is an aspect of the process of biological evolution as it has actually occurred, and is to us part of the same mysterious totality as earthquakes, volcanic eruptions, storms, hurricanes, and tidal waves. The very fact that it is mysterious may, however, itself have value. We shall come presently to the positive role of mystery, according to the Irenaean theodicy.

To summarize thus far:

(1) The divine intention in relation to humankind, according to our hypothesis, is to create perfect finite personal beings in filial relationship with their Maker.

(2) For humans to be created already in this perfect state is logically impossible, because in its spiritual aspect it involves coming freely to an uncoerced consciousness of God from a situation of epistemic distance, and in its moral aspect, freely choosing the good.

(3) Accordingly, the human being was initially created through the evolutionary process, as a spiritually and morally immature creature, and as part of a religiously ambiguous and ethically demanding world.

(4) Thus, that one is morally imperfect (i.e., that there is moral evil), and that the world is a challenging and even dangerous environment (i.e., that there is natural evil), are necessary aspects of the present stage of the process through which God is gradually creating perfected finite persons.

In terms of this hypothesis, as we have developed it thus far, then, both the basic moral evil in the human heart and the natural evils of the world are compatible with the existence of a Creator who is unlimited in both goodness and power. But is the hypothesis plausible as well as possible? The principal threat to its plausibility comes, I think, from the sheer amount and intensity of both moral and natural evil. One can readily accept the principle that in order to arrive at a freely chosen goodness one must start out in a state of moral immaturity and imperfection. But are the depths of demonic malice and cruelty that each generation has experienced necessary, such as we have seen above all in the twentieth century in the Nazi attempt to exterminate the Jewish population of Europe? Can any future fulfillment be worth such horrors? Consider Dostoyevsky's haunting question: "Imagine that you are creating a fabric of human destiny with the object of making men happy in the end, giving them peace and rest at last, but that it was essential and inevitable to torture to death only one tiny creature—that baby beating its breast with its fist, for instance—and to found that edifice on its unavenged tears, would you consent to be the architect on those conditions?"[3] The theistic answer is one that may be true but which takes so large a view that it baffles the imagination. Intellectually one may be able to see, but emotionally one cannot be expected to feel, its truth; and in that sense it cannot satisfy us. For the theistic answer is that if we take with full seriousness the value of human freedom and responsibility, as essential to the eventual creation of perfected children of God, then we cannot consistently want God to revoke that freedom when its wrong exercise becomes intolerable to us. From our vantage point within the historical process, we may indeed cry out to God to revoke his gift of freedom, or to overrule it by some secret or open intervention. Such a cry must have come from millions caught in the Jewish Holocaust, and in the more recent laying waste of Korea, Vietnam, Rwanda, and Kosovo, and from the victims of racism in many parts of the world. And the thought that humankind's moral freedom is indivisible and can lead eventually to a consummation of limitless value which could never be attained without that freedom, and which is worth any finite suffering in the course of its creation, can be of no comfort to those who are now in the midst of that suffering. But while fully acknowledging this, I nevertheless want to insist that this eschatological answer may well be true. Expressed in religious language it tells us to trust in God even in the midst of deep suffering, for in the end we shall participate in the divine kingdom.

Again, we may grant that a world that is to be a person-making environment cannot be a pain-free paradise but must contain challenges and dangers, with real possibilities of many kinds of accident and disaster, and the pain and suffering which they bring. But need it contain the worst forms of disease and catastrophe? And need misfortune fall upon us with such heartbreaking indiscriminateness? Once again some answers may well be true, but truth in this area may nevertheless offer little in the way of pastoral balm.

We can see that a pain-free paradise would not constitute a person-making environment. But we cannot profess to see that the world's actual pains are just the amount needed and no more. However, at this point we meet the paradox that if we *could* see that, then the world would no longer serve a person-making purpose! For if we were right earlier in concluding that such a purpose requires a religiously ambiguous world, in which God is not evident, then God's purpose for the world must not be evident within it. That the world is as it is must be to us a mystery which, according to the Irenaean theodicy, is itself an essential aspect of its person-making character.

But one of the most daunting and even terrifying features of the world is that calamity strikes indiscriminately. In the incidence of disease, accident, disaster, and tragedy, no justice can be found. The righteous as well as the unrighteous are alike struck down by illness and afflicted by misfortune. There is no security in goodness, for the good are as likely as the wicked to suffer "the slings and arrows of outrageous fortune." From the time of Job this fact has set a glaring question mark against the goodness of God. But let us suppose that things were otherwise. Let us suppose that, misfortune came upon humankind, not haphazardly and therefore unjustly, but justly and therefore not haphazardly. Let us suppose that, instead of coming without regard to moral considerations, misfortune was proportioned to desert, so that the sinner was punished and the virtuous rewarded. Would such a dispensation serve a person-making purpose? Surely not. For wrong deeds would obviously bring disaster upon the agent while good deeds would bring health and prosperity. In such a world truly moral action, action done because it is right, would be impossible. The fact that natural evil is not morally directed, but is a hazard that comes by chance, is thus an intrinsic feature of a person-making world.

In other words, the very mystery of natural evil, the very fact that disasters afflict human beings in contingent, undirected and haphazard ways, is itself a necessary feature of a world that calls forth mutual aid and builds up mutual caring and love. Thus on the one hand to say that God sends misfortune upon individuals, so that their death, maiming, starvation, or ruin is God's will for them would be completely wrong. But on the other hand God has set us in a world containing unpredictable contingencies and dangers—in which unexpected and undeserved calamities may occur to anyone—because only in such a world can mutual caring and love be elicited. As an abstract philosophical hypothesis, this may offer little comfort. But translated into religious language it tells us that God's good purpose enfolds the entire process of this world, with all its good and bad contingencies, and that even amidst tragic calamity and suffering we are still within the sphere of God's love and are moving towards the divine kingdom.

But there is one further all-important aspect of the Irenaean type of theodicy, without which all the foregoing would lose its plausibility. This is the eschatological aspect. Our hypothesis depicts persons as still in the course of creation towards an end-state of perfected personal community in the divine kingdom. This end-state is conceived of as one in which individual egoity has been transcended in communal unity before God. In the present phase of that creative process the naturally self-centered human animal has the opportunity freely to respond to God's noncoercive self-disclosures, through the work of prophets and saints, through the resulting religious traditions, and through the individual's religious experience. Such response always has an ethical aspect; the growing awareness of God is at the same time a growing awareness of the moral claim that God's presence makes upon the way in which we live.

This person-making process, leading eventually to perfect human community, is obviously not completed on this earth. It is not completed in the life of the individual—or at best only in the few who have attained sanctification, or *moksha*, or nirvana on this earth. Clearly the enormous majority of men and women die without reaching such levels. As Eric Fromm has said, "The tragedy in the life of most of us is that we die before we are fully born."[4] Therefore if we are ever to reach the full realization of the potentialities of our human nature, this fulfillment can only come in a continuation of our lives in another sphere of existence after bodily death. The perfect all-embracing human community, in which self-regarding concern has been transcended in mutual love, not only has evidently not been realized in this world, but never can be, since hundreds of generations of human beings have already lived and died and accordingly could not be part of any ideal community established at some future moment of earthly history. Thus if the unity of humankind in God's presence is ever to be realized it will have to be in some sphere of existence other than our earth. In short, the fulfillment of the divine purpose, as it is postulated in the Irenaean type of theodicy, presupposes each person's survival, in some form, of bodily death, and further living and growing towards that end-state. Without such an eschatological fulfillment, this theodicy would collapse.

A theodicy that presupposes and requires an eschatology will thereby be rendered implausible in the minds of many people today. The belief, however, in the reality of a limitlessly loving and powerful deity must incorporate some kind of eschatology according to which God holds in being the creatures whom he has made for fellowship with God, beyond bodily death, and brings them into the eternal fellowship that he has intended for them.[5] I have tried elsewhere to argue that such an eschatology is a necessary corollary of ethical monotheism; to argue for the realistic possibility of an after-life or lives, despite the philosophical and empirical arguments against this; and even to spell out some of the general features that human life after death may possibly have.[6] Since this task is very large, far exceeding the bounds of this paper, I shall not attempt to repeat it here but must refer the reader to my existing discussion of it. That extended discussion constitutes my answer to the question of whether an Irenaean theodicy, with its eschatology, is not as implausible as an Augustinian theodicy, with its human or angelic fall. (If the Irenaean theodicy is implausible, then the latter is doubly implausible; for it also involves an eschatology!)

One particular aspect of eschatology, however, must receive some treatment here, however brief and inadequate: the issue of "universal salvation" versus "heaven and hell" (or perhaps "annihilation" instead of "hell"). If the justification of evil within the creative process lies in the limitless and eternal good of the end-state to which it leads, then the completeness of the justification must depend upon the completeness, or universality, of the salvation achieved. Only if it includes the entire human race can it justify the sins and sufferings of the entire human race throughout all history. But, having given us cognitive freedom, which in turn makes moral freedom possible, can the Creator bring it about that in the end all will freely turn to him in love and trust? The issue is very difficult, but I believe that reconciling a full affirmation of human freedom with a belief in the ultimate universal success of God's creative work is in fact possible. We have to accept that creaturely freedom always occurs within the limits of a basic nature that we did not ourselves choose, as is entailed by the fact of having been created. If a real though limited freedom does not preclude our being endowed with a certain nature, it also does not preclude our being endowed with a basic Godward bias, so that, quoting from another side of St. Augustine's thought, "our hearts are restless until they find their rest in Thee."[7] If Augustine is correct, sooner or later, in our own time and in our own way, we shall all freely come to God; and universal salvation can be affirmed, not as a logical necessity but as the contingent but predictable outcome of the process of the universe, interpreted theistically. Once again, I have tried to present this argument more fully elsewhere, and to consider various objections to it.[8]

On this view the human, endowed with a real though limited freedom, is basically formed for relationship with God and destined ultimately to find the fulfillment of his or her nature in that relationship. This outlook does not seem to me excessively paradoxical. On the contrary, given the theistic postulate, this view seems to offer a very probable account of our human situation. If so, we can rejoice, for this situation gives meaning to our temporal existence as the long process through which we are being created, by our own free responses to life's mixture of good and evil, into "children of God" who "inherit eternal life."

CRITIQUE BY DAVID RAY GRIFFIN

I begin my response to Hick by emphasizing my agreement with his formal statements about theodicy. The task, as he says, is to construct a hypothesis about the nature of the universe, a hypothesis that, besides being (1) consistent with the data of the religious tradition it represents, is also (2) *plausible*, which means that it must be internally coherent, consistent with the world's moral and natural evil, and consistent with the world's character as known through scientific enquiry. Given the state of philosophy of religion today, this formal agreement is no small matter.

Otherwise, however, I must confess to being disappointed that, although Hick's position has changed more radically than that of any of the other contributors to the first edition of this book, his essay for this edition is, aside from a few additions, simply a reissue of his earlier one. This is especially problematic in light of the fact that in the meantime Hick has produced a new idea of Ultimate Reality that relativizes the idea of God contained in his earlier work. If we call the earlier position $Hick_1$ and the later position $Hick_2$, the question is: After we have read $Hick_2$, how can we be expected to take $Hick_1$ seriously?

According to the somewhat Kantian hypothesis suggested by $Hick_2$, the ideas of deity in the various religions are various phenomenal manifestations of Ultimate Reality, which he calls the Real, about which we can say little. "[T]he Real *an sich*," says $Hick_2$, "cannot be said to be one or many, person or thing, substance or process, good or evil, purposive or non-purposive."[9] Although some purely *formal* properties, such as "being a reference of a term" and "being that than which no greater can be conceived," can be attributed to the Real, we cannot apply *substantial* properties, such as "being good," "being powerful," and "having knowledge."[10] Accordingly, although the theodicy offered by $Hick_1$ was based on the idea of "a limitlessly good and limitlessly powerful Being," $Hick_2$ has said that this idea of God refers only to a phenomenal manifestation of an Ultimate Reality that in itself (*an sich*) cannot be said to be "good," "powerful," or even—since it cannot be said to be "one"— "a Being." $Hick_2$ has thereby said, in effect, that the theodicy offered by $Hick_1$ can no longer be taken as a plausible account of what is really going on in the universe. Indeed, $Hick_2$ has explicitly said that his earlier theodicy, with its language of "a personal being carrying out intentions through time," must be considered "mythological" because such language "cannot apply to the ultimate transcendent Reality in itself."[11] It is difficult to know, therefore, what point there would be in discussing that theodicy one more time (I have critiques in *God, Power, and Evil* and *Evil Revisited* as well as the first edition of this book). What I am calling for is the emergence of $Hick_3$, who will tell us how we are to understand the relation between $Hick_1$ and $Hick_2$.

Perhaps $Hick_3$ will say that, although we cannot *know* this, it is *possible* that one of the phenomenal manifestations of the Real corresponds to it more closely than the others—and that this may be true of the picture painted by $Hick_1$. This move would require him, however, to reject the gnostic version of Kantianism articulated by $Hick_2$, according to which one claims to *know* that personalistic language cannot apply to Ultimate Reality in itself, in favor of an agnostic Kantianism, which simply says that we cannot know whether it does or not.

If this line were to be taken by Hick$_3$, then I would like him to answer some questions about the theodicy republished here. For one thing, in my prior critique, I pointed out, as I did again in my essay for this edition, that the granting of freedom to human beings by this theodicy's God is arguably selfish, because this God is the only one who derives any real benefit from it. The omnipotent creator accepted by Hick$_1$ could have programmed us always to do good while giving us the illusion that we were doing so freely. Only God would know otherwise. The sole reason not to do so is God's wish to have the satisfaction of knowing that when we obey God, we do so *freely*. Hick previously replied that such deception would imply a moral limitation in God. But Hick$_1$'s entire theodicy, insofar as it is oriented around the idea that the divine being deliberately put "epistemic distance" between itself and human beings, involves deception by making the world seem "as if there were no God." Why is this deception, which has resulted in most of the evils of human history, acceptable, whereas the deception about freedom, through which all those evils could have been avoided, would be unacceptable?

I do agree, to be sure, than any kind of deception would be morally problematic. The deeper problem with the theodicy of Hick$_1$ is that it must even face the question of which kind would be worse. The deeper problem, in other words, is its idea of divine omnipotence, according to which every general feature of our world is arbitrary in the sense of being freely chosen by the divine will. Hick$_1$ criticized the Augustinian theodicy for being "implausible" in light of our evolutionary picture of the world. But the evolutionary account of the origin of our world renders implausible not merely the idea of an early "fall from perfection" but the very idea of a supernatural creator who could have chosen to create a world similar to ours in some way other than an evolutionary process taking billions of years, who could have chosen to make such a world far less dangerous, and who now could choose occasionally to suspend its causal structure. Given the fact that Hick$_1$'s neo-Irenaean theodicy presupposes this idea no less fully than does Davis's neo-Augustinian theodicy, I cannot regard it as much more plausible. I wonder what Hick thinks nowadays.

Another respect in which I was disappointed by Hick's decision simply to reissue his earlier essay is that he has thereby republished his early view that what he calls the Augustinian and Irenaean approaches are the only two types of theodicy within Christian thought worth serious attention. This narrowness reflected the deep-seated conviction of Hick$_1$ that the Christian God has the kind of power implied by the doctrine of *creatio ex nihilo*. "To solve the problem of evil by means of the theory . . . of a finite deity who does the best he can with a material, intractable and coeternal with himself," said young

Hick, "is to have abandoned the basic premise of Hebrew-Christian monotheism."[12] Given this view, which led him to call any theology that denies the infinite power of God "sub-Christian,"[13] he was unable to take seriously the possibility that process theism, with its doctrine of creation out of chaos, could provide a viable theodicy for Christians. Shortly after the publication of the first edition of the present book, however, he included in a new edition of his *Philosophy of Religion* a section on "process theodicy," calling it one of the "three main Christian responses to the problem of evil."[14] After this development, it was disappointing to have Hick, almost two decades later, seemingly endorse his earlier view that only those theodicies that accept the traditional doctrine of omnipotence can be taken seriously by Christianity and other biblically based religions.

I would think, in any case, that for two reasons Hick should now take this third option even more seriously than he did in the past. First, the emerging scholarly consensus, as reflected in my essay, is that insofar as there is a biblical doctrine of creation, it involves creation out of chaos, not creation out of absolute nothingness. This consensus is very different from that which existed when the position of Hick$_1$ was taking shape. Second, insofar as Christian, Jewish, and Islamic theologies come into harmony with the biblical doctrine on this issue, they will also be brought into harmony with virtually all the other religious cosmogonies of humanity. In light of Hick's admirable concern for a theodicy that is globally viable—which, although not addressed in the body of his essay, is reflected in his (new) note about Marilyn Adams's position—this point should not seem unimportant to him. Given the fact that the global theology suggested by Hick$_2$ has been widely considered problematic, perhaps Hick$_3$ could develop a more viable global theology on the idea of creation out of chaos?

To reinforce the need for some such Hick$_3$, I will point out one more problem in Hick$_2$, which involves the fact that while relegating his earlier doctrine of God to the category of the mythological, he has retained his earlier eschatology. In the interests of this eschatology, Hick$_2$ has opposed any view according to which language about ultimate reality is not intended to refer to something that exists independently of our thoughts and language about it. The ultimate problem with this nonrealist view, Hick$_2$ says, is that "it cannot credibly claim to represent the message of the great spiritual traditions," namely, their "ultimate optimism" that all human beings will eventually reach fulfillment.[15] His reason for this judgment is that those who reject the realist use of religious language fail to describe the nature of the universe in such a way as to make this fulfillment possible, because for such thinkers "God/Brahman/the Dharmakaya are human ideas, existing only *in mente*."[16]

Although this is true, the position of Hick$_2$ has the same consequence, because there is no significant difference between saying that the word "God" refers to nothing outside our imaginations and saying that it refers to something about which we can know absolutely nothing. If, as Hick$_2$ says, the properties of "having knowledge" and "being powerful" do not apply to the Real in itself, we have no basis for believing that there is an Ultimate Reality that knows what is going on and, even if it did, could do anything about it. And if it is not characterized by the property of "being good," we have no reason for assuming that it would be interested in bringing all sentient beings to fulfillment. It would seem, therefore, that Hick needs a theology of religious pluralism that is able to apply personal and causal language to our creator.

CRITIQUE BY D. Z. PHILLIPS

According to Augustine, human life is a fallen state, lived at an inevitable distance from God. John Hick wants to offer us an alternative: a theodicy, the seeds of which he finds in Irenaeus. God, he argues, created us as immature beings, so that we may participate in an evolutionary process towards our ultimate perfection. He regards the Augustinian view and his own as two large-scale hypotheses about the nature and process of the universe. He finds his own view more credible that the Augustinian alternative. I want to reject this conclusion for two reasons: first, Augustine's view is not a hypothesis; second, Hick's alternative contains insuperable conceptual difficulties.

In his criticism of Augustine's so-called hypothesis, Hick says that most people regard the story of Adam and Eve as a myth rather than as history. But if this is so, Hick ought to recognize that myth and history are separate *conceptual* categories. One may erode the other, but myth cannot be criticized as though it were poor history. But Hick does precisely that when he says that no historical evidence exists for the Fall in the distant past. Again, if Hick says that myth belongs to a prescientific age, he cannot criticize it as though it were a poor scientific hypothesis. These criticisms confuse the categories.

Augustine's myth of the Fall offers us, not a hypothesis, but a way of understanding human life as something that has imperfection at the heart of it. Secular thought often concurs with that aspect of it. Camus, in *The Plague*, reminds us of the foolishness of any modern city that thinks itself free of the possibility of plague. Camus regards as foolish the main alternative to Augustinianism since the Enlightenment, namely, the humanistic hope in the perfectibility of human beings. Humankind was said to go through necessary stages of development, each one being an advance on the preceding stage. Two world wars shattered this optimism. Optimistic humanism is as dead in our world as any ideology could be. I say "ideology" because this optimism was never a genuine hypothesis. Its pretension in attempting to be one involved a condescending attitude to so-called primitive peoples. Thus, rain dances, which celebrated the coming of rain, were regarded by many early anthropologists as understandable mistaken hypotheses about the causes of rainfall. At dawn, rites celebrated the coming of a new day. If we ask whether our conception of "a new day" has progressed, is the answer obvious? One cannot ask, free of any context, whether we have progressed. We must always ask, "Progressed with respect to what?"

Against this background, I find Hick's *general* evolutionary account of human progress a rather curious phenomenon. Wittgenstein said that if, despite dire circumstances, someone says, "I remain optimistic," he could admire the spirit of the remark. What he thought confused is any attempt to turn such optimism into some kind of theory or hypothesis. Hick has a two-stage account of human progress. At the end of the first stage, he tells us, humans have emerged, from a long evolutionary process, as creatures with an innate tendency to think of the world in supernatural terms. We can say that primitive peoples *did* wonder at the world. To say they *had* to is a philosophical superstition.

In the second stage of human progress, Hick argues, human beings evolve towards the divine likeness. If the evolutionary model is to be preserved, earlier generations must be regarded as the means to our progress. This assumption involves the instrumentalism that Roth and I find objectionable. There is a tension between it and the values in human relationships. Tennyson struggled with this tension in *In Memoriam*. Tennyson praises Hallam, his dead friend. He does not want to say that he could have had a better friend. In a vain attempt to reconcile this with evolution, he said that God had created Hallam before his time in the evolutionary process! Similar tensions appear in Hick. His evolutionary framework is hard to reconcile with his admiration for Kant's insistence that human beings should always be treated as ends, and never simply as means. The same tension necessitates Hick's assurance that evolution continues after death. The obvious failures of the process on earth need rectifying in the hereafter.

The presence of failures on earth brings us back to Roth's questions about the cost-effectiveness of God's plan. Hick asks whether it justifies the horrors we have witnessed. He does not see that the moral objection is not to the effectiveness of the plan, but to the very conception of it. As a result, he misses the point of Dostoyevsky's anti-utilitarian protest against such a plan. As Kierkegaard says in *Purity of Heart*, if the means in our actions are not as morally important as our ends, the heterogeneous means will flow in between in confusing and corrupting fashion. Thus, if my moral development is offered as the justification for the sufferings of others, such a justification leads towards, not away from, an egocentricity and self-centeredness which, according to Hick, religious belief is meant to transcend.

Hick's answer to evils, however horrendous, is to say that we should trust that everything will work out for the best after death. What "the ultimate end" is baffles our imagination. I cannot pursue, here, the formidable difficulty of treating death as though it were a state, like unconsciousness. I recommend Rush Rhees's "Death and Immortality" in his collection, *On Religion and Philosophy*. But I shall comment on what Hick does say about "the state" he envisions. The state is supposed to be perfect, or still on the way to it. He has defined "maturity," however, as making wise decisions when faced by inferior alternatives. Since such "decisions" and "inferior alternatives" make no sense "after death," a perfect state must, on Hick's terms, exclude maturity. I do not accept, for one moment, Hick's conception of maturity, since we frequently praise people for the fact that inferior alternatives, to which we are prone, do not even occur to them. But I am simply bringing out implications in Hick's terminology.

For Hick, life after death is perfected *human* life. To be that, it must be a matter of husbands, wives, parents, children, friends, lovers, etc., etc. I have seen no suggestion that the contexts in which these relationships have their sense—the family, for example—survive death. But these contexts are logically related to the possibility of what we mean by human life, and to the development Hick speaks of. Without them, one is left asking: "Development of *what*?" If the reply is: "It is different there," we ask: "Why should suffering here be regarded as necessary for something different there?" The conception of development, in any moral sense, would have to be jettisoned. I cannot *become* a better son after death unless I meet my mother, or *become* a better husband unless I meet my wife. But I cannot meet them, in Hick's sense, if the concepts of family and marriage have no application.

Perhaps such details are thought to be unimportant. "We'll survive," it may be said, "but we don't know how." This recourse to ignorance hides a conceptual bankruptcy. In Beckett's *Waiting for Godot*, one of the tramps, to relieve their boredom, says to the other, "Suppose we repented?" The other asks, "Repented what?" The first replies: "Oh . . . we wouldn't have to go into the details." But I'm afraid we do: details about "myth," "progress," "innate tendencies," "moral action," "moral development," "human life," and "survival after death." Details are not a matter of abstract logic, but a concern for the sense in our words, in our hopes and aspirations, in our fears and disappointments, and in the very lives we lead.

CRITIQUE BY STEPHEN T. DAVIS

Of the theodicies presented in this book (besides my own, of course) Hick's is the one with which I am in most sympathy. The main reason is that Hick (like me and unlike the others) tries to retain rational belief in "a limitlessly good and limitlessly powerful being."

Moreover, I agree with Hick on several other important points: that there is a sense in which God is ultimately responsible for the state of the world and a sense in which human beings are responsible for their own evil deeds; that human beings were created as free, morally neutral creatures in a religiously ambiguous world; that eschatology is crucial to theodicy; that moral values (and thus moral growth) could not exist without pain and suffering; and that in the midst of life's ambiguities and suffering, people must trust in God. In addition, I am persuaded by much that Hick says about natural evil.

However, I do have several reservations about Hick's theodicy, some of which are more important than others. Let me mention four.

(1) I accept that in this book Hick is writing as a Christian theologian and not a global theologian. He is trying to provide a theodicy largely for Christians, or at least a theodicy that makes Christian assumptions. But his own views on religious pluralism and religious experience have been developed in great detail since 1981, especially in *An Interpretation of Religion* (1989) and *The Fifth Dimension* (1999). One cannot help wondering whether his present theodicy is consistent with the theory suggested in those works, especially since in Hick's official view, all that we can literally know about the Real is that it exists and is the ground of human religious experience. I confess that in the light of that stance, I anticipated changes in Hick's theodicy, especially along the lines of some of its central claims being only metaphorically or phenomenally true. That is, I expected something like what Hick has already done in the area of christology, in his *The Metaphor of God Incarnate* (1993). I will leave it to Hick, in his response, to clear up the difficulty (if he wishes to do so).

(2) I am dubious about Hick's hope of a gradual spiritual evolution till human beings reach a full state of God-consciousness. Since I see no convincing evidence that the human race is improving morally or spiritually, I prefer to hope for a sudden spiritual revolution in the eschaton. Now I am not accusing Hick of nineteenth-century theological optimism; he knows that God's "person-making" process "is not completed on this earth." Most people only attain it after death, he says. But if people are as morally and spiritually free after death as they are now—as Hick claims—then the evidence of how people behave here and now does not give me much hope that the human race will gradually improve till all are the God-conscious "persons" God intended. My own view is that at a decisive point in history God will seize the initiative and will give those who say yes to him a new "heart of flesh" (Ezek. 11:19–20). God will, in short, suddenly transform us into "new persons."

(3) I believe Hick also faces what I call the "cost-effective" criticism of the free-will defense (see my main essay), and I am curious how he would answer

it. Perhaps, as he claims, virtues that are freely learned on one's own are intrinsically more valuable than virtues bestowed as a gift of God. But is this excess virtue worth the price we pay for it, i.e., the great evils in the world that human freedom has produced? Perhaps, also, given the physical and psychological laws at work in the world, free kittens and persons develop adaptive behavior patterns in our inimical world much more readily than unfree ones. But surely an omnipotent being is not bound by these laws. Surely such a being could have made us grow and learn in a much less painful, harsh, and destructive world.

(4) My final criticism of Hick concerns his commitment to universalism. By way of introduction to this point, I would like to call attention to Hick's requirement that, in order to be acceptable, a theodicy must be "consistent with the data . . . of the religious tradition on which it is based." I strongly agree with this. My complaint is that I do not believe universalism is consistent with the data of the Christian tradition. But before speaking further about universalism, let me briefly move to a related general question that I, as a theologically conservative Christian, would like to address not only to Hick but to other contributors to this book as well. My question is this: If fidelity to the teachings of the Bible and to the Christian religious tradition no longer plays the normative role it once did in developing theological propositions that are acceptable to Christians, what will play such a role?

Both from what they officially say and from what they presuppose, clearly none of my fellow contributors feels any strong need to be guided in theology by scripture or Christian tradition. They do not feel particularly bound in any normative sense to do theology either on the basis of the Protestant methodological principle of *sola scriptura* or the Catholic principle of "scripture and tradition." How then do we determine what is and what is not allowable in Christian theology? This question is serious. Can a person come up with any thesis, however bizarre, and push it on Christians? What if some future theologian says that the devil created God or that Jesus Christ was an astronaut from Tralfalmadore or even that God wants all redheaded people to move to Borneo? In an age of religious charlatans like Jim Jones (who reportedly told his followers, "I'm the nearest thing to God you'll ever see"), I would have thought we needed far more, not less, adherence to the Bible and to the Christian religious tradition. This, I believe, is our only epistemological protection against religious figures and theologians who stray from the truth.

Let me say a word about universalism and the Bible. The Bible does teach that it is God's will that everyone be saved (Rom. 11:32; 1 Tim. 2:4; 2 Peter 3:9) and that the work of God's grace in Christ was designed for the salvation of everyone (Titus 2:11; Heb. 2:9; 1 John 2:2). Pauline thought also includes the notion of God's ultimate victory and of the eventual reconciliation of everything to him (Rom. 8:19–21; 1 Cor. 15:22–28; 2 Cor. 5:19; Eph. 1:10, 20–23; Col. 1:19–20). But none of this implies universalism. Universalists say that a few texts explicitly predict the salvation of everyone (John 12:32; Rom. 5:18; Phil. 2:9–11). But on the assumption—which I am prepared to make—that Paul and the author of the Fourth Gospel do not blatantly contradict themselves, we can see that universalists fail to interpret these texts correctly, for these same biblical authors can also make the statements found in John 3:17–18, Romans 5:18–19, and 1 Timothy 4:10 (assuming 1 Timothy is Pauline). The first shows, contrary to the universalist's interpretation of the "all" passages in the Fourth Gospel, that the Son's being the savior of the world, whatever precisely it means, is quite consistent with some people being condemned. The second shows that Paul's doctrine that "all" are acquitted and have life, whatever precisely it means, does not entail universalism, for it can equally well be stated (as if in Hebrew parallelism) in terms of "many." And the third shows that the sense in which God is the savior of "all people" is not the same sense in which God is the savior of "those who believe." God is the savior of all, but he is *especially* the savior of those who believe.

Let me confess that I would like universalism to be true. I would find it comforting to believe that all people will be saved, and Hick may be correct that the problem of evil is less intractable for the universalist than for the nonuniversalist. (Although not meant as an argument against universalism, I know from my experience of teaching Hick's theodicy in Philosophy of Religion courses that not all people are attracted to universalism. I have found that many of my Jewish students, for example, reject Hick's theory on the grounds that "I don't want Hitler and the other Holocaust murderers to be present in heaven.") But as a matter of theological method, we cannot affirm a doctrine just because we would like it to be true. The plain teaching of scripture, I believe, is that some will be condemned to eternal separation from God (see, for example, Matthew 7:13, 12:32, 25:41; 2 Cor. 5:10; and 2 Thessalonians 1:8–9). And the reality of hell seems inextricably tied to such major themes in New Testament theology as God, sin, judgment, atonement, and reconciliation. That is enough for me, that is why I cannot affirm universalism.

But how can a just and good God condemn someone to eternal torment? In the first place, I do not believe hell is a place of torment or fire. New Testament metaphors that seem to suggest these characteristics of hell are merely metaphors. Indeed, many quite different metaphors for hell are found in the New Testament. For example, Mark 9:48 describes hell as a place where "their worm never dies" and "the fire is never quenched." Why take the second literally and not the first? I would say both are metaphors of the terrible nature and eternality of hell. Second, I believe the citizens of hell are there because they freely choose to be there. Unless one bows to God and makes God's will one's own, heaven is too much to bear and one chooses hell. Thus that God allows them to live forever in hell is not only just but loving. Third, hell may have the effect on many of hardening their resolve never to repent; sin may voluntarily continue; and if it is right for evil-doers to be punished for the evil deeds they do here and now, this will be true of the evil deeds they do after death. Fourth, Christians believe their salvation is a matter of sheer grace; we deserve to be condemned, but out of love rather than sheer justice God forgives us and reconciles us to God. If hell is inconsistent with God's love, then our salvation is not a matter of grace but rather is a matter of our justly being freed from a penalty we don't really deserve.

CRITIQUE BY JOHN K. ROTH

Three features of Hick's theodicy attract me. I concur with his emphasis on God's omnipotence. I share his belief that theodicies are doomed unless they include an eschatological dimension that points to personal life beyond death. I also agree that demonstrations of logical possibility take us hardly anywhere. Far more decisive is the degree to which a theodicy is plausible.

By Hick's reckoning, a theodicy's plausibility rises or falls to the extent that the theory fits facts. Unfortunately, even if one accepts that qualification, what is plausible to one person may be a snare and a delusion to another. No doubt John Hick has a possible theodicy. However, because I find it falling short by its own criterion, his perspective is not one that I can accept. In a word, Hick's theodicy is just too good to be true.

Hick rightly calls the Holocaust an instance of "demonic malice and cruelty." His theodicy requires him to reconcile that event with other crucial claims. They include these affirmations: (1) God is not only "limitlessly powerful" but also "limitlessly good and loving." (2) This God has created human life in an evolutionary setting where progress toward person-making is the aim and where achievement of person-perfecting is the end. Hick's theodicy is implausible to me because I am convinced that his claims about God's goodness cannot stand the onslaught of what he calls the principal threat to his own perspective: "the sheer amount and intensity of horrendous evil."

Hick's theory tends to keep the most wanton qualities of evil at arm's length. Some hardship and pain may make persons stronger and better, but Hick, I think, sees the world too much as a schoolroom when it is actually more like a dangerous alley. How is the Holocaust compatible with the plan of person-perfecting that he describes? How does Auschwitz fit the claim that divine intent ensures evolutionary progress where human character is concerned? In the Holocaust, persons were ruined and destroyed more than they were made or perfected. Auschwitz is waste, the very antithesis of providential design and purpose in God's economy.

Hick's Irenaean theodicy banks on life after death to redeem waste and to justify God's limitless love and goodness. Presumably God's heavenly persuasion will reconcile everything and everybody; all experience will figure into our ultimate perfection. Still, how will that process work in relation to waste that cannot be undone any more than it did not have to be? Much explanation—from Hick, if not from God—is needed if it is going to be plausible that "God's good purpose enfolds the entire process of this world ... and that even amidst tragic calamity and suffering we are still within the sphere of divine love and moving toward the divine kingdom." The arguments may not be God's, but Hick does offer examples of how that explanation might unfold. They are plausible if one wants to legitimate evil.

John Hick is critical of some free-will defenses for God. Yet his own theodicy belongs to that genre. According to Hick, persons-in-the-making must be free. Indeed they must be free to do all manner of evil. In addition, if men and women are to grow into a genuinely loving relationship with God, human freedom will entail both an "epistemic distance" from God and a pilgrimage through moral dilemmas and natural difficulties in which failure, pain, and untimely death are live options.

The general outline could be correct: If God's intention is to create a world with "person-making character," that world may have to be at least partly mysterious to us, lest its lack of ambiguity would undercut God's "person-making purpose." If we are fully to become God's children, our environment may have to be "broadly the kind of world of which we find ourselves to be a part." Their breadth, however, makes such claims insufficient. It will not do for Hick to take what may be a wiser course and to admit that some facts cannot be reconciled with God's limitless goodness and love. But so long as he stays with his general approach, the effect is precisely to leave unjustified the grisly details and the structures that produce them. Unfortunately, when he does move to consider those details, his theory fares no better. The reason is that Hick must defend evil, and he cannot do so without condoning—even if only inadvertently or unintentionally—what happened to its victims.

For instance, Hick notes that there is "intolerable" evil. He mentions this reality, however, not to reveal its sheer waste but to mitigate evil by relativizing it. In a world of person-making freedom, Hick at least implies, people can always find something to fault no matter how good things are. There will always be some evil, something that is "worst" and therefore intolerable. Since we must have some "intolerable" evil in order to become the perfected persons we are destined to be, the further implication appears to be that we ought not to protest very much.

Such implications, unintended though they may be, lurk in Hick's apologies. Those implications do everyone a disservice. Most people will not protest hardship, or even pain, if they can clearly see a commensurate benefit. Moreover, it is not impossible that there could be a world with commensurability between hardship and benefit, even if this present one cannot qualify. On Hick's terms, though, moral value would be diminished in that case, for virtue would never be its own reward. In a theodicy so heavily dependent on an eschatological resolution for the problem of evil, it is questionable whether virtue will ever be its own reward in the final analysis, but however that dilemma comes out, Hick's apologies still seem to be offered at the expense of evil's victims.

Correctly, Hick acknowledges that his theodicy may take "so large a view that it baffles the imagination," but at the end of the day he joins the company of Leibniz and urges contentment with the metaphysical structure of our current world, if not with the details of our experience. Thus, he argues that if one lets faith, if not reason, prevail, we will not want God "to revoke . . . freedom when its wrong exercise becomes intolerable to us." Hick makes this claim on the grounds that our taking "with full seriousness the value of human freedom and responsibility" will enable us to see that "humankind's moral freedom is indivisible, and can lead eventually to a consummation of limitless value which could never be attained without that freedom."

Is it clear, however, that moral freedom is or must be indivisible, or that such indivisibility is all that good? The moral fabric of human existence, for example, depends on intervention, on stopping people from doing certain things. On the other hand, Hick's vaunted indivisibility allows freedom to make all hell break loose. Apparently God will not intervene to stop this waste, but that fact does little to enhance the plausibility of God's limitless love and goodness—unless "limitless" implies something very strange in this case. Rather the waste of permissiveness, God's and ours, in allowing freedom to be indivisible augurs against God's benevolence. True, if some "limitless value" (whatever that might be) results from indivisible liberty, we can be more tranquil. The problem, though, is to imagine how evil's waste will fit. If our epistemic distance from God were less, we might understand more, but Hick also suggests that if we knew too much now, the risk factors in our lives would be curtailed and the grandeur of our character might be diminished. Such excuses, I fear, defend evil too much.

If Hick is correct, my fear is groundless. Waste will waste away. Evil will be transcended, rendered inconsequential, forgotten so that neither God nor humanity is in any way permanently soiled. There shall be pie in the sky by and by—a whole one, not just a slice. This theodicy is nice. Its plausibility, however, must be judged in terms of how nice life seems to be. John Hick finds it nice enough to justify calling God's love and goodness limitless. The sheer amount and intensity of evil's waste make me demur.

REJOINDER

This book was conceived as a Claremont product, so that we writers all know one another as friends and colleagues. And so it seems quite natural to conduct this part of the discussion in dialogue form. The reader must remember, however, that when I am presenting the others' criticisms, I have in fact (except when quoting them) written their parts myself, so that I alone am responsible for what "they" say in this imaginary dialogue.

John: I see that both of you, David and Steve, point out that since the first edition of our book twenty years ago I have developed a more global understanding of religion and that this sets my theodicy in a new light.

Steve: Yes. We wonder why you have not now worked out a new theodicy on the basis of that new global understanding?

John: Well, the book was designed, wasn't it, to illustrate the range of specifically Christian responses to the problem of evil? As you wrote in your original Introduction: "For our purposes, let us say that a theodicy is *any* response to the problem of evil from the perspective of Judeo-Christian religious belief, broadly construed." I assumed that the new edition was to serve the same purpose. An attempt at a global theodicy would have been a quite different project. But I still hold that among Christian theodicies the Irenaean type is the most viable.

David: Okay. But now that we have raised the global question, let's discuss it.

John: Yes, let's—though without crowding out discussion of the Irenaean theodicy itself. As you know, I've come to see the world religions' different conceptions of the ultimate, the absolutely real, as different human images formed in response to the universal presence of the Real. So I see the idea of the divine trinity, the second person of whom became incarnate as Jesus of Nazareth; and the Jewish concept of a unitary (not triune) God who has chosen the Jewish race as his specially treasured people; and the Islamic concept of the strictly unitary Allah who is self-revealed in the Qur'an; and likewise the non- or transpersonal concepts of the ultimate as Brahman, or the Tao, or the Dharmakaya, etc., as respectively *personae* and *impersonae* of the ultimate.

David: Right. So this means that there is no "limitlessly good and limitlessly powerful Being" who is a "personal being carrying out intentions through time" and who has created the world, with all its evils—thereby also creating the theodicy problem. All that, you say, is a myth. So why not simply abandon the myth and start again?

John: Well, you have to take note of the sense in which I am using "myth"—not the popular idea of myth as falsehood. In my sense of the term there can be true myths, and people of different religions may each be living within different true myths. As I say in the book that you and Steve both refer to, "A statement or a set of statements about X is mythologically true if it is not literally true but nevertheless tends to evoke an appropriate dispositional attitude to X."[17] And the Ireneaen theodicy "may be—and I believe it is—mythologically true. That is to say, it may be the case that seeking to bring good out of evil, both through one's own personal bearing of suffering and mutual caring in face of disasters, and by cherishing an ultimate hope beyond this life, is appropriate to the actual character of our situation in the presence of the Real." So in speaking of the Christian story as mythological I'm not dismissing it as false and misleading, but on the contrary recommending it as a valid guide for life.

Steve: Yes, but you also say that it's only one among several equally valid guides?

John: Right. As an analogy, when we make a two-dimensional map of the earth, which is itself a three-dimensional globe, we have to distort it. You can't get three dimensions into two without distortion, and the cartographers' different projections are different but equally valid ways of doing this systematically. So if a map made in one projection is accurate, it doesn't follow that one made in a different projection is inaccurate. If they're properly made they're both accurate, and yet they both distort. I think of the theologies or worldviews of the different religions as being like these different projections. They all have to distort in trying to express the infinite divine reality within our limited human systems of ideas. And the fact that our Christian map enables us to travel successfully through life in response to the Ultimately Real does not mean that the religious maps used by other faiths, although different, may not also do that, and this applies to the theodicies that are part of those theologies.

David: But how can you know that the attitude evoked by the Irenaean theodicy is appropriate? After all, "there is no significant difference between saying that the word 'God' refers to nothing outside our imaginations and saying that it refers to something about which we can know absolutely nothing." So would not agnosticism be preferable at this point?

John: I don't hold that the word "God" refers to "nothing outside our imaginations." But I accept the basic epistemological principle that, in Aquinas's words, "Things known are in the knower according to the mode of the knower."[18] So a particular God figure, such as our distinctively Christian one, is the form in which the presence of the Ultimately Real comes to human consciousnesses trained by that tradition.

Steve: But what could lead anyone to such an unbiblical and unorthodox position?

John: Well, let's start out from the basic faith that human religious experience is not purely imaginative but is at the same time a range of responses to a transcendent reality. Can that reality be identified with the specific deity or absolute of any one of the world religions to the exclusion of the others? No, because they all produce forms of religious experience that are integral to forms of religious life which seem, so far as we can tell, to be more or less equally "salvific," i.e., transforming men and women from natural self-centeredness to a new orientation centered in the Transcendent or the Real as known to them. So we arrive at a two-level model consisting of the ultimate reality in itself and its various manifestations within human experience. The ultimate reality is what it is, but what it is lies beyond the scope of our human conceptualities. But on the other hand, from our human point of view, as it is experienced by us, the witness of the religions is that it is benign. So the status of the Christian God is as one major authentic manifestation of the in-relation-to-humanity benign Ultimate.

David: But surely that reduces any theodicy, including the Irenaean, to a purely imaginative creation?

John: No, the suggestion is that they are mythologically true stories. The world faiths all teach an accepting attitude to unavoidable suffering, whether as submission to the will of God, or as trust in a mysterious divine providence, or as occurring within an ultimately benign universal process; and all teach a cosmic optimism that gives us hope for the ultimate future. I recommend the Irenaean type of theodicy as our Christian version of this.

David: Well, anyway, let me turn now to my main criticism of the Irenaean theodicy itself, namely that "the granting of freedom to human beings by this theodicy's God is arguably selfish, because this God is the only one who derives any real benefit from it. The omnipotent creator . . . could have programmed us always to do good while giving us the illusion that we were doing so freely. . . . The sole reason not to do so is to have the satisfaction of knowing that when we obey God, we do so freely." So why did not God create beings who are perfectly good and perfectly happy—a creation with no complications such as free will introduces?

John: A good question. Shall we ask the Creator?

David: Let's. May we ask you, O Lord, why did you not create such beings?

The Lord: How do you know I didn't?

David: You mean that you did?

The Lord: Of course I did. Haven't you heard of the endless millions of angels? They are not imaginary funny creatures with wings but precisely the good and happy beings you ask about.

David: Oh. But still we humans are not angels. So may I ask why you also created us?

The Lord: Because while the unchosen and unachieved goodness and happiness of my angels—and there can't be too many of them—is an intrinsically good element in my universe, the freely chosen goodness of free finite persons is (in my divine opinion) also an intrinsic good, and one that leads in the end to a different and higher quality of happiness. So I choose to have them both in my universe. Okay?

David: If you say so, Lord. (Having returned to earth:) John, turning back to you, I also asked in my critique why you discussed the Augustinian and Irenaean theodicies but ignored the process option?

John: I haven't in fact ignored it. But remember that before your own *God, Power and Evil* in 1976 the process option was little known outside process circles. But in the editions of my *Philosophy of Religion* since then, there has been what I regard as a substantial criticism of it. And of course while I was at Claremont, you and I had many both public and private debates about it.

Steve: (Speaking as editor) All right. My turn now. I also have criticisms of your theodicy, John. You seem to speak of "a gradual spiritual evolution till humans reach a full state of God-consciousness." But for my part, "I see no convincing evidence that the human race is improving morally or spiritually."

John: Well, neither as a matter of fact do I. But I don't think in terms of a natural evolution—I'll come back to that when I discuss with Dewi—but of growth through many lives. So the progress made by each individual in the course of this life goes with that individual into the next. It does not accumulate from generation to generation within this world, and so it does not show in the course of world history.

Steve: But this idea that in further lives we shall all gradually grow spiritually towards an eventual universal "salvation" is, surely, both speculative and, I'm sorry to say, quite unbiblical. The Bible teaches that "some will be condemned to eternal separation from God."

John: Frankly, I don't mind if it's unbiblical. To my mind the biblical eschatology, in for example the Book of Revelation, is itself speculative, as indeed are all conceptions of the final end. The question is, what speculation seems most probable? And it seems to me a reasonable expectation that in the infinite resourcefulness of infinite love working in unlimited time, God will eventually succeed in drawing us all into the divine Kingdom. However, I know that the fact that this is not a biblical teaching rules it out for you.

Steve: Yes, this lack of faithfulness to the Bible's my basic difficulty with all of you. None of you seems to feel "any strong need to be guided in theology by scripture or Christian tradition," whereas I certainly do.

John: Yes, that's how it must seem from a conservative-evangelical point of view. But I think the rest of us see Christianity as a developing tradition, and one within which many different kinds of theological theory have emerged and will continue to emerge, going far beyond the presuppositions of the ancient world reflected in the Bible. And so we all in practice use the scriptures selectively— including, I'll bet, yourself. But of course that's a big subject.

Steve: Okay. Well, another criticism concerns the cost-benefit balance of the Irenaean theodicy: Is not the sheer amount of evil in the world too great to be justified even by the creation of freely virtuous beings?

John: Yes, this is a problem, isn't it, and as much for your theodicy as for mine, since we both take essentially the same line at this point? But I think you have given the right answer in your own chapter: "What the free-will defender must insist upon is, first, that the amount of evil that in the end will exist will be outweighed by the good that will exist; and second, that this favorable balance of good over evil was obtainable by God in no other way." The only thing I would add to this is that (as I suggested in my own chapter) the very fact that we cannot see how the extent of evil in the course of the world is going to be engulfed by the limitlessly good end that is gradually being achieved is itself a necessary aspect of the cognitive distance that creates our freedom in relation to God.

Steve: Yes, I'm familiar with that argument. But perhaps we had better let the other John in now.

John R.:   Thanks. To me, your theodicy "is just too good to be true." And of course I point to the Holocaust as the rock on what all theodicies founder. You don't deal with this in your chapter, and so you "leave unjustified the grisly details and the structures" that produce such utterly devilish evils. To make your theodicy work you find yourself having to "defend evil, and [you] cannot do so without condoning—even if only inadvertently or unintentionally—what happens to its victims." Isn't this a fair criticism?

John H.:   No, I don't really think it is. I do respect your determination not to let me, or indeed God, forget the victims of the Holocaust. But surely you accept that it was humans, not God, who were responsible for that appalling crime? So the question is whether God should at some point have withdrawn our human free will and moral responsibility. But wouldn't this have been to cancel our humanity?

John R.: Perhaps, but your theodicy seems to me to imply that because this freedom is so valuable "we ought not to protest very much" about such evils as the Holocaust.

John H.: Of course we should protest against such evils—not, however, against God but against those who perpetrate them. And right uses of our human freedom must counter wrong uses of it. But to protest against the gift of free will itself, which your position seems to imply, is to my mind to claim that God made a mistake in creating finite free beings, which I can't accept.

John R.: But in saying that, you are assuming that "humankind's moral freedom is indivisible." But is it? Should not God use his own freedom to intervene and prevent at least the worst human sins, which waste so many human lives? However, "God does not intervene to stop this waste, [and] that fact does little to enhance the plausibility of God's limitless love and goodness."

John H.: It seems to me that once you ask God to intervene to prevent some specific evil you are in principle asking him, or her, to rescind our human freedom and responsibility. Was God supposed to change Hitler's nature, or to have engineered his sudden death, at a certain point in history? But the forces leading to the Holocaust ramify out far beyond that one man. God would have had to override the freedom not only of Hitler and the Nazis, but all participants in the widespread secular anti-Semitism of nineteenth- and twentieth-century Europe, which itself was rooted in nearly two thousand years of Christian anti-Semitism. Further, having prevented this particular evil, God would be equally obliged to prevent all other very great human evils. The Jewish Holocaust particularly concerns and appalls you and me because it came out of the heart of Christian Europe and because we have many Jewish friends. But numerically there have been even greater evils. Even more millions were killed by Stalin in Russia and by Pol Pot in Cambodia. Where should a miraculously intervening God have stopped? Only, it would seem, when human free will had been abolished.

John R.: Nevertheless, my sense of outrage that God should have allowed such things to happen remains undiminished.

John H.: Okay. Well, now I must respond to Dewi.

Dewi: Yes, I think your whole theodicy program is misconceived, and indeed that all such projects are.

John: I know you do. But coming to specifics that can be debated, you (like Steve) speak of my "evolutionary model." But the reason that

I have myself avoided the word "evolution" is that it could so easily suggest an automatic progression. What I speak of is individual moral and spiritual growth through the experience of life as we know it. This does not in any way entail that "earlier generations must be regarded as the means to our progress." We each live in our own generation in the world as it is in our time. Nor does it in any way mean that "my moral development is offered as the justification of the sufferings of others." These are misconceptions.

Dewi: Well, it's not a misconception, is it, that you have to appeal to an afterlife to make your theodicy work? For you, "The obvious failures of the process on earth need rectifying in the hereafter."

John: But a great number of people do make significant spiritual progress as they live through youth, maturity, and old age—though needless to say everyone still has a very great deal further to go. So it doesn't follow that this life has been a failure to be rectified in another. Rather, the next life continues the process. It's also true that many who die young or who find themselves in terribly adverse life circumstances are able to make little or no progress in this life, and that some actually regress. But that does not entail that they will not fare better in future lives. We all have to live amid the unforeseeable contingencies of history and help one another as best we can.

Dewi: But in your hereafter there is no more making of decisions within imperfect situations and so no more moral and spiritual growth.

John: Not so. You seem to be working with the traditional Christian picture of an eternal existence after death with no further possibility of further choices and responses, no living within a real environment. But I have rejected that picture (in *Death and Eternal Life*) and instead see this present life as one of many lives in many worlds.

Dewi: I see, though I don't think you mentioned that in your present chapter. But in those future lives will I still be the same Dewi Phillips, still Welsh, still the same husband and father, with the same friends, still a Wittgensteinian, still a lover of funny stories, still in a world in which all this make sense?

John: The kind of afterlife belief that seems to me most plausible—it's familiar in Buddhist and Hindu philosophy, from which I have learned—suggests that it's not the present conscious self that lives again but a deeper element of our nature, which is expressed in a new personality each time. But the editor is about to cut us off, so let me just refer you to a much fuller discussion of this in my *Death and Eternal Life*.

Dewi: Okay. You are thinking in such different terms, particularly in taking literally the idea of further lives beyond this one, that it is difficult to find common ground. All such speculation seems to me irrelevant to true religion. It's very frustrating!

John: Yes, that's my own feeling, too. I think we start from fundamentally different conceptions of philosophy, so that our arguments pass one another by. So what do you say to having a drink instead?

Dewi: Good idea. Have you heard the story about . . . ?

3

Free Will and Evil

Stephen T. Davis

Let me begin with the central assumptions that control what I will say in this essay. I approach the problem of evil—as I approach all philosophical and theological problems—wearing, as it were, two hats. I am both an analytic philosopher and an evangelical Christian. As an analytic philosopher, trained in logic and twentieth-century linguistic philosophy, I am interested in the rigor and soundness of the arguments I encounter. My controlling presuppositions are that people ought to believe what it is rational for them to believe, and that human reason is a normative guide to all belief and action.[1]

As an evangelical Christian, I accept orthodox Christian claims about God, Christ, human beings, human history, and human destiny. I believe that all truth is from God and is consistent with the existence, goodness, and omnipotence of God. So I accept each of the following claims:

(1) God is omnipotent;
(2) God is perfectly good;

and

(3) Evil exists.

As I approach the problem of evil my aim is to find a solution that is both philosophically defensible and consistent with these (and other) central Christian claims. Indeed, I do not believe the problem of evil can be solved with the resources provided by bare theism; it can only be solved, in my opinion, from a perspective that makes use of Christian doctrine, especially Christian soteriology and eschatology.

So I am not attracted to any "solution" that denies that evil exists—e.g., which claims that evil is some sort of illusion or metaphysically unreal thing.

Nor am I attracted to any "solution" that denies God's omnipotence—e.g., that says that God is not powerful enough to prevent evil. Nor am I attracted to any "solution" that denies that God is wholly good—e.g., that says that God has an evil or demonic side, which sometimes expresses itself in malevolent acts.

Let me distinguish between two aspects of the problem of evil, the logical problem of evil (LPE) and the emotive problem of evil (EPE). We will discuss the EPE later, but let us call the LPE the problem of showing that (1), (2), and (3) are logically consistent. That this is one serious aspect of the problem is clear. At one time, twentieth-century critics of theism were much inclined to suggest that (1), (2), and (3) form an inconsistent triad. That is, they claimed that it cannot be the case that (1), (2), and (3) are all true; the truth of any two of these statements—so they said—implies the falsity of the third. Thus, the rational theist must give up at least one of (1), (2), and (3).[2]

I will argue, then, that (1), (2), and (3) are consistent and can all be rationally believed. I will do so by means of the so-called free-will defense (FWD), a line of argument that was developed classically by Augustine (354–430 A.D.)[3] and has been skillfully defended in our time by Alvin Plantinga. Indeed, I think it is largely due to the work of Plantinga that one rarely hears any longer the problem of evil presented as if it were a purely logical problem, as if theists are contradicting themselves.

It is crucial to the FWD to ask what were God's aims in creating the universe. According to free-will defenders, God had two main aims. First, God wanted to create the best universe God could, i.e., a universe with the best possible balance of moral and natural good over moral and natural evil. Second, God wanted to create a world in which created rational agents (e.g., human beings) would decide freely to love and obey God. Accordingly, God created what was originally an evil-free world, and God created humans with the facility of free moral choice, with what philosophers call *libertarian freedom*.

Let us say that human beings have libertarian freedom and are accordingly *free moral agents* if and only if in the case of the decisions they make:

> (4) their choices are not coerced;

and

> (5) they have genuine alternatives.

And let us say that X has genuine alternatives in those cases where X's decisions and actions are not causally determined, i.e., where it is in X's power, under a given set of antecedent conditions, to do something or not do it. Typically, these conditions will hold in cases of equally strong desires (to do something and not to do it) or in cases of moral temptation, i.e., where a strong desire to do something is in conflict with a belief that not doing it would be best.[4]

Obviously, in making human beings free, God ran the risk that they would go wrong. The possibility of freely doing evil is the inevitable companion of the possibility of freely doing good. Unfortunately, human beings did just this: they fell into sin. So God is not to be blamed for the existence of moral evil. We are. Of course God is indirectly responsible for evil in the sense that God created the conditions given which evil could come into existence. But it was not necessary that evil exist. The nonexistence of evil was possible; humans could have chosen to obey God. Sadly, they didn't.

Why then did God create free moral agents in the first place? Does it not look as if God's plan went wrong, as if God's righteous desires were thwarted? Not so, says the free-will defender. God's policy decision to make us free was wise, for it will turn out better in the long run that we act freely, even if we sometimes err, than it would have turned out had we been created as innocent automata, programmed always to do the good. God's decision will turn out wise because the good that will in the end result from it will outweigh the evil that will in the end result from it.[5] In the eschaton it will be evident that God chose the best course and that the favorable balance of good over evil that will then exist was obtainable by God in no other way or in no morally preferable way.

In response to the problem of evil, some theists have argued that this is "the best of all possible worlds." Must free-will defenders make this claim? I believe not. In the first place, it is not clear that the notion of *the best of all possible worlds* is coherent. Take the notion of the *tallest conceivable human*. This notion is incoherent because, no matter how tall we conceive a tall human to be, we can always conceptually add another inch and thus prove that this person was not, after all, the tallest conceivable human. Just so, it may be argued, the notion of *the best of all possible worlds* is incoherent. For any possible world, no matter how much pleasure and happiness it contains, we can always think of a better one, i.e., a world with slightly more pleasure and happiness.[6] Accordingly, there logically cannot exist such a world, and the free-will defender need not claim that this world is the best of all possible worlds.

But even if this argument is fallacious, even if the notion is coherent, the FWD still need not claim that this is the best of all possible worlds, because better worlds than this world certainly seem conceivable. For example, so far as I can tell, this world would have been morally better (would have contained less moral evil) had Hitler not hated Jews. The death of six million Jews in the Holocaust, I believe, was based on decisions made by free and morally responsible human agents, Hitler and others. So the FWD must say that the amount of good and evil that exists in the world is partially up to us and not entirely up to God. If so, it becomes easy to imagine worlds better than this one—e.g., a world otherwise as much as possible like this one except that no Nazi Holocaust occurs. Accordingly, this world is not the best of all possible worlds.

What the free-will defender must insist upon is, first, that the amount of evil that in the end will exist will be outweighed by the good that will exist, and, second, that this favorable balance of good over evil was obtainable by God in no other way. But let us return to propositions (1), (2), and (3), which the LPE critic says form an inconsistent set. Is this true? How does the FWD answer this charge? Let me restructure the problem slightly. It will be less cumbersome to work with two rather than three propositions. So let us now ask whether

(3) Evil exists

is consistent with the conjunction of (1) and (2), which we can call

(6) God is omnipotent and God is perfectly good.

People who push the LPE will claim that (3) and (6) are inconsistent—if one is true the other must be false. Is this true?

Alvin Plantinga has used in this connection a recognized procedure for proving that two propositions are logically consistent.[7] We can prove that (3) and (6) are consistent if the FWD can provide us with a third proposition (we'll call it [7]), which has three properties. First, it must be possibly true. Second, it must be consistent with (6). Third, in conjunction with (6), it must entail (3). The proposition that the FWD suggests will be something like this:

(7) All the moral evil that exists in the world is due to the choices of free moral agents whom God created, and no other world which God could have created would have had a better balance of good over evil than the actual world will have.

What (7) says is that God's policy decision to create free moral agents will turn out to be wise and that it was not within God's power to have created a better world. Now (7) certainly seems possibly true (it need not, at this point, be true, although free-will defenders consider it true); I can detect no contradiction or incoherence in (7). And (7) seems consistent with (6)—I can see no reason to consider them inconsistent, at any rate. And the conjunction of (6) and (7) does indeed entail (3). (Since [7] entails [3] all by itself, obviously the conjunction of [6] and [7] does, too.) Thus (3) and (6) are consistent, and the LPE is apparently solved. A rational person can believe that God is omnipotent, that God is perfectly good, and that evil exists.

The intuitive point here is that the LPE cannot by itself rule out the possibility of God having an overriding reason for allowing the amount of moral evil that exists in the world. Indeed, Christians claim that God does in fact have such a reason, which explains why the numerous divine interventions to prevent evil that are called for by critics of theism do not occur. Both human free will and our sense of moral responsibility for each other would be meaningless if God were constantly interrupting in the indicated way.[8]

However, three serious objections must be dealt with before we can consider the LPE solved. The first asks why an omnipotent creator could not create free beings who always freely choose the good. This outcome certainly seems logically possible: it is obviously possible for a person freely to choose the good on one occasion; if so, why not choose good on all occasions? And if this is possible for one free person, why not for every free person? And if all this accordingly is logically possible (i.e., God creating a world peopled only by beings who always freely choose the good), it seems that a perfectly good creator would certainly create such a world. But since God obviously did not do so, at least some of the assertions that theists make about God must be false.[9]

One claim being made here is surely true: although it is highly improbable, it does seem logically possible that all free moral agents always freely choose the good. The sentence, "Jones is free and Jones never sins," is not necessarily false. Nor is the sentence, "Jones and all other free moral agents never sin." But given the definition of "free" stated earlier, it follows that had this possibility been actualized—i.e., had the moral agents whom God created never sinned—it would have been a pleasant accident. God would not have brought it about, nor would God be responsible for it. For if the agents were really free, no one could have caused them to behave as they did.

Accordingly, the other claim being made by the critic—that it is logically possible for God to create free moral agents such that they always freely choose the good—is false. "Jones is a free moral agent whom God creates in such a way that Jones never sins" is necessarily false. There is a logical tension between an agent's being free vis-à-vis certain acts and that agent's somehow being influenced by God always to behave in a certain way regarding those acts. Again we see that given God's decision to create free moral agents, the condition of the world is in part up to those agents and not entirely up to God. Some logically possible worlds are not creatable, not even by an omnipotent being. If there is a given free moral agent, say Jones, who in a given situation will freely decide to sin, it is not in God's power to create a relevantly similar world in which Jones is free and Jones does not sin.[10]

The second objection can be stated as follows: "If the whole creation was originally perfectly morally good, then human beings, as originally created, were perfectly morally good. But then how do we explain the fact that people sin? A fall into sin seems logically impossible for a perfectly morally good being; a person sins only if that person has a moral flaw. Since humans do sin, it follows that they were not originally created perfectly morally good, and thus God is directly responsible for moral evil."[11]

Several points here are true. I agree: (1) that a perfectly morally good being will never sin; (2) that there was no evil in the original creation; and (3) that Genesis 1:31 says of God's entire creation (which includes human beings) that "it was very good." But despite these points, the above objection does not stand. The FWD is not committed to the claim that humans were created perfectly morally good. The biblical expression "very good" quite obviously does not mean *perfectly morally good*. How could created things like the moon or Mount Baldy or the eucalyptus tree outside my office be perfectly morally good? Clearly they cannot, and so "very good" must mean something else. I would suggest God judged the creation to be very good in that it was a harmonious, beautiful, smoothly working cosmos rather than the ugly, churning chaos over which the Spirit of God had moved (Gen. 1:2). Human beings too were created good in *this* sense. But since God wanted them to be free moral agents, God must have created them as spiritually immature, morally neutral creatures, capable of choosing either good or evil. That is just what the FWD says God did.

The third objection concerns natural evil. The FWD defense—so it is said—may well be able to account for the presence of moral evil but not the presence of natural evil. Proposition (7) contains the statement, "All the *moral* evil that exists in the world is due to the choices of free moral agents whom God created." But this obviously does not cover natural evils like the pain and suffering caused by earthquakes, disease, or famine. Accordingly, the FWD fails.

At this point the free-will defender must go beyond the bounds of the free-will defense, which is indeed at its strongest when dealing with moral evil.[12] Given God's aims in creation as outlined above, creating a world with a coherent system of natural causes and effects is in God's interests. In such a world, natural events can in principle be understood, explained, and even predicted (although humanly unpredictable events can occur), some of them good and some of them bad. In other words, it is in God's interests to create a world in which pain results from nonhuman causes. This implies that divine interventions in the world—say, to prevent an earthquake or the outbreak of a disease—must be rare. If the world is to be regular and lawlike, such interventions can hardly be frequent or numerous. In the vast majority of cases, God must stay out of the way and let nature take its course. Otherwise, the result would be an irregular and almost totally unpredictable world.

One way to see this point is to imagine a world in which human beings suffer no pain, i.e., in which human experience is only pleasurable. In such a world, there would be little or no sense of morality, of some things being good and others evil. There would be little sense that our decisions and actions have consequences. There would be no compassion for others or occasion to help others. There would be no courage or heroism. There would be no reason for moral growth or improving one's soul. There would be no spiritual longing for moral excellence or for a better world. There would be little felt reason to love and obey God. There would be no growth through suffering.

In other words, as Richard Swinburne has argued, certain goods are such that God's creating a world in which natural evil exists is the only way, or the morally best permissible way, for God to make them possible."[13] Moreover, spiritual good for human beings arises in the existence of at least some natural evil. Pain shows us that something is wrong with our lives, that something more is needed. Thus Eleonore Stump says, "Natural evil—the pain of disease, the intermittent and unpredictable destruction of natural disasters, the decay of old age, the imminence of death—takes away a person's satisfaction with himself. It tends to humble him, show him his frailty, make him reflect on the transience of temporal goods, and turn his affections towards otherworldly things, away from the things of this world."[14]

Now what this argument does, if successful, is establish that, given God's aims in creation, some natural evil must exist. Whether the argument justifies the amount of natural evil that actually exists is still an open question. And of course God must limit the amount of natural evil that humans experience; we can imagine worlds of universal, prolonged, and intense suffering due to natural evil that would be inconsistent with God's goodness and God's aims. Moreover (as I will argue later), human beings must have a way to be compensated for their undeserved sufferings.

All three objections to the FWD as a solution to the LPE apparently fail. Those who push the LPE argue that theists contradict themselves by believing in the omnipotence and goodness of God and the existence of evil. We can now see that this is not true. The FWD successfully rebuts this charge.

But even if it is true that theism is logically consistent, there is the other difficulty that remains, viz., what I call the emotive problem of evil (EPE). This difficulty, too, concerns the proposition:

(8) God is omnipotent and God is good and evil exists,

which is, of course, simply the conjunction of (1), (2), and (3). Now against (8), someone might says something like this:[15]

> Perhaps it is true that there is no logical inconsistency in (8), but the problem of evil, when grasped in its full depth, is deeper than a mere logical exercise. A cold logical approach that merely shows the consistency of (8) fails to touch the problem at its deepest nerve. To show that (8) is consistent does little to convince people

to believe (8). To show that (8) is possibly true does not show that it is true or even probably true, i.e., it does little to show that people should believe, despite evil, in divine omnipotence and perfect goodness.

But what exactly does the EPE come to? This conclusion is not altogether clear from the previouis lines. Let me suggest some possible interpretations.

Words such as these are sometimes expressed with deep emotion. Perhaps the EPE means something like this: the existence of evil in the world somehow makes us deeply feel that

(6) God is omnipotent and God is perfectly good

is false. Because of evil, we find (6) hard to believe. Now obviously some people do find (6) hard to believe. But despite that point, detecting any real difficulty for theism here is hard. By itself, the fact that because of evil certain people find (6) hard to believe is no more serious an objection to theism than, say, the following comment: "You theists believe in God but somehow I can't."

But perhaps the EPE amounts to something more than this. Perhaps the claim is that the existence of evil makes (6) improbable or implausible, that the existence of evil constitutes strong evidence against (6). But the problem here is that seeing how any probabilistic judgments can be made is difficult. And this is for the obvious reason that we do not seem to be in a position to make a probability judgment about the truth of the FWD.[16] As I have claimed, the FWD claims that (8) is consistent (at least so far as moral evil is concerned) because proposition (7) is possibly true:

(7) All the moral evil that exists in the world is due to the choices of free moral agents whom God created, and no other world which God could have created would have had a better balance of good over evil than the actual world will have.

If we knew that (7) was false or improbable we might have good reason to deny (6). But in fact we do not know that (7) is false or improbable, and so we do not seem to be in a position to say that (6) is false or improbable.

There seems to be no way for us to argue analogically either. We might be able to do so if we knew that this were true:

(9) There are ninety universes in which evil exists but no good, omnipotent God and only ten universes in which evil and a good, omnipotent God both exist.

If (9) were known to be true we might be able to make a probability estimate— we might hold that because of (9), the probability is .1 that (6) is true. But in fact (9) is not only not known to be true, it does not even make good sense.

Since the term *universe* is all-inclusive (nothing except perhaps God lies outside "the universe"), no other universes than ours exist with which we can compare it.[17]

Possibly other interpretations of the EPE are more threatening to theism than these. I cannot think of any, however, and so I conclude that the EPE poses no philosophical difficulty for theism. (By the expression "philosophical difficulty for p," where p is some proposition or claim, I mean some reason to consider p either logically inconsistent or else disconfirmed by the available evidence.) If the theist's problem when confronted with the LPE is the apologetic task of responding to the critic's charge that theism is inconsistent, then if the LPE can be solved (by the FWD or any other argument), I see no added philosophical difficulty for theism in the EPE. I have shown that (8) is consistent, and so I believe that this task has been accomplished.

What does remain is what we might call an "evangelistic difficulty." By the expression, "evangelistic difficulty for p," I mean the difficulty of convincing people who do not believe p to believe p. In this case, we are talking about the difficulty of convincing people who (given the presence of evil in the world) do not believe

(6) God is omnipotent and God is perfectly good

instead to believe it. All philosophical difficulties are evangelistic (it is normally hard to convince someone to accept an incoherent or improbable claim), but not all evangelistic difficulties are philosophical (e.g., the difficulty we might have trying to convince a patient in a mental hospital to accept the belief that he is not Napoleon).

Now, trying to convince people to believe (6) may indeed be a serious problem. But evangelism is not philosophy. If philosophers have successfully defended theism against the charge that

(8) God is omnipotent and God is good and evil exists

is inconsistent or improbable, it is not easy to see what else they can or must do. They may not be able to convert a person who says, "Sorry, but because of evil I just can't see how a good and omnipotent God can possibly exist." But they can point out that this person's inability to believe does not in itself constitute a good reason for anybody else to reject (6). Thus, I conclude, the EPE may pose difficulties for theism, but not philosophical difficulties.

What my argument has established thus far—I believe—is that

(6) God is omnipotent and God is perfectly good

is consistent, both logically and probabilistically, with the presence of evil in the world. But that conclusion is insufficient for the purposes of theodicy.

What must be established is that (6) is consistent not just with the existence of evil but with the existence of the amount of moral and natural evil in the world.

At first glance, the FWD seems less embarrassed than other theodicies by the amount of moral evil that exists. The free-will defender will simply say of all morally evil events that they are due not to God (or at least not directly to God) but rather to created free moral agents who chose to do evil. But at a deeper level the FWD still seems open to the objection that it flounders against the huge amount of suffering that exists. The question can still be raised whether the moral freedom that the FWD says God gave us was worth the cost. This is an especially riveting question when viewed in relation to moral monsters like Hitler and Stalin. To put the question in economic terms: Is human freedom cost-effective? Why didn't God create a world of less freedom and thus less murder? Why didn't God place us in an environment that provides fewer opportunities or temptations to do wrong? Why didn't God provide us with a morally stronger psychological endowment? Why didn't God create us with an inability to kill other human beings?

Christians believe that we are now living in an interim time, the time between the incarnation of Christ, in the first century, and his return, at the end of history. We hold that in Christ's death and resurrection, our redemption was accomplished and all the forces that oppose God's rule—forces like sin, suffering, death, the devil, hatred, injustice, racism, etc.—were decisively defeated. Yet, like the Nazis in the ten months subsequent to the Allied success in Normandy in 1944, those forces fight on. They are still present in the world. Their final defeat will only occur when Christ returns. So we live in a time when evil is rampant and we wait for our final redemption.

One of the most disheartened books in the Bible is the book called Lamentations. It has been traditionally ascribed to the prophet Jeremiah (probably because of 2 Chron. 35:25); but whether it was written by him or not, its dirges over the fallen city of Jerusalem after its destruction by Babylon in 586 B.C. are very much in the spirit of Jeremiah's oracles:

> Is it nothing to you, all you who pass by?
>   Look and see
> if there is any sorrow like my sorrow,
>   which was brought upon me,
> which the LORD inflicted
>   on the day of his fierce anger.
>
>   (Lam. 1:12)

The Israelites were waiting for their national redemption, just as we human beings wait for the redemption of the world. And while we wait, we suffer.

Is there spiritual value to be found in waiting? Apparently the prophet thought so. In chapter 3, he declares:

> The LORD is good to those who wait for him,
>   to the soul that seeks him.
> It is good that one should wait quietly
>   for the salvation of the LORD.
>   (Lam. 3:25–26)

This last sentence forms part of the Roman Catholic liturgy on Holy Saturday, when Christians are waiting for the good news of Easter. Jewish readers of Lamentations were enjoined to wait for the salvation of the Lord, i.e., the rescue of Israel from Babylonian captivity. Similarly, Christians are enjoined, in the midst of the suffering of Good Friday, the darkness of Holy Saturday, and the pain of daily life, to wait for our redemption. The blessedness of waiting for our salvation is also an important concept in the Psalms (Ps. 39:1; 130:1–6) and in the Pauline literature (Rom. 8:23–25; 1 Cor. 1:7; Gal. 5:5; Titus 2:13).

Here the free-will defender will wish to make two preliminary points about our present suffering; neither of them is alone sufficient to solve the theodicy problem, but both are important nonetheless. First, suffering, and the waiting it almost always includes, can be spiritually uplifting. Of course, pain does not always help people to rise to new moral and spiritual heights—sometimes it destroys personality. But that it can produce spiritual good is important; this has always been a major emphasis of the Eastern Orthodox Christian tradition. Suffering can be a stimulus to spiritual growth, an invitation to trust in God more fully. When we suffer we are often vulnerable and malleable, so suffering can be a kind of wake-up call that we need to grow spiritually. It can lead to repentance. Perhaps for this reason, most people who come to faith as adults do so in the midst of some personal crisis. Suffering can teach us, train us, make us wise. Indeed, some kinds of spiritual wisdom and maturity are probably obtainable only through suffering.

Second, God is with us in our suffering, loving us and caring for us. I take it that this lesson is the intent of Paul's eloquent outburst about nothing being able to separate us from the love of God. He asks:

> If God is for us, who is against us? He who did not withhold his own Son, but gave him up for all of us, will he not with him also give us everything else? Who will bring any charge against God's elect? It is God who justifies. Who is to condemn? . . . Who will separate us from the love of Christ? (Rom. 8:31–35)

Paul concludes on the ringing note that nothing—and that includes all human pains and fears—"will be able to separate us from the love of God in Christ Jesus our Lord" (Rom. 8:39).

The basic claim of my theodicy is that God will redeem all evil. There are two ways in which this will be done: First, some evil will be used causally by

God to help produce the great good of the kingdom of God. Second, in the kingdom of God all evil will be overcome, transcended, made to pale into insignificance. Let me discuss these two points in turn.

On the first, I must define some terms. Let us say that *gratuitous evil* is any painful event that makes the world worse, all things considered, because it occurs. Some painful events are such that it is better, all things considered, that they occur. Think of the suffering that athletes endure in order to bring their bodies to fitness. Think of the pain of a surgery that returns a patient to health and strength. Let us say that in all such cases the evil that occurs has been *justified*. That is, the evil has been rendered worthwhile; it has been shown to have produced a greater good. Now *unjustified* evil is gratuitous evil, evil that the world, in the long run and all things considered, would have been better without. And an important question when discussing the problem of evil is whether any gratuitous evil occurs. I am inclined to say that it does, but I also believe the problem posed by gratuitous evil can be solved.

My first claim is that some evil is redeemed because God uses it to produce greater goods, especially the great good of the eschaton. God has a marvelous ability to outsmart us and bring good out of evil. Let me adapt a metaphor used in another context by P. T. Geach.[18] Suppose I were to play chess against Gary Kasparov. Now I know how to play chess; I have played the game many times, and I fully understand the rules, but I am no expert. In playing a match against Gary Kasparov, I would be able to use my free will, to make this move or that, as I thought best. But one thing would be certain: no matter what moves I decided to make, Gary Kasparov would find a way to outsmart me and defeat me in the end. Similarly, human beings have the freedom to resist God and to cause great suffering in the world. But at least some of those free decisions and some of that suffering can be used by God to help advance the divine purposes.

Now, we cannot always tell, in the case of any episode of suffering, precisely how God will use it to produce greater goods or to bring about the eschaton. Indeed, we can rarely do that. We almost never know why God allowed some specific evil. Virtually every Christian, however, can testify that this very thing occurs. We can look back at past events that, at the time they occurred, we considered gratuitous evils and that later turned out to have led to outweighing goods.

The second point is that in the kingdom of God, all evil will be overcome. People will be able to look back from the perspective of the kingdom of God and see that their past sufferings, no matter how severe, prolonged, or undeserved, have been overcome and no longer matter. As Paul says, "I consider that the sufferings of this present time are not worth comparing with the glory about to be revealed to us" (Rom. 8:18).

Let me tell a true story. This was years ago, during my first week in junior high school. I had skipped a grade in grammar school, so I was a ten-year-old seventh grader, very small and twerpy and uncool. One day my mother made me wear a pair of pants that were embarrassingly out of the style worn by chic junior high schoolers of the day. Walking across campus, I felt conspicuous and slightly ridiculous. My fears were not assuaged when I was stopped in the hall by three mammoth ninth graders, one of whom said to me (his voice dripping with sarcasm): "Gee kid, I wish I had a pair of pants like *that*."

That episode was humiliating. If I could have crawled into a hole and disappeared, I would have done so. But here is the point: Today, many years later, I recall this event without any suffering at all. It was painful at the time, but I've grown up. I've gone on to more important things; I no longer care what ninth graders think about what I wear. That episode is now more amusing than painful.

Similarly (so I say), in the kingdom of God, when redemption is complete, all previous sufferings will pale into insignificance next to "the glory that is to be revealed to us." The biblical vision is that despite the pain that all people have endured, and despite the horrible pain that some people have endured, the vision of the face of God that we will then experience will make all previous suffering such that the pain will no longer matter. We may not at present be able fully to realize or even conceptualize the infinite goodness of the kingdom of God and the way that it will overwhelm all previous evil. But given that we are dealing with infinite goods produced by a transcendent God, our inability to understand this point is just what we should expect.[19]

Let me now consider one last objection to the FWD. I will call it the "foreknowledge" objection. Its several forms can be expressed as a series of questions: (a) Why didn't God foresee, via middle knowledge, which free persons, if created, would be morally perfect and which would be morally imperfect and then opt to create only those in the first group? (b) If morally imperfect people must exist for some reason, why didn't God then foresee, via middle knowledge, which morally imperfect persons would end up part of the blessed and which ones part of the damned and then opt to create only those in the first group? (c) If members of the set of the damned must exist for some reason, why didn't God foresee, via middle knowledge, which members of that set would be run-of-the-mill sinners and which would be heinous moral monsters and then opt to create only those in the first group?

(a) In response to the first question, I have already admitted that it is logically possible for free moral agents never to sin; I only insisted that if this occurred it would be a happy accident from God's perspective. Now in response to this first form of the foreknowledge objection, Plantinga raises the possibility of what he calls "transworld depravity."[20] This depravity is the contingent property of any being who would do at least one morally wrong action in every possible world that God strongly actualized. Plantinga claims that it is logically possible that no matter what possible world God strongly actualized, every free human agent would go morally wrong at least once. This seems to me quite correct: it is possible and does help show that the LPE can be answered.

But in the context of the EPE, we must ask whether the claim that all possible human agents whom God could have created suffer from transworld depravity is not just possibly true but true. And I believe the answer is that this claim is not true. There are, in my opinion, possible worlds in which even Hitler never sins, e.g., those in which he dies at the age of two days. However, there is a weakened kind of transworld depravity from which I believe all free human agents, possible or actual, do indeed suffer. I believe in a kind of transworld depravity for all free human agents who (1) live long enough to make a significant number of moral choices, and (2) live in worlds relevantly similar to this world. And the main relevant similarity is that the world be one that God has designed with the same purposes in mind that (as I claimed earlier) God had in mind in creating this world. I believe it is highly probable that any free human agent who must make a significant number of moral choices in a world relevantly like ours will eventually go wrong.

So the answer to the first question is: given God's intention to create a world in which free human agents would freely say yes to God, it may well be that the category of morally perfect human agents is an empty set (with the exception of Jesus Christ). Given the pervasive influence of evil in the actual world, I seriously doubt that any free human agent who reaches an age of moral and spiritual responsibility (whatever it is) will remain morally innocent for long. Of course, by creating a very different sort of world, God could have ensured that moral evil would have no pervasive influence in it. But given God's aims in creation, God had to run the risk that evil would exist and even run rampant, and unfortunately it did.

(b) Why didn't God create only people whom God could foresee would be part of the blessed? Now some theologians answer this question by denying the existence of any damned, or any eternally damned, i.e., by embracing universalism. Much as I would like to follow this line, I do not believe any biblical Christian can do so. Universalism is far too clearly inconsistent with scripture to constitute a viable option to people who have a high regard for its theological authority.[21]

Moreover, serious problems of personal identity are present here. Suppose that John Jones Sr. is in the actual world part of the damned, and that his son, John Jones Jr., is in the actual world part of the blessed. So the objection we are discussing amounts to asking why God, foreseeing all this, did not opt to create John Jones Jr. but not John Jones Sr. The answer is clear: John Jones Jr.

just *is* the son of John Jones Sr. John Jones Jr. could not exist, could not be John Jones Jr., without being the son of John Jones Sr.

Two further questions are relevant here: Do souls as coherent individuals preexist their embodied lives? And, can souls at birth be packaged, so to speak, in any number of ways? People who strongly suspect, as I do, that the answer to both questions is "no" will deny that God could have created John Jones Jr. without having created John Jones Sr. To ask God to do so is to ask God to do the logically impossible. Why then did God create people whom God foreknew would be damned? Because that was the price of creating people who would be saved.

Moreover, once we rid ourselves of common misconceptions about hell, its existence can be seen as compatible with a perfectly good God. I do believe that hell exists, but I do not hold that it is a place where protesting people are led against their will to be tortured vengefully. I believe that the people who will end up separated from God freely choose hell and would be unhappy in God's presence. Having lived their lives apart from God, they will choose—eternally—to go on doing so. So it is not a bad thing that they do not spend eternity in the presence of God. People who will prove to be incorrigibly evil will never come to the point of desiring the beatific vision. Furthermore, I do not believe that hell is a place of torture. Biblical metaphors that seem to some to suggest so point, I believe, to the deep regret the citizens of hell will feel that they are not able to live in the presence of God, the source of all life, light, and love. Though they freely choose hell and could not be happy in paradise, I believe they will clearly understand what they have chosen to miss.

(c) Why did not God avoid creating those human beings, like Hitler and Stalin, whom God could foresee would be moral monsters? And here I have no compelling answer apart from the general line of my theodicy, viz., that God's policy of not intervening in the indicated ways will turn out best in the end. This relates to a point I made earlier: so far as particularly heinous events that occur, Christians need not feel that they must be able to explain why God allowed them to occur. A general answer to the theodicy problem, if successful, will suffice. That this is true is proved by the fact that every main contributor to this book gives a general answer to this question; not one of them claims to be able to explain precisely why God allows this or that particularly evil event to occur.

Ultimately, it comes down to trust. Some folk trust in God and some do not; the ones who do trust in God choose not to question God inordinately (Isa. 45:9–11). They believe God has the answers to many questions that now appear unanswerable. Christians, then, believe that God has good reasons for allowing particularly evil people to exist and particularly evil events to occur.

Christians do not always claim to know what those reasons are, but they trust in God nonetheless.

Thus, again, we see that an aspect of the emotive problem of evil remains a problem: the difficulty the believer has in convincing the nonbeliever to accept God's perfect goodness and omnipotence. This leads me to conclude as follows about the problem of evil: on a philosophical level, the LPE can be solved but the evangelistic aspect of the EPE cannot. That is, I have no philosophical tools for convincing people who because of evil deny (6) instead to affirm (6). Perhaps other tools are at the disposal of Christian philosophers: perhaps we can preach to them or pray for them. But at this point Christian philosophy comes to the end of its tether and can do no more for faith.

I am arguing that the problem of evil is not as serious an intellectual difficulty for Christian faith as it may first appear. This is because if I am right, God has an acceptable moral reason for allowing evil. That reason is constituted by two facts: some evil will be used by God to produce greater good (either greater earthly goods or the omni-good of the kingdom of God); and all evil will be overcome and transcended in the eschaton. In the kingdom of God, the blessed will experience a world in which all tears will be wiped away, all diseases will be healed, all crimes will be forgiven, all injustice will be repaid, all questions will be answered, all relationships will be restored, and all suffering will be redeemed.

In conclusion, I do not claim to have suggested in this essay a theodicy that solves the problem of evil in the sense that Sherlock Holmes solved mysteries, or in the sense that certain moves solve a chess problem. I have no "solution" that will be acceptable to those who do not share my philosophical and especially theological assumptions. No matter what one says about the theodicy problem, an air of puzzlement always remains. As Paul says in Romans 11:33, "O the depth of the riches and wisdom and knowledge of God! How unsearchable are his judgments and how inscrutable his ways!" God is a transcendent being, and so there is mystery inherent in anything we want to say about God. So what I am claiming is to have provided a theodicy that is sufficiently plausible to Christians as to disarm the problem of evil as a daunting intellectual objection to Christianity. That problem, I claim, does not amount to a refutation of belief in a perfectly good and all-powerful God.

If Christianity is true, then given what it says about God's transcendence and our cognitive limits, we would expect that there will be evils that we cannot explain (but God can) and goods so great that we cannot comprehend them (although God can). So the fact that there are mysteries in theodicy and that many of the relevant truths are quite beyond our ken is not a last-ditch attempt to save a theology from criticism but rather exactly what that theology should lead us to expect.

Let me conclude by indicating briefly why I find the FWD attractive. The first and most obvious reason is that the FWD is a theodicy that unlike others in this book does not require theists to give up any of their crucial beliefs. Second, the FWD is a theodicy that grows out of the witness of the Christian scriptures. It is not the arbitrary invention of some theorist. Rather, it emerges from two great biblical stories: the story of the moral freedom of God's creatures and of the contingent entry of evil into the world in Genesis 2 and 3, and the story of God's final triumph over all the forces of sin, disorder, hatred, and death in the book of Revelation and the theology of Paul. Finally, as noted, the FWD is a theodicy that recognizes its limits. There are such things as mysteries; not all questions can be answered.

There is a level at which faith as trust in God is necessary in theodicy. Free-will defenders are quite prepared to admit that they cannot answer some questions, or cannot answer them very well. They trust that some day they will know the answers, as God now knows them. "For now we see in a mirror, dimly, but then we will see face to face. Now I know only in part; then I will know fully" (1 Cor. 13:12).

CRITIQUE BY D. Z. PHILLIPS

In my criticisms of John Roth and John Hick, I have called attention to a morally problematic instrumentalism that looms large in the views of the latter, but which can also be seen in the former. Whatever of this, however, it may be claimed that contemporary philosophers of religion have solved what Stephen T. Davis calls the *logical* problem of evil. That is to say, it can be shown that there is no logical inconsistency in believing in the omnipotence, love, and goodness of God in the face of evil. Davis distinguishes between the logical problem of evil and the emotive problem of evil. The latter is the problem of how to move people to appropriate the logically consistent religious belief in their lives.

In this critique, I want to argue that the logical problem of evil has not been solved. To anticipate: We cannot argue that emotions and values are emotive extras to logical issues, if it can be shown that there are internal relations between certain values and emotions and concept-formation in religion.

On the one hand, Davis argues that God's gift of human life is a free gift. He concludes, quite rightly, that to speak of God *seeing to it* that people always reach the right decisions freely is incoherent. On the other hand, Davis says that God's gift has a purpose. He wants human beings to love and obey him. The gift, to that extent, has strings attached; it is *for* something. I have called attention to what it makes sense to regard as a higher conception of love, one

in which the gift is not for anything. This approach avoids the instrumentalism which, even on Davis's view, still makes creation look like an egocentric
exercise. My main point, however, is that the love I am talking about logically
cannot be possessed by a God who has a plan up his sleeve.

Davis's attempt to solve the logical problem of evil consists in combining
the free-will defense with the view that God cannot achieve his purposes by
any other means. This must be distinguished from the view that this is the best
of all possible worlds. A better world than the one we have is easy to imagine:
one without Hitler or Stalin, for example. Nevertheless, Davis argues, this
world may be necessary for God to achieve his purposes. We cannot know
whether this is so since, as Hume argued, we have no experience of universes
being made. But it is not irrational, therefore, to take this matter on trust.
Here, Camus says, secular revolutionaries and religious apologists unite in
placing "the solution" in an unspecifiable future. Meanwhile, the millions continue to suffer.

Does this picture violate the logical character of certain aspects of moral
discourse? The notion of "moral responsibility" keeps reappearing in this context. Davis says that we could not develop moral responsibility if there were
no sufferings to respond to. That is a sound logical point. But it does not follow at all that such development justifies or gives point to the sufferings. A logical relation becomes an immoral motivation, one that distorts *the logic* of
moral responsibility. In moral responsibility I am concerned with the sufferings of others. In Davis's analysis, the sufferings subserve my development.

When Davis worries, as Roth does, over whether God's plan is cost-
effective, he does not pause to consider whether *the logic* of the language of
management, or accountancy, should be imported into human relationships. I
do not suppose for one moment that Davis, when not philosophizing, would
say that all was well with Job since he ended up with more children at the end
that he started out with (as though the children were like replaceable spare
parts—technological barbarism in the realm of the spirit). To say, with Davis,
that we are ignorant of whether God's plan is cost-effective is simply to
immerse ourselves further in the impropriety of this whole way of thinking—
a way of thinking that is *logically* inappropriate in morality and religion.

Apparently, God's plan does not work for everyone. Some end up in hell.
Davis's better nature breaks through, and he wishes that this were not so. Is it
not troublesome to think that his nature is better than his God's? I am not pit-
ting a human desire against God's will, but finding a decency present in a
human being that seems to be absent in his God. Neither am I denying belief
in hell. Wittgenstein said that there was no seriousness without that belief—
the belief that I have it within me to damn myself. But here, there is an internal, not an external, relation between hell and who we are. When Faustus asks

Mephistopheles, when he appears, "How comes it then that thou art out of hell?" Marlowe has him reply, "Why, this is hell, nor am I out of it."

The instrumentalism present in Hick and Roth runs through Davis's analysis. A person who used another in this way would be subject to moral reproach. Should we not say the same of a God who acts in the same way? Such a God could not be said to be perfectly good. As I have shown, the logic of moral responsibility, and of certain aspects of human relationships, makes such an ascription *logically* inappropriate. For this reason, Davis cannot be said to have solved the logical problem of evil.

It may be argued that my demands have been too stringent. We have to make hard choices in life. Davis suggests that, given his purposes, the same may be true of God. Unfortunately, the analogy does not hold. There are, of course, terrible dilemmas and choices. Think of William Styron's *Sophie's Choice*, where a mother can save the life of one of her children only by handing the other over to the Gestapo. She cannot absolve herself from what she has done in making her choice, though she is an object of pity and compassion for us. She comes out with blood on her hands. Does God come out with blood on his hands, an object of pity and compassion for the rest of us?

In moral dilemmas, we may not regard the unfulfilled obligation as an excusable exception, given the obligations we have fulfilled. We may still feel the need to do penance for the harm that doing the right thing has involved. We may still stand in need of forgiveness. The "no other way" does not excuse us. When Davis says that God may have no other way to achieve his purposes than that which involves the sufferings in this world, does God stand unexcused, in need of penance and forgiveness? The unacceptability of these conclusions for believers shows that we have been pursuing a false analogy. The consequence, however, is that recourse to moral dilemmas and an emphasis on God's hard choice do not rescue Davis from his failure to solve the logical problem of evil.

CRITIQUE BY JOHN HICK

Davis represents what is probably the most vigorous philosophical contribution to the theodicy discussion during the last couple of decades, a contribution associated above all with Alvin Plantinga. While fully agreeing with the emphasis on human free will as our clue to the problem of moral evil, I nevertheless see problems in Davis's treatment both of this and of natural evil.

To begin with the latter, I would like to ask for more clarification on a change from Davis's first to his second edition essay. In the first edition (pp. 74–75) he held that it could be true that, in Plantinga's words, "Satan rebelled against God and has been wreaking whatever havoc he can. The result is natural evil. So the natural evil we find is due to the free actions of nonhuman spirits," as Augustine had taught. In this new edition Davis takes the different path of treating natural evil as, in effect, necessary for human soul-making. But in note 12 he adds that he still believes "that the devil exists and is possibly responsible for natural evil," but for apologetic purposes is omitting this from his present argument. Now "possibly" in "is possibly responsible . . ." is compatible with the devil having nothing whatever to do with natural evil in our world. The bare unrealized logical possibility would then be irrelevant. For that it is logically possible that natural evil is due to the devil, but that actually it is not due to the devil, does not help a theodicy of natural evil. The devil can only help (i.e., help a theodicy!) if it is claimed that he is in fact the cause of natural evil. So let us suppose that this is what Davis intends. My question then is how this is to be combined with the treatment of natural evil in his present paper. It seems that (a) natural evil is necessary for the fulfillment of God's purpose for humanity, but (b) natural evil is caused by something strongly contrary to God's will, namely the fall of Satan. How do these two statements fit together?

One other request for clarification. Davis says several times that God can and, he implies, does sometimes intervene miraculously on earth: "divine interventions in the world—say, to prevent an earthquake or the outbreak of a disease—must be rare. . . . In the vast majority of cases God must stay out of the way and let nature take her course" lest the regular order of nature be visibly undermined. But such divine interventions are evidently not excluded by Davis provided they are not too frequent or, perhaps more importantly, not visible—for if they are never humanly known, need there be any limit to their number? But if this is so it is proper to ask of some great natural catastrophe, of which major examples occur somewhere in the world every year, why God did not intervene "behind the scenes" to prevent it from ever coming about? To hold, as Davis does, that it is "okay" from God's point of view secretly to intervene miraculously on earth, but that in the majority of cases God decides not to do so, has perilous implications for his theodicy, for it implies that God specifically decides to allow *this* great human catastrophe but not *that*. Can this really be what Davis intends?

Concerning moral evil, Davis relies on the idea of the fall of humanity: "The nonexistence of evil was possible; humans could have chosen to obey God. Sadly, they didn't." He seems here to be referring to a historical fall involving a pre-fallen human state at a certain period in the past, as affirmed in the Bible, before humans had chosen not to obey God. But this is as implausible today as the idea that natural evils are the work of devils. Just as we know too much about natural law to believe that devils are causing storms and earthquakes, so we also know too much about the evolution of *homo sapiens* out of earlier forms of animal life to believe in a paradisal state of human society in the distant past. Davis acknowledges that "God must have created them [i.e., humans] as spiritually immature." However he does not think that they would also be morally immature, but rather "morally neutral creatures, capable of choosing good or evil." He seems to suppose that the earliest specimens of *homo sapiens* had no survival instinct causing them to seek their own self-preservation at the expense, whenever necessary, of others. And can we separate spiritual and moral states so completely? Surely we have to recognize that humans emerged from the process of biological evolution as intelligent animals, programmed to seek their survival within a harsh environment, and thus with the basic self-centeredness that is the origin of "sin," and also, at the same time, as spiritual beings with a potentiality to transcend their natural human egoism; and that human life has been the story of the interplay of these two aspects of our nature, worked out in the theater of earthly history.

I do not believe that all this is best taken up into theodicy by clinging to the biblical myth of the Fall, but rather by seeing humanity as created through the evolutionary process as a morally as well as spiritually immature creature who is to come through the soul-making process that Davis describes to an ultimate fulfillment in God's kingdom.

CRITIQUE BY DAVID RAY GRIFFIN

I applaud the fact that Davis, like Hick and myself, intends to affirm all three dimensions of the problem of evil—understood as genuine evil, God's perfect goodness, and God's perfect power. My question is only whether Davis really succeeds with this intention.

I begin with whether Davis really affirms the existence of evil. He certainly intends to. Besides asserting that he is "not attracted to any 'solution' which denies that evil exists," he says that "this is not the best of all possible worlds." Furthermore, defining "gratuitous evil" in the same way as I have defined "genuine evil"—namely, as "evil that the world, in the long run and all things considered, would have been better without"—he affirms that such evil occurs. In the end, however, he seems to deny it. He says we have no good reason to consider false the idea that "no other world which God could have created would have had a better balance of good over evil than the actual world we have" (which seems to contradict his earlier assertion that we can "imagine worlds better than this one"). And his affirmation of gratuitous evil seems to be contradicted by his claim that "all evil will be overcome and transcended in the eschaton" so that it "will no longer matter."

If these latter statements really do amount to a denial of genuine evil, there would be no logical difficulty in affirming God's perfect goodness while retaining divine omnipotence as traditionally understood. It is not clear, however, that Davis's attempt to portray his God as perfectly good succeeds.

One problem involves his free-will defense. As a historical point, it is misleading for Davis to trace the libertarian version of this argument back to Augustine, because in his later writings, at least, Augustine rejected libertarian freedom (as I showed in *God, Power, and Evil*), affirming instead that form of "compatibilism" according to which human freedom is compatible with divine determinism. More important is the fact that Davis himself evidently affirms this type of compatibilism with regard to Jesus, thereby undermining his free-will defense. That is, Davis first claims that "it is [not] logically possible for God to create free moral agents such that they always freely choose the good," which means that if some free moral agents never sinned it would be "a pleasant accident." But later, when suggesting that "the category of morally perfect human agents is an empty set," Davis adds: "(with the exception of Jesus Christ)." If there *is* one exception—that is, if Davis affirms with Christian orthodoxy that Jesus was fully human and yet not only morally perfect but also *divinely guaranteed* to be such—then Davis's free-will defense collapses. Having accepted compatibilism in one case, he is in the same boat with Augustine, being unable to claim that God could not have made an entire race of beings who are morally free and yet guaranteed never to sin. His claim that "God has to run the risk that evil would exist and even run rampant" is thereby undermined.

Even aside from this problem, Davis's free-will defense is problematic. For one thing, to explain "why the numerous divine interventions to prevent evil that are called for by critics of theism do not occur," he says that our freedom and moral responsibility "would be meaningless if God were constantly interrupting." But most critics of classical theism argue not that its omnipotent being should intervene "constantly" but only that it should do so occasionally, to prevent particularly horrendous events. They argue, in other words, that there could be some happier middle ground between *always* and *never* interrupting.

Davis's attempt to defend the goodness of his omnipotent deity is also undermined by his retention of belief in a literal hell. Although Davis says that "[t]he basic claim of [his] theodicy is that God will redeem all evil," by which he means that "in the Kingdom of God, all evil will be overcome," he rejects the idea of universal salvation, holding instead that some people will spend eternity in hell. If Davis holds that being a Christian is a necessary condition for entrance into God's presence, it would seem that a majority of the human race would be excluded. In any case, even if only a small percentage go to hell, it would seem that *all* evil will not be redeemed. Davis seeks to overcome the apparent contradiction by saying that the damned "would be unhappy in God's presence" and therefore freely choose hell. But then he speaks of "the deep regret the citizens of hell will feel that they are not able to live in the presence of God." A universe in which some of the souls created by God suffer eternal regret does not sound like a universe in which all evil has been overcome.

Davis's attempt to portray his omnipotent creator as perfectly good is further undermined by evil that is produced by nonhuman creatures, which by Davis's hypothesis have no freedom. While admitting that the free-will defense is weaker with regard to such evil, Davis resorts to the standard soul-building defense, suggesting that all the pain due to nonhuman causes serves God's interest in promoting human morality, compassion, courage, and love for God. One problem with this suggestion is that it ignores all the pain caused by nonhuman causes in all the nonhuman animals, which, Davis's silence about them suggests, are not involved in a soul-building journey. Davis's free-will theodicy, like Hick's, at best provides an answer for *one* of the many species of animals on this planet. This "at best," furthermore, is not good enough for many people, including Roth, Phillips, and myself.

The difference between Davis and me on whether his theodicy really defends the goodness of our creator can be discussed in terms of faith and reason. I agree with Davis's statement that "people ought to believe what it is rational for them to believe." But I find too limited his conception of what is required to show that his beliefs are rational for him. I am, frankly, not quite certain what Davis's position on this issue is. On the one hand, some of his statements seem to suggest that he has defended the rationality of his position if he has shown it not to be inconsistent. On the other hand, he agrees that he needs to answer the charge that his position is *improbable* or *implausible*. But then he seems to minimize the importance of this issue by suggesting that it is a merely "emotive" or "evangelistic," as distinct from a philosophical, issue, and also by claiming that "we do not seem to be in a position to make a probability judgment about the truth of the [free-will defense]." Two paragraphs later, however, he seems to claim to have defended his theism against the charge that it is improbable, and by the end of the paper he claims "to have provided a theodicy that is sufficiently plausible to Christians." The apparent contradiction is perhaps overcome by the phrase "to Christians," the point being that his solution "will be acceptable [only] to those who . . . share [his] philosophical and especially theological assumptions."

With that statement, in any case, we come to the heart of the issue, which is that Davis's conception of showing his position to be rational does *not* include showing his basic philosophical and theological assumptions to be rational from any perspective other than his own. I do agree with the view, which he evidently shares with Plantinga, that our thinking is necessarily based on "faith" in the sense of starting from assumptions that cannot directly be shown to be true. But I maintain that we need to show the rationality of our faith-assumptions indirectly by showing that a system of thought based on them can fulfill the standard rational criteria of self-consistency and adequacy to all the available evidence.

I find Davis's position here especially weak. He fully admits that "there are questions that [he] cannot answer, or cannot answer very well." But he seeks to suggest that this fact does not undermine his position by adding: "There are such things as mysteries; not all questions can be answered." This is true. But it is essential to distinguish between two completely different kinds of mystery: natural and artificial. There are many questions about the world, such as how our universe began, how evolution occurs, and how spiders know how to spin their webs, to which we do not have, and may never have, adequate answers. These are *natural* mysteries, being simply given to us by the phenomena. But the word "mystery" is often applied to puzzles that are created by particular human beliefs, such as the puzzles as to how evolution could have occurred *on the assumption that it was not divinely guided*, how mind and body can interact *on the assumption that the body is composed of insentient bits of matter*, and how the existence of a loving creator is compatible with the world's evils *on the assumption that there are no limitations on the creator's power other than purely logical ones*. These are *artificial* mysteries, created by human constructions. The fact that there are natural mysteries, which we must simply accept, provides no excuse for tolerating artificial mysteries. Because we have created them—whether we originated them or simply accepted them from previous human beings—we are responsible for them in the sense of being accountable for all the questions they raise. To the extent, therefore, that Davis's hypothesis about the nature of reality creates unanswerable questions, that hypothesis is undermined.

Most of the problems of Christian theology, I contend, have been created by the traditional doctrine of divine omnipotence. With regard to the problem of evil in particular, Davis's position negatively illustrates, I believe, my claim that we must fully surrender this doctrine if we, while recognizing that genuine evil occurs, are to hold without any inconsistency or equivocation that our creator is unambiguously loving, *wholly* for us—*all* of us. Davis's consideration of this option is limited to his statement that he is "[not] attracted to any 'solution' that denies God's omnipotence." Perhaps one reason Davis finds this option unattractive is that he thinks that to deny divine omnipotence as traditionally conceived would be to say that God is not perfect in power, that God has less power than it is possible for one being to have—as suggested by his statement that to deny omnipotence is to say that "God is not powerful enough to prevent evil." We process theologians, however, argue that the traditional doctrine of ommipotence is incoherent, so that it does not provide a standard by which to call imperfect a creator without coercive power.

CRITIQUE BY JOHN K. ROTH

Stephen Davis's office is near mine. Usually we are not far apart on philosophical issues either, but for a long time our views about theodicy have differed. Since I am linked with what he calls "the emotive problem of evil" (EPE), a position that poses—he thinks—"evangelistic" but not "philosophical" difficulties, I shall concentrate on that part of his essay.

Philosophically, Davis believes, it is sufficient for him to accomplish a defensive apologetic task. Committed to the proposition that God is both omnipotent and perfectly good in spite of a world full of evil, he finds no logical inconsistency in that belief package. Because the logical possibility of a theory says little about its plausibility, I will not contest Davis's logical analysis. A second dimension of his position, however, is much more problematic.

That dimension involves Davis's contention that his position is not "disconfirmed by the available evidence." If that case can be made, he believes, all philosophical difficulties are set aside. The only remaining problems are evangelistic. To make his case, Davis modifies the approach he took in *Encountering Evil*'s first edition. There, he relied on what I called the "I Just Don't Know Defense." It emphasized a version of the idea that God's ways are not our ways, but somehow everything will work out all right in the end. Presently, "Free Will and Evil" still includes that outlook, but it has been superseded by another: namely, that the problem of evil can solved only by "use of Christian doctrine, especially Christian soteriology and eschatology." This development, however, does not rescue Davis's handling of "available evidence."

According to Davis, God wanted to create "the best possible balance of moral and natural good over moral and natural evil." Although humanity's sinful abuse of freedom bollixed original perfection, "evil . . . will be outweighed by the good" nonetheless. The Holocaust, Davis asserts, occurred because human freedom was badly used. In the first version of "Free Will and Evil," Davis confessed that Auschwitz was quite beyond him when it came to showing how that place of horrendous evil figures into God's benignly cost-effective economy. In the present edition, Davis's more explicit reliance on Christian apologetics is apparent when he acknowledges that no "solution" to that problem "will be acceptable to those who do not share my philosophical and especially theological assumptions." Those assumptions include (1) that "some evil will be used by God to produce greater good" and (2) that "all evil will be over-come and transcended in the eschaton." The latter outcome seems to entail that the overcoming and transcending of evil will be complete and perfect, for Davis assures us further that "all questions will be answered." Davis's theod-icy is extremely optimistic, and not least because apparently God's answers—will they be essentially Christian answers?—are to be fully persuasive to all who encounter them.

Although all questions will be answered eventually, Davis conveniently retains ignorance as his ally by amplifying his confessional emphasis. To the question of whether cancer's immediate elimination, for example, would enhance the best possible balance of good over evil—or I assume we could think of the nonoccurrence of the Holocaust in this same regard—Davis says not only that there are "evils that we cannot explain (but God can)" but also that there are "goods so great that we cannot comprehend them (although God can)." Such an outcome, he adds, is "exactly what [Christian] theology should lead us to expect."

Meanwhile, Davis's theodicy depends on a free-will defense (FWD), which leads him to acknowledge crucial questions that he puts in economic terms: Is the moral freedom that God gave humankind worth the cost? "Is human free-dom cost effective?" His response both avoids the particularity of history's destruction and, again, retreats to ignorance—"we almost never know," he says, "why some specific evil was allowed by God"—as it also advances a tra-ditional Christian confession: "All the forces that oppose God's rule" have been "decisively defeated" in "Christ's death and resurrection," but we live in "an interim time," waiting for "our final redemption." Such waiting, Davis claims, can be "spiritually uplifting," and when the promised redemption does arrive "all previous suffering . . . will no longer matter."

Davis began by saying that no theodicy could be adequate if it denied evil's existence. Unfortunately, his view approaches what can be called "soft denial" by coming dangerously close to trivializing suffering—Davis's schoolboy example comes to mind—for in the long run suffering "will no longer matter." Before we accept Davis's word about this matter, however, perhaps the Jewish families gassed at Treblinka should be consulted—if they can be—and that example would be only one of a staggering number of particular instances that could be mentioned.

Davis's combination of an appeal to ignorance and a Christian confession-alism is unpersuasive, but not because emotion has carried me away. To the contrary, although Davis tries to shore up his position by denying that prob-ability judgments and analogical arguments can dislodge the possible truth of his basic outlook, this defense still remains problematic. It does because Davis fails to take seriously enough how much evidence really exists to show that an optimal balance of good over evil could be much enhanced by the elimination of cancer now, or by God's direct intervention to check the freedom that can unleash genocide. Otherwise how are we to understand the huge amounts of money, time, and energy spent annually in trying to rid human life of such waste?

From a human point of view, such efforts are not made primarily because they are morally edifying in and of themselves, or because we are playing along with God's ability to "outsmart" us by bringing some greater good out of evil. Instead, such efforts are made because most people are convinced beyond any reasonable doubt that cancer ought not to be. Likewise, some people work equally hard to forestall repetitions of genocide. Why? Is it not because the preponderance of available evidence is so plain?

Mass murder wastes and destroys so much that many people find reasons good and sufficient enough to deny that evil can be entirely outweighed or completely overcome by God, perfectly good or not. Nevertheless, Davis tries an eschatological argument: "In the eschaton it will be evident that God chose the best course and that the favorable balance of good over evil that will then exist was obtainable by God in no other way or in no morally preferable way." Unfortunately, the evidence available here and now, not in some promised eschaton, convincingly attests that a perfectly good God would never have permitted such waste in the first place.

Davis has the problem backwards. He would make the skeptic responsible to show how cancer and the Holocaust render improbable the claim that "God is omnipotent and God is perfectly good." Sufficient evidence to do so is available for anyone who will see it. Accumulating massively over the centuries, it consists of millions who have suffered without justification and died without peace, to say nothing of their agonizing but unanswered questions. If God is omnipotent, God's "perfect" goodness is problematic every day, and God's goodness, though it may be improved, will not be rendered perfect by a "redemption" that makes "all previous suffering such that it will no longer matter."

The fundamental issue raised by Davis's essay is what counts as evidence. Davis's persuasive powers may be considerable, but I doubt that he can accomplish the evangelistic task of getting me to assent to his creed. The reason he will not be able to do so is because I see evidence in terms of waste that makes it abundantly clear that there is no credible, pragmatic sense of "perfectly good" that I could attach to God. To reduce such disagreement to a matter of "evangelistic difficulty," moreover, involves a conveniently limited notion of "philosophical difficulty" that Davis may accept but I do not. Philosophy does not end with analysis of logical consistency and metaphysical possibility. At those points, philosophy has scarcely begun, because history's slaughter bench compels philosophical attention even more.

Davis admits that evil and suffering pose problems, but from a fortress of Christian orthodoxy, buttressed by appeals to ignorance, he calls upon the skeptics to show him wrong. Of course, if one has already concluded that there cannot be sufficient damning evidence because we do not—indeed cannot—know enough to judge, and if, besides, we can trust God to make everything perfectly right, there is definitely an impasse. Short of testimony that heaven alone can give, we should ask Davis, is there anything that could possibly count as sufficient evidence that his propositions about God's omnipotence and perfect goodness are mistaken? I suspect that he must say, "I just don't know," pronounce an inconsistent "absolutely not," or appeal again to his Christian orthodoxy to support his theodicy. Meanwhile Auschwitz can be visited, cancer kills, racked and ruined lives cry out in anguish on every hand. How ignorant can we be? How trusting should we be?

Davis's conclusion says that his theodicy has three advantages. It does not require one to give up the belief that God is omnipotent and perfectly good. Maintaining that belief, however, would be an advantage only if the belief makes good sense, and where God's perfect goodness is concerned, I am unable to follow Davis's lead. In that regard, I am not alone. Evidence gives me company, and that fact creates not just an evangelistic but a philosophical difficulty for Davis's theodicy. Second, Davis says, his theodicy grows out of Christian scripture. But so do many others, and, in addition, the New Testament is not theodicy's sole source. Scripture—Christian or not—does not contain some single theodicy alone. In fact, that inconclusive outcome is itself one facet of the problem of evil. It could even imply God's intention that there should be multiple theories about the divine—and us—no one of which will or can be adequate for everybody. Third, Davis notes that his theodicy recognizes its limits. Here I agree and disagree. Granted, Davis rightly recognizes that there is much that we cannot explain or understand, but at the same time a problem remains: Does Davis's confessionalism and his appeal to ignorance legitimate evil too much? According to Davis, all evil—instrumental or gratuitous, justified or unjustified—gets encompassed by God's perfection, which entails that people will eventually see that "their past sufferings, no matter how severe, prolonged, or undeserved, have been overcome and no longer matter." But should it ever be true that Auschwitz no longer matters?

According to Davis, "the problem of evil is not as serious an intellectual difficulty for Christian faith as it may first appear." As a Christian, I dissent, especially if we are to interpret freedom, evil, and suffering in terms of God's perfect goodness and omnipotence. Like John Hick, Stephen Davis has a whole pie in the sky by and by, at least for some folks. But if the price for even a slice turns out to be a free-will defense of God that makes the suffering of our earthly lives matter so little, then will you, should you, freely want any?

REJOINDER

As in 1981, I enjoyed reading the critiques of my colleagues, and learned from them. Several points caused me to think deeply about what I want to say.

(1) *The IJDK Defense*. Phillips, Griffin, and especially Roth hit hard on what Roth calls my use of the "I just don't know" defense. Roth says that in my theodicy I "appeal to ignorance." And it certainly is a fault in a theory if there are too many questions that it cannot answer. But in the 1981 edition I confess I was slightly irritated at this point being raised against me. My opinion then was that I was simply being honest in admitting that there were questions whose answers I did not know. My irritation was due to the fact that I also believed that there were equally as many points in the theodicies of the other contributors where they, too, were ignorant—they just did not own up to the fact. That is still my view. In Roth's antitheodicy, for example, is God going to be able to overcome evil? RJDN. Why does God's evil side predominate on some occasions (and produce events like the Holocaust) while on other occasions God's good side predominates (and produces events like the resurrection of Jesus)? RJDN. Is trust in Roth's partly demonic God worth the risk? RJDK.[22] So I confess I was surprised at being attacked at this point.

Obviously we know some things and we don't know other things. The same is true about issues in philosophical theology. I would claim to know what I believe God has revealed and what I can learn from others or figure out for myself. All the rest is ignorance. In my present theodicy, there is just one question that I admit I cannot answer, viz., why God allows certain terribly evil events to occur, or certain terribly evil people to exist. The general answer, of course, is that God's policy in creating this sort of world, with these sorts of natural laws and this degree of human freedom, will turn out best in the long run. But I do not know why God did not step in to prevent African slavery or destroy Hitler at birth. But no other contributor to this book (with the possible exception of Griffin, whose God is largely powerless to do such things) can adequately explain this either.

In this connection, Hick and Griffin both ask about divine interventions in human affairs. Griffin accepts my argument that rules out—given God's purposes in creation—frequent divine interventions to prevent evil events from occurring; he asks instead why God does not occasionally intervene. But I think God does occasionally intervene, and is morally justified in intervening when and where God does intervene. But the question then is: Why didn't God intervene to prevent the Holocaust (or other horrendous events)? (Hick himself faces this same problem; I do not know whether Hick thinks God ever does intervene miraculously in human affairs, but Hick's God certainly has the ability to do so.) And here we have reached the point where I am unable to give a secure answer. We can speculate about God's reasons, but that accomplishes little. Reformed Christians—believing, as we do, in the sovereignty of God—stress God's freedom to act as God wants to act. God has no obligation to keep our lives tranquil and trouble-free. Hick considers the idea perilous, but I do indeed think that God decides to intervene on some occasions and not others. Moreover (as I argued in my main essay), given that God is God and that we are mere humans, we should expect that there will be mysteries and unanswered questions about God's actions.

(2) *Phillips on the LPE.* Phillips claims that I have not solved the logical problem of evil. This is the form of the problem of evil that says that theists are contradicting themselves in believing in the existence both of evil and of a good and all-powerful God. The short way with this problem, of course, is simply to point out the possibility (and that is all it takes, a mere possibility) that God has a good moral reason for allowing evil. Since that is a possibility (and free-will defenders think it is also an actuality), there is no contradiction. *QED.*

But at this point I have a problem. Although I think I understand the various points Phillips goes on to make against me (and I will endeavor to answer them momentarily), I do not understand what they have to do with any failure on my part to solve the LPE. Indeed, in my opinion, in the previous paragraph I just solved it. (I also did so, at greater length, in my main essay.) The LPE is no longer credible as an objection to theism. So far as I can tell, I never said anything to deny that there are, as Phillips insists, "internal relations between certain values and emotions and concept-formation in religion." I rather suppose that there are internal relations between certain emotions and (say) the formation of the concept of "evil" in religion. But how that negates my solution to the LPE is quite beyond me.

Phillips says that I argue that "God's gift of human life is a free gift." I don't actually recall arguing for that point, but depending on what is meant by "free," I have no objection to it. But Phillips thinks that if life is a free gift from God, it can't have any strings attached. That is, the gift cannot have a purpose. On the "higher conception" of love that Phillips has in mind, the gift cannot be "for" anything; this sort of love is not possessed by "a God who has a plan up his sleeve." But here I must object. I don't claim to know where Phillips's higher conception of divine love comes from, but it is no part of biblical religion. In both Judaism and Christianity, God gave human beings life for a purpose, viz., that they come to love and obey and glorify God in their lives. God's gift of life—as indeed God's gift of grace—is certainly free. But free does not mean that no strings are attached, that the gift has no purpose. "Free" just means it is unearned.

Parents occasionally allow their children to suffer for the sake of increasing their maturity and sense of moral responsibility. Phillips claims it would be immoral if God did analogous things to humans. But I do not see why. Now I do not justify all suffering by saying that it makes us better people, although it sometimes does that very thing. (I know that it does, because it has happened to me.) But much of the suffering that people endure cannot be justified in that way at all, as I noted in my main essay. And contrary to Phillips, moral virtue normally requires both some degree of suffering and genuine concern for others in their suffering. Recognizing the fact that people sometimes grow morally through suffering need not and should not lessen in the slightest one's genuine concern for suffering people.

Perhaps Phillips's deepest reason for denying that I have solved the LPE has to do with his charge against me (and Hick and Roth) of instrumentalism. I take it that something is instrumentally good if it is a means to, or causally contributes to, something else that is intrinsically good. Thus, as I suppose, instrumentalism in this context is understood by Phillips as the attempt to justify human suffering as a means to something greater. And it is clear that Phillips finds this idea morally objectionable and untrue to the logic of moral responsibility. But I am afraid I don't, and I'm not sure what else can be said here.

(3) *Getting the problem of evil backward.* Roth argues that "the evidence available here and now . . . convincingly attests that a perfectly good God would never have permitted such waste in the first place." He then goes on to argue that I've got the theodicy problem backward: he says I put the burden of proof on the skeptic to show that the waste that exists could not have been allowed by a good and all-powerful God. Presumably Roth thinks the burden is on me to show that my theology is rational in the light of evil. He even asks whether anything could possibly happen that I would count as sufficient evidence against my view of God.

Well, obviously there are different versions of, and different ways of understanding, the problem of evil. For Roth, I suppose, it is something like this: In the light of evil, what sort of God should we believe in? But for me it is different; I approach the problem of evil with an already existing belief in a good and all-powerful God. So the problem of evil for me amounts to this: Does the existence of evil rationally require me to alter my beliefs, either by abandoning God's omnipotence (as in my view Griffin does), by abandoning God's perfect goodness (as Roth himself does), or by denying God's existence? Roth's irritation with me is simply a function of our approaching the problem of evil with different sets of assumptions. Moreover, I do not see how the evidence of waste in the world, massive as it is, shows that a perfectly good God could never have allowed it. Sadly, Roth and I are at an impasse here. I argue that in the light of the eschaton a perfectly good God morally can allow the waste that we see in human history. To counter this, Roth keeps pointing out how terrible and massive the waste is. And I keep looking for an argument why this admitted amount of waste—whatever amount it is—could not have been allowed by God. He thinks I am looking at the evidence blindly; I think he is not producing an argument.

And contrary to Roth's pointed query, yes, there are conceivable events that if they occurred would make me change my beliefs. For example, if human suffering became massive, universal, and destructive of morality and the practice of religion, it would be extremely difficult for me to continue believing in a good and all-powerful God. But I can hardly be faulted for the fact that such an event has not yet occurred.

(4) *How can all evil be redeemed if hell exists?* Let me make three points in response to this question from Griffin. First, I believe that all evil has already been redeemed in the life, death, and resurrection of Christ. But evil still exists, and will continue to run rampant until the eschaton. Second, some evil, although redeemed, will doubtless continue to exist in hell, just in the sense that its denizens will steadfastly refuse to obey and honor God. Finally, evil is redeemed in two senses: (a) some evil will be used by God causally to help bring about the eschaton (outsmarting the evil intentions of human beings and the devil); and (b) all evil will be overcome, transcended, made to pale into insignificance. Yes, hell will continue to exist, but will pale into insignificance. It will have no more influence on the world. And contrary to Phillips's ruminations about my remarks on hell, God's goodness (and, yes, God's decency) is infinitely greater than mine in part precisely because God's desire that no one end up in hell is infinitely stronger than mine.

(5) *The devil and natural evil.* Hick asks me for further explanation of the footnote in which I talk about the shift in my approach to natural evil since 1981. The truth is that I have never thought of earthquakes and famines as direct works of the devil. This is in part because we have available perfectly adequate naturalistic explanations of the occurrence of most such events. Also, I believe the devil's program, so to speak, is not to make people suffer but to convince them to refuse to honor and obey God. (Sometimes suffering can cause people to do that, but often it only brings them closer to God.) So making people suffer is not the best use of the devil's energies. I have always been attracted to Hick-like explanations of natural evil. But in 1981, in an effort to provide some variety in the book, I followed the Augustine line. Now as I have

explained, in response to the logical problem of evil, all that the theist needs is a possibly true statement that is consistent with "God is omnipotent and God is good" and together with "God is omnipotent and God is good" entails "Evil exists." I believed in 1981 and still believe that "The devil causes natural evil" is possibly true, and accordingly can be used as part of the statement we are looking for to respond to the LPE. I made it clear in 1981—and wish to stress again—that even if the devil is responsible for natural evil (or some of it), that fact does not go far in theodicy. God is still ultimately responsible.

(6) *Natural and artificial mysteries.* I can accept Griffin's distinction between two sorts of mysteries, but here we arrive at a fundamental difference between us. Let me illustrate this difference by asking about certain foundational Christian doctrines, e.g., the incarnation and the Trinity. These doctrines certainly amount to mysteries, or have mysteries imbedded in them; virtually every theologian in the tradition has said so. But would Griffin call them natural or artificial mysteries? They don't amount to natural questions about the world (or answers to them) like, How do spiders know how to spin? So one assumes Griffin would call them artificial. That is, they are mysteries that are produced by particular human beliefs, in this case beliefs like, "Jesus was truly divine and truly human" and "The Father is God; the Son is God; the Holy Spirit is God; and there is only one God."

Where do those beliefs come from, the culprit beliefs that are responsible for producing these artificial mysteries? Obviously, theologically orthodox Christians believe them because they hold that God has revealed them. I do not know whether Griffin believes in divine revelation, or whether he believes the scriptures of the Old and New Testaments have any relationship whatsoever to divine revelation. But I believe that God is self-revealed to human beings, and that the Bible is the preeminent and normative place to find that revelation. I accept that God is all-powerful—the item Griffin thinks causes most of the problems of theology—because I see myself as part of a community that lives under an epistemic obligation to accept it. That is why I expressed no more than the hope that I have produced a theodicy that is acceptable to those who share my assumptions.

Of course one must show that one's beliefs are not just coherent but plausible. Part of my effort in this book and elsewhere has been to demonstrate the coherence of Christian beliefs not because I think that is sufficient but because many critics have argued that they are incoherent.

(7) *Two contradictions.* Griffin thinks he has found two outright contradictions in my account, but he hasn't. On the first, I do indeed affirm the existence of gratuitous or genuine evil, i.e., events that the world (even in the long run and even in the light of the eschaton) would have been better without. My affirmation of the existence of gratuitous evil would only be contradicted by a

claim to the effect that all apparent evils will turn out really good (in some hidden way). But I deny that. We can imagine worlds better than this one (a world with no Holocaust, for example). But that does not contradict the claim that had God created a world with different initial conditions (different natural and psychological laws, for example) things would have turned out worse than they will in fact turn out. On the second, who says that Jesus was "divinely guaranteed" not to sin? I certainly didn't. I think it was a real and genuine possibility for Jesus to have sinned; he was entirely free to succumb to the devil's entreaties (Matt. 4:1–11). To deny that, in my view, amounts to a version of docetism. Christians consider Jesus sinless precisely because he resisted those and all other temptations.

(8) *Five animadversions.* (a) *Cancer and the Holocaust.* In response to Roth on this point, let me simply say that it is not cancer or the Holocaust that I was justifying. They are genuine evils. I was justifying God's decision to create a world in which cancer and the Holocaust can and do occur. (b) Reacting to my claims that one day all evil will be redeemed and that God is perfectly good despite the Holocaust, Roth says that we should allow the people who suffered at Treblinka to decide whether this is true. Now I see this point mainly as a rhetorical device on Roth's part, and at the level of rhetoric it is an effective one. But, as Roth knows, many survivors emerged from the Holocaust with their faith in the goodness of God intact. But, more importantly, although I have no wish ever to say anything to lessen the respect we must have for those who suffered in the Holocaust, their absolute authority is limited to telling us as witnesses what actually occurred. They are not in any more (or less) authoritative a position than Roth, me, or any other thoughtful person to rule on the theological implications of what they experienced.

(c) Griffin wonders whether I hold that you have to be a Christian to go to heaven. That raises a question that I have no business answering; who will be saved and who will not is a mystery that is in the hands of God, not me. But the claim that orthodox Christians hold that "You have to be a Christian to go to heaven" is a red herring. We do not in fact hold that. Haven't traditional Christians always held that people like Abraham and Sarah and Jacob and Rachel and Isaiah will be present in the kingdom of God? And they were certainly not Christians. They were never baptized or joined the church or accepted Jesus as their savior. (I do hold, however, that anyone who will be saved is reconciled to God only because of the life, death, and resurrection of Jesus.) (d) Roth says that I legitimate evil, or at least come close to doing so. I reply that one does that when one argues that all apparent evil is not really evil. I do not say that. And I reject entirely the idea that only those who deny God's perfect goodness can avoid trivializing evil. Roth asks whether it should ever be the case that Auschwitz no longer matters. I sincerely hope so. This is one reason that I do not affirm the timelessness of either God or heaven. I hope events like the Holocaust recede further and further into the past rather than remain an aspect of an "eternal present moment." (e) Griffin asks about the suffering of animals. This is a point none of us has said much about, and I entirely agree that it an important aspect of the problem of evil. My answer to it would be along the lines of what I said about natural evil. Given God's aims in creation, creating this sort of world with these sorts of natural laws (and thus this sort of competition for scarce resources at the human and animal level) was in God's best interests.

(9) *Trust in God.* Is God trustworthy? I continue to believe so. Jeremiah, Job, and Jesus were all people who endured wholly undeserved suffering. Each in the face of disaster asked God tough questions, just as we sometimes do. But each in the end rested his case and trusted in God (see Job 1:21; 13:15; Lam. 3:21–26; Luke 22:42; 23:26). Those are my exemplars. I will cast my lot with them.

4

Creation out of Nothing, Creation out of Chaos, and the Problem of Evil

David Ray Griffin

"When God began to create the heaven and the earth, the world was without form and void." According to most scholars of the Hebrew Bible, this is the best translation of Genesis 1:1–2a.[1] The prevalent translation, however, has been something like that of the Revised Standard Version, which renders it, "In the beginning God created the heavens and the earth. The earth was without form and void." The latter rendition, by indicating that the earth's being "without form and void" comes *after* God's initial creative activity, suggests that our universe was created out of nothing (*ex nihilo*). The former rendering suggests a version of the view articulated not only in most cosmogonies of the Ancient Near East but also in Plato's *Timaeus*, namely, that our universe was created out of a primeval chaos.

These alternative ways of understanding the origin of our universe suggest different conceptions of divine power. "Creation out of chaos" suggests that the "material" from which our world was created had some power of its own, so that it would not be wholly subject to the divine will. Plato explicitly makes this point, saying that the creator willed that everything should be good "as far as possible."[2] The idea that our universe was created out of nothing—which, to accommodate Genesis 1:1–2, often involves a "two-stage" theory, according to which God first created the raw material out of nothing, then used it to create our world—suggests that the divine Creator is absolutely omnipotent: The basic elements of the world, owing their existence wholly to the Creator's will, would have no *inherent* power with which to offer any resistance. This understanding is expressed by Millard Erickson, a contemporary Calvinist theologian, who says: "God did not work with something which was in existence. He brought into existence the very raw material which he employed. If this were not the case, God would . . . have been limited by having to

108

work with the intrinsic characteristics of the raw material which he employed."[3] Erickson's view, that God is *not* limited by anything, is expressed in
his conviction that "God's will is never frustrated. What he chooses to do, he
accomplishes."[4]

The difference between these two views is crucial for the question whether
the world's evil is compatible with the idea that it is the product of a perfectly
good creator. The idea of divine power suggested by *creatio ex nihilo* makes it
difficult to give an affirmative answer. If, as Erickson says, God's will is never
frustrated, then the Jewish Holocaust, in which 6 million Jews were murdered,
must ultimately have been in harmony with the divine will. It was Jewish theologian Richard Rubenstein's realization of this point that led him to declare
that *After Auschwitz* no Jew—and, by implication, no morally sensitive person—should believe in the God who determines the course of history.[5] The
idea of creation out of chaos, however, suggests that the creatures have some
power that is not fully controllable by divine power, so that we should not
expect the course of history to wholly reflect the divine will.

The theodicy developed in this essay is a version of this latter view. As a
Christian theologian, I offer it as a theodicy for Christians while hoping that
it will be found helpful by Jews, Muslims, and members of other theistic traditions as well. It is widely assumed, however, that such a theodicy should be
considered unacceptable by adherents of the biblically based religions because
the doctrine that our universe was created out of absolutely nothing is the biblical position. In the first section, I will show otherwise. In the second section,
I will suggest that this doctrine makes a satisfactory solution to the problem
of evil impossible. In the final section, I will lay out a theodicy based on the
process philosophy of Alfred North Whitehead, who returned to the position
of Plato and many early Christian theologians.

The Origin of the Doctrine of *Creatio ex Nihilo*

Is the Doctrine of *Creatio ex Nihilo* in the Bible?

Although it is widely assumed that the doctrine of *creatio ex nihilo* is the biblical doctrine, or is at least reflected in some biblical passages, this view is now
rejected by leading scholars. I will here employ the books of two such scholars, Jon Levenson's *Creation and the Persistence of Evil* and Gerhard May's *Creatio ex Nihilo*.[6]

If "properly understood," says Levenson, Genesis 1:1–2:3 "cannot be
invoked in support of the developed Jewish, Christian, and Muslim doctrine
of *creatio ex nihilo*."[7] One problem with the traditional translation of the opening verse—"In the beginning God created the heavens and the earth"—is that

later verses say that the heaven was created on the second day, the earth on the third.[8] This inconsistency is removed if the first verse is taken as a temporal clause, "When God began to create the heaven and the earth," and the second verse as saying that the world was a formless waste.[9] Another count against the idea that Genesis 1 implies *creatio ex nihilo* is the fact that the waters and the darkness are not said to be created.[10]

With regard to the Hebrew Bible more generally, Levenson argues that the assumption that it is based on the idea of *creatio ex nihilo* has led to the distorted, overly optimistic view that God is in complete control.[11] "The persistence of evil" in the title of Levenson's book reflects the idea that chaos was only circumscribed, not annihilated, with the result that it constantly threatens to erupt.[12]

Gerhard May also argues, independently of Levenson,[13] that the doctrine of *creatio ex nihilo* is nowhere to be found in the Hebrew Bible. Because that judgment is now commonplace, far more important is May's conclusion that this doctrine is also not found in intertestamental Judaism. The main evidence for the contrary view has always been 2 Maccabees 7:28, which says that God created the world and humanity "out of non-being." May argues, however, that this formula does not necessarily imply *creatio ex nihilo* in the strict sense.[14] In the fourth century B.C., for example, the Greek philosopher Xenophon said that parents "bring forth their children out of non-being," and in the first century A.D., the hellenistic Jewish philosopher Philo spoke of God as creating "out of non-being," even though Philo accepted the existence of a preexistent matter alongside God.[15] The formula *creatio ex nihilo*, in other words, was simply an "unreflective, everyday way of saying that through the act of creation something arose which did not previously exist."[16] As such, it did not imply the doctrine of *creatio ex nihilo* in the strict sense, according to which the very stuff of which this world is composed was itself created out of nothing (which is the sense in which *creatio ex nihilo* will be used in the remainder of this essay).

This denial that *creatio ex nihilo* was developed in pre-Christian Judaism is especially important because many scholars have argued that "primitive Christianity found the doctrine ready-made in the Jewish tradition," so that "[o]ne would be able to presuppose it for the New Testament."[17] On this basis, several passages in the New Testament, such as John 1:3, Romans 4:17, Colossians 1:16, and Hebrews 11:3, have been taken as evidence that the doctrine of *creatio ex nihilo* was held by first-century Christians. Having undermined this basis, May argues that neither these nor any other passages in the New Testament provide evidence for this doctrine.[18] May's testimony is especially important because he cannot be suspected of slanting the biblical evidence to support his own position.

Is the Doctrine of *Creatio ex Nihilo* Necessitated by Christian Faith?

May's own position is that although the doctrine of *creatio ex nihilo* is nowhere explicitly formulated in the Bible, it is implicit in the biblical view in the sense that once biblically based thinkers were exposed to the Greek idea that our world was formed by the creator out of some preexistent stuff, the doctrine of *creatio ex nihilo* was seen to be necessary to protect the biblical view of divine power.[19] The exposure to this Greek idea came in the form of Middle Platonism, according to which, although the *ordered* cosmos originated in time, there are "three principles"—namely, God, the Ideas, and Matter—that are co-eternal.[20] May's contention is that "as soon as Christian thought engaged in a critical debate with the philosophical doctrine of principles," the contrary doctrine of *creatio ex nihilo* "sooner or later had to be drawn from the biblical belief in creation."[21]

May's contention, however, begs the question of *why* Christian thinkers came to engage in "critical debate" with Middle Platonism's doctrine of principles. Although May claims that the rejection of the Platonic doctrine of principles in favor of the doctrine of *creatio ex nihilo* reflected an "inner necessity,"[22] this claim is contradicted by his own account.

One problem with May's claim is that the idea of creation out of chaos was accepted by Jewish thinkers for many centuries. Nothing in May's account challenges Levenson's view that creation out of chaos was the standard Jewish position. May points out, furthermore, that the theology of hellenistic Judaism in general and Philo in particular saw no contradiction between the biblical doctrine of God's power and "the acceptance of a matter that had not originated in time."[23] He points out, in fact, that *creatio ex nihilo* was not accepted by Jewish thinkers until the Middle Ages.[24] May's contention that the Platonic view contradicts the true biblical view can be maintained only by means of the question-begging claim that these Jewish thinkers were insufficiently critical.[25]

Although May believes that Christian thinkers had reason to be more critical,[26] he points out that many second-century theologians considered "orthodox" by later standards, including Justin Martyr, Athenagoras, and Clement of Alexandria, held that the "acceptance of an unformed matter was entirely reconcilable with biblical monotheism."[27] Justin even argued that Plato "took over the doctrine that God made the cosmos out of unoriginate matter from the opening verses of Genesis."[28] May contends that when Christian theologians finally developed the doctrine of *creatio ex nihilo*, they did so "partly to express opposition" to Middle Platonism.[29] But if there had been something about *this position as such* that was antithetical to the monotheism of the Bible in general and Christian faith in particular, we should expect opposition to have been expressed from the outset.

May's account shows, however, that when some Christian theologians began rejecting the idea of creation out of chaos in the latter part of the second century, they did so because of the threat raised by Marcion's version of gnosticism.[30] Besides accepting the eternity of matter, Marcion regarded it as evil. Our world is filled with evil, argued Marcion, because it was formed out of evil matter by the Hebrew Bible's Creator-God, who is different from the supreme God revealed in Jesus.[31] Marcion thereby contradicted not only the monotheism of Christian faith but its conviction that the world is essentially good, only contingently evil. As May points out, it was because of Marcion that the church not only began to fence itself off from heretical tendencies but also to include among those tendencies the idea that our world was created out of unformed matter.[32]

Endorsing this inclusion, May says: "Marcion's teaching that matter and the world created from it were bad and hateful could only make it obvious in an impressive way what dangerous dualistic consequences could develop from the philosophical doctrine of the pre-existence of matter."[33] The phrase to emphasize here is "*could* develop." That philosophical doctrine did not *necessarily* have any "dangerous dualistic consequences." May himself points out, in fact, that most philosophers who affirmed the existence of uncreated matter defined it as being "without qualities," so that it could not coherently be said to be essentially either good *or* evil.[34] Marcion's idea that matter is essentially evil was, far from being a logical implication from the idea of formless matter, actually an incoherent addition to it. Thanks to Marcion, nevertheless, the idea of uncreated matter became subject to guilt by association, with the result that Christian theologians began attacking the idea of uncreated matter as such.[35]

The Platonic Christian theologian who was the primary victim of this development was Hermogenes, who otherwise might be recognized as one of the greatest Christian thinkers of the period. Hermogenes, May points out, was "emphatically anxious to ensure the absolute goodness of the creator God."[36] In employing the idea of unoriginate matter, his primary concern was to explain the origin of evil in a way that protected that absolute goodness.[37] Although Hermogenes' own writings are no longer extant, his basic idea seems to be that "the ground of the evil present in the world" is "the trace of the original disorder of matter remaining in every created thing."[38] If, by contrast, we supposed God to have created our world out of nothing, we could have no coherent explanation, "because as perfect Goodness [God] could only have created good, so the origin of evil would not be explained."[39] The idea of *creatio ex nihilo*, by saying that God is the source of literally everything, including evil, would threaten the perfect goodness of God.

Besides showing that the doctrine of creation out of chaos protected the absolute goodness of the Creator, Hermogenes argued that it was otherwise perfectly acceptable from the perspective of Christian faith. His contention that Genesis 1:2 supported creation out of chaos followed, May points out, "a widespread expository tradition."[40] Also, far from regarding matter itself as evil, Hermogenes pointed out that "matter before its ordering is without qualities" and therefore "neither good nor evil."[41] If Hermogenes' theology is to be called "dualistic," therefore, it was clearly not the Manichean, Marcionite type of dualism. It was not even dualistic in a weaker sense: "Hermogenes emphatically declared that matter cannot be a principle of equal rank ontologically with God. God is Lord over matter."[42] Apart from the polemical, fencing-off mind-set created by the Marcionite episode, accordingly, there was evidently nothing in Hermogenes's position that would have provoked charges of heresy.

As it was, however, "When Hermogenes put forward his ideas, literary polemic against him seems to have begun almost immediately."[43] May's account shows that Hermogenes's position never had a chance:

> In the last decades of the second century the process by which the Catholic Church fenced itself off from the gnostic heretics was in full swing, and with it there was a critical reaction against philosophical reinterpretations of Christian doctrine and especially against all forms of intellectual syncretism. In this historical situation a synthesis of Christianity and Platonism, such as Hermogenes was attempting, could no longer be pursued; to undertake it was, in the atmosphere of anti-gnostic theology, immediately to incur the verdict of heresy.[44]

The reverse side of this rejection of Platonic Christianity was the adoption of the fateful doctrine of creation out of nothing: "Theophilus of Antioch, the earliest opponent of Hermogenes, is the first church theologian known to us— and this is certainly no accident—to use unambiguously the substance and the terminology of the doctrine of *creatio ex nihilo*."[45] Theophilus's polemical writings on this issue influenced not only Hippolytus and Tertullian,[46] but probably also Irenaeus, the other founder, along with Theophilus himself, "of the church doctrine of *creatio ex nihilo*."[47] This rejection of creation out of chaos, which had been the understanding of the biblical tradition for over a millennium, occurred very suddenly: "For Tertullian and Hippolytus [and Origen] it is already the fixed Christian position that God created the world out of absolutely nothing."[48]

Given the context and suddenness of this change, we should ask if it was precipitate. In spite of being in favor of the change, May makes many comments that suggest that its implications were insufficiently thought through. For example, after pointing out that the doctrine of *creatio ex nihilo*, which removes all restrictions on God's creative activity by declaring "the free decision of God's will [to be] the sole ground of creation," was bound to make the biblical concept of God "a philosophical problem," May adds: "But this is a question far beyond Theophilus."[49] Also, while praising Irenaeus's rejection of the Platonic view that God can only will "the best possible" in favor of the "absolute freedom and omnipotence of the biblical God," which "must rule and dominate in everything" so that "everything else must give way to it,"[50] May adds that "[b]eyond the demands of the controversy with gnosticism cosmological questions scarcely worried Irenaeus" and that his position was "only attainable because Irenaeus is quite unaware of philosophical problems."[51]

The move to the doctrine of creation out of absolute nothingness, I suggest, *was* precipitate. Spearheaded by theologians who, besides being uninterested in taking a circumspect view because of their single-minded focus on the threat from Marcionite gnosticism, were perhaps intellectually unequipped to do so, this adoption of *creatio ex nihilo* was made without due regard to the warning by Hermogenes about the threat to Christian faith implicit in *this* doctrine—the threat to the perfect goodness of God. The history of theodicy would bear out his warning that, if God is said to have created the world out of absolute nothingness, the origin of evil cannot be explained, at least without implying that God's goodness is less than perfect.

Creatio ex Nihilo and Traditional Theism's Problem of Evil

In line with widespread usage, I use the term "traditional theism" to refer to the doctrine of God as a personal being whose attributes include not only perfect goodness but also omnipotence (all-powerfulness), with the nature of this omnipotence clarified by the assertion that this being created our universe out of absolute nothingness. A central question of critics of this doctrine is whether the perfect goodness is contradicted by the implications of the omnipotence in light of the world's evil. This "problem of evil" can be formulated thus:

(1) God is, by definition, omnipotent and perfectly good.
(2) Being omnipotent, God could unilaterally prevent all evil.
(3) Being perfectly good, God would want to prevent all evil.
(4) However, evil does occur.
(5) Therefore, God (thus defined) does not exist.

The special difficulty created for traditional theism by its acceptance of the doctrine of *creatio ex nihilo* is indicated by the word "unilaterally" in the second premise. Without that doctrine, the idea that God is *all*-powerful could be taken to mean, for example, that God is the only being who exerts power over all other things, that God is the *supreme* power of the universe, far more powerful than anything else, or even that God is *perfect* in power, having all the power that it is *possible* for one being to have. None of these definitions would entail that God essentially has *all* the power in the universe, so that any power possessed by any other beings would be wholly derivative from, and thereby wholly controllable by, God's power. Accordingly, any or all of these conceptions of "divine omnipotence" could be held without implying that God could *unilaterally* prevent all evil. Evil could be explained, as Hermogenes suggested, in terms of power to resist the divine will inherent in the creatures, a power that they have by virtue of the "primordial stuff" from which they were made. The doctrine of *creatio ex nihilo*, however, closes off that option by implying (1) that the creatures have no inherent power with which to offer any resistance to the divine will, and (2) that there are no metaphysical principles, inherent in the nature of things, descriptive of the kinds of relations that necessarily obtain either between God and the creatures or among the creatures themselves.

These two implications lie behind the traditional doctrine of omnipotence, according to which God can unilaterally bring about any possible state of affairs, providing that such states of affairs do not contain anything self-contradictory, such as round squares, or anything that could not without self-contradiction be unilaterally brought about by God, such as the free decisions of creatures. The most important implication of this view is that God could unilaterally bring about a world that is just like ours except for being free of at least most of those things that we normally consider unnecessary evils, such as cancer, earthquakes, hurricanes, nuclear weapons, rape, murder, and genocide. Traditional theism's problem of evil is why our world has these (and many other) seemingly unnecessary evils. In considering the possible answers, we need to distinguish between two versions of traditional theism: the all-determining and the free-will versions.

Traditional All-Determining Theism

According to this first version, as its name indicates, literally every event and feature of the world—whether in the physical world or the human mind—is fully determined by God. Although advocates of this position affirm that human beings are free in the sense of being responsible for their actions, their freedom is said somehow to be compatible with all their actions, thoughts, and feelings being fully determined by God. How can advocates of this position, such as Augustine, Thomas Aquinas, Luther, Calvin, Leibniz, and Karl Barth, avoid the conclusion of the above argument, that "God does not exist"? I can here give only summary statements of their approaches, which I have discussed at length elsewhere.[52]

One approach has been to reject the third premise, that God would *want* to avoid all evil. Many evils, such theologians point out, lead to great goods that would have been impossible without the evils: Pain created by the dentist is necessary for healthy teeth later on; poverty provides the opportunity for charity; sin against others provides them the opportunity for forgiveness; suffering can promote compassion; and so on. Although this answer may initially seem convincing, it really amounts only to the observation that many things that seem evil at first glance, which we can call *prima facie* evils, are not *genuine* evils, defined as occurrences that make the universe worse than it might have been, all things considered. Many *prima facie* evils, in other words, are *only apparently* evil. This is certainly true. But this observation would provide a solution to the problem of evil only if it were claimed that *every* instance of *prima facie* evil is only apparently evil, so that there would be no genuine evil. With that claim, however, the all-determining theist would be denying not the third premise, but the fourth one, that "evil does occur."

The confusion as to what is being denied can be avoided by inserting the word "genuine" before "evil" in premises 2, 3, and 4. While this insertion will not affect the second premise, it turns the third premise into a truism, because a perfectly good being is by definition one who would want to prevent all genuine evil, meaning anything that would make the world worse than it might have been. All-determining theists can logically avoid the conclusion that God does not exist, therefore, only by denying the fourth premise, that "genuine evil exists"—which is what Leibniz does in declaring this to be "the best of all possible worlds."[53]

However, as I have argued elsewhere,[54] this denial is not one that we can make consistently—that is, without contradicting what we presuppose in practice—because in our daily living we all presuppose that less than optimal events occur. The same is true for the closely related idea that we have genuine freedom (which all-determining theism denies in effect by redefining freedom to make it compatible with divine determinism): We all in practice presuppose that we have a degree of freedom in the sense that, after we choose A, it is true that we could have chosen B or C. The denial that any genuine evil occurs also contradicts the very nature of religion, which, in providing a way to overcome (genuine) evil, presupposes that it occurs. Because we cannot help presupposing that genuine evil occurs even if we verbally deny it, all-determining theism, by implying that God has unnecessarily brought about genuine evil, in effect denies the perfect goodness of God, as Hermogenes warned.

The only way to avoid this implication is to deny that the ordinary rules of logic apply in theology. This approach has been employed in Christian theology by Karl Barth and Emil Brunner and in Jewish theology by Emil Facken-heim.[55] One problem with this approach is that it gives up the very task of theo-logy, which is that of applying logos, or rational thought, to our image of God. Also, if we exempt our own thinking from the basic rules of logical implication, we must, in fairness, do this for opposing schemes of thought. Rational argumentation would no longer be possible.

Traditional Free-Will Theism

Some traditional theists, recognizing that all-determining theism cannot pro-vide a satisfactory answer to the problem of evil, have developed a free-will version. It holds that although God *essentially* has all the power, God has, through a self-limitation on this power, *voluntarily* given freedom to at least some of the creatures (human beings and perhaps some other rational creatures, such as angels), freedom with which they can act contrary to the will of God. This idea of a voluntary self-limitation on divine omnipotence is necessary because free-will theists (rightly) reject the "compatibilism" of all-determining theism, according to which creaturely freedom is somehow compatible with divine determinism. The basic idea is that although this freedom allows gen-uine evils to occur—namely, sin and the evils resulting therefrom—*the fact that* such evils occur is itself not genuinely evil, because a world with genuinely free creatures, who can freely choose the right and the good and thereby freely develop moral and religious virtues, is a better world than a world that, while sin-free, is devoid of the values made possible by genuine freedom. This ver-sion of traditional theism, by allowing for both genuine freedom and genuine evil, can provide a more satisfactory answer to the problem of evil than can the all-determining version. But it still has several problems; I can here mention only three (which I have discussed more extensively elsewhere).[56]

First, because advocates of traditional free-will theism usually regard human beings as the only earthly creatures with freedom, it provides no answer to the question of what is usually called "natural evil," meaning the forms of evil that are not due to human volition, such as the suffering in the prehuman evolu-tionary process; the fact that the face of the Earth is susceptible to earthquakes, tornadoes, and hurricanes; the fact that human beings and other animals are susceptible to cancer and other diseases; and the fact that the Earth contains the elements to produce nuclear weapons and other weapons of mass destruc-tion. The doctrine of *creatio ex nihilo* implies that God could have created a world supportive of human life that would not have had all these dangers.

A second problem is that, according to the hypothesis of traditional free-will theism, God could intervene to prevent any specific instance of evil. God could have diverted every bullet headed toward a human being "too young to die." God could have prevented any of the massacres that have occurred. God could, in fact, prevent any sinful human intention from producing its intended effects. And God could prevent any disease or any natural disaster from producing permanent injury or premature death. This position, therefore, retains the assumption of traditional theism that has led millions to question the existence or at least the goodness of a divine being. If there were a Superman who could prevent all these kinds of events but refused to do so—perhaps on the grounds that doing so would "prevent opportunities for human growth"—we would certainly question his moral goodness. A Superman, of course, could not prevent all genuine evils, because, being finite, he could not be everywhere at once. But the God of traditional theism, being ubiquitous, does not have this excuse.

A third problem for traditional free-will theism is based on its position that even the freedom of human beings is an entirely gratuitous gift of God, not necessitated by anything in the nature of things (except the purely logical point that only genuinely free creatures can develop virtues that presuppose freedom). According to this position, God could have created beings identical with ourselves, except that they would not have really been free to sin. They could have enjoyed all the kinds of values that we enjoy, from friendship and family to music and philosophy, except those that involve or presuppose genuine evil. They could even have believed that they were really acting freely while always doing good. Only God would know otherwise. It is only God, accordingly, who gains anything from the fact that creatures have genuine freedom. Granting this freedom, from which most of the world's ills result, would thereby seem to be a very selfish decision.

Even if we grant that our world, with its genuine freedom and correlative genuine evils, was the best choice, it would still be the case, to return to the second problem, that this freedom could always be temporarily interrupted. Defenders of this position rightly point out that, given our normal understanding of human beings as genuinely free, God's interruption of someone's freedom would mean that that person in that moment would not be fully human. To have violated Hitler's freedom would have violated his full humanity. In response, however, the critic can ask: Would not this violation have been a small price to pay to have prevented Hitler from violating the freedom and humanity of millions of other people? A similar question arises every time human beings use their freedom to rob, injure, rape, murder, and otherwise violate the freedom and humanity of other human beings: Can we consider perfectly good and loving an omnipotent being who, having the power to prevent such acts, does not do so?

Faced with these problems, some traditional free-will theists simply say that, although they cannot explain why God allows so much evil, they need not do so. "If God is good and powerful as the theist believes," says Alvin Plantinga, "then he will indeed have a good reason for permitting evil; but why suppose the theist must be in a position to figure out what it is?"[57] Plantinga's answer here is part of his claim that theists need not offer a *theodicy*, which would attempt to provide a *plausible* explanation for the world's evils, but can rest content with a *defense*, which merely shows that there is no logical contradiction between holding that "evil exists" and that "God is omnipotent, omniscient, and wholly good." As long as a proffered explanation shows how these two propositions *might* be consistent, says Plantinga, the fact that it is implausible "is utterly beside the point."[58] The main problem with this approach is that its contentment with such a minimalist view of theological rationality seems to be based on the assumption that traditional theism is somehow in a privileged position. I have argued, by contrast, that traditional theism is no longer in such a position, so that it must, like any other position, commend itself in terms of plausibility as well as self-consistency.[59] But that is what it has been unable to do—at least without smuggling in assumptions that are inconsistent with the doctrine of *creatio ex nihilo*.[60]

Neither version of traditional theism, in sum, provides a position that shows the world's evils to be compatible with the perfect goodness of God.

A Process Theodicy

Having suggested that traditional theism has an insoluble problem of evil because of its acceptance of the (postbiblical) doctrine of *creatio ex nihilo*, I will now provide a brief account of the approach I favor, which involves a nontraditional version of theism usually known as "process theism" (because it is integral to the "process philosophy" articulated primarily by Alfred North Whitehead).[61] This type of theism shares much in common with traditional theism, affirming the existence of a personal creator who is perfect in both power and goodness, but it is nontraditional in affirming a contemporary version of the biblical and Platonic notion of creation out of chaos and thereby a different understanding of divine power. Although the brief account provided here will necessarily leave many questions unanswered, the interested reader can consult the more extensive accounts that I have provided elsewhere.[62] I will first explain how creation out of chaos is understood, then lay out some implications for the problem of evil.

Creation out of Chaos: A Process Version

In the ancient visions of creation out of chaos, the "stuff" out of which our world was created was generally thought of as passive matter. As such, it could be understood to offer resistance to the divine will and thereby to provide a reason for imperfections in the natural world. But it provided little if any basis for explaining distinctively human evil.

In process theism, by contrast, the stuff out of which our world was created is not what we normally think of as "stuff" at all, but creative activity. This idea is based in part on recent physics, according to which what we think of as "matter" consists of energy. Generalizing the notion of energy, Whitehead refers to the stuff embodied in all things as "creativity." On this basis, the long-standing dualism between "physical nature" and "human experience" could be overcome: All things, from electrons to living cells to human souls, could be understood as embodiments of creativity, or creative activity.

A crucial feature of this nondualistic worldview is a new understanding of the basic units of which the world is composed. In line with the view that the "stuff" of which things are composed is not stuff-like, Whitehead also held that the basic "things" are not thing-like: Rather than being enduring substances, they are momentary *events*. The creative activity embodied in each event takes two forms. One form is the influence of an event on subsequent events, which involves what physics describes as the transfer of energy. This creative activity is efficient causation, the causal influence of one actuality on others. After these other events receive this causal influence, however, they then exercise the other kind of creativity, which is final causation, in the sense of self-determination, insofar as they decide precisely how to respond to the various causal influences upon them. These decisions then become the basis for their efficient causation upon subsequent events.

We are aware that we make such decisions in every moment, insofar as we hold ourselves responsible for how we respond to the various situations we confront. We also commonly attribute a degree of spontaneity to other animals. Whitehead's view is that we can intelligibly attribute at least some iota of such spontaneity all the way down, to the subatomic level, suggesting that it accounts for the lack of complete determinism discerned by quantum physics. Accordingly, rather than an absolute dualism between "humanity," with its freedom, and "nature," assumed to be rigidly determined, process philosophy suggests, in line with the evolutionary nature of our world, a series of more or less radical differences of degree. In other words, the evolutionary process, in successively bringing forth atoms, molecules, prokaryotic cells, eukaryotic cells, multicelled animals, mammals, and human beings, has brought forth beings with increasingly greater freedom.

Given this initial overview of the position, we can now ask how it conceives the beginning of our universe as the bringing of order out of chaos. If the ultimate units of our world are not enduring things, but momentary events, then enduring individuals, such as electrons, photons, and quarks, would already constitute an evolved type of order, in which a particular form of existence is repeated rapidly. Prior to the emergence of these "enduring objects," the realm of finitude would have consisted entirely of extremely trivial events— even more trivial than the types of events of which quarks now consist— happening at random. To say that these events happen "at random" is to say that they do not belong to enduring objects. Without enduring objects, the development of higher forms of existence would have been impossible. Accordingly, the creation of elementary enduring objects, such as quarks, photons, electrons, protons, neutrons, and neutrinos, was the necessary first step in the creation of our universe.

Prior to the emergence of these enduring objects, there would have been no "things," in the ordinary sense of *enduring* things. For those who like the phrase, then, it can be said that our world was created out of "no-thing." It was not, however, created *ex nihilo* in the sense that this phrase took on in post-biblical times, to mean the absolute beginning of finite existence. Finite events were happening, but they constituted a chaos, not a cosmos, because none of the events were yet ordered into the forms of contingent order lying at the root of our universe. The realm of finitude did not, accordingly, have forms of energy such as quarks, electrons, and photons (which would be a contemporary way of understanding the suggestion of Genesis 1:2 that the world was "formless"). This does not mean, however, that the realm of finitude was devoid of power or energy in the most general sense. Rather, each of the events embodied creativity, understood as the most fundamental type of power or energy, having the potential to be transmuted into the contingent forms of energy constituting our universe. This description of the precosmic chaos still applies, in fact, to most of the universe today, insofar as it mostly consists of "empty space," meaning space that is empty of standing enduring objects (as distinct from forms of radiation passing through). Whitehead's view that it is *not* empty of events embodying creative power is consistent with the view of recent physics that the "vacuum" contains enormous energy.

Those whose thinking has been shaped by the idea of *creatio ex nihilo* will be inclined, at this point, to ask where this chaos of events came from. They may contend that it must have been created by God. What, however, is the self-evident truth behind this "must"? It cannot be simply that "everything that exists must have been created," or else we would have to ask who created God. We do not ask this question, however, because part of what we mean by "God" is "a being who exists necessarily." This point leads to the correct formulation of the self-evident truth involved, which is that "everything that exists contingently, rather than necessarily, must have been created." Traditional theists are quite right to hold that *something* must exist necessarily: Given the intuition that a universe could have never arisen out of a complete absence of anything actual (*ex nihilo nihil fit*), there must be something actual that exists eternally and thereby necessarily. The question, however, is what this something is.

Western minds have been shaped by many centuries of traditional theism, with its idea that the universe of finite existents was created *ex nihilo*, to assume that this something was God alone, without a realm of finitude. One can at least equally well assume, however, that what exists necessarily is God-with-a-realm-of-finite-existents. In fact, as May points out, Hermogenes used the biblical designation of God as "Lord" to support this view, arguing that "God was in his unchangeableness always Lord, and so there must have been from eternity something for him to be Lord of."[63] Whitehead's position embodies an analogous idea: that it is the very nature of God, as the supreme embodiment of creativity, to interact with finite embodiments of it, both influencing and being influenced by worldly events. Or, in Charles Hartshorne's language, God is by nature the soul of the world.[64] The necessary existence of God, therefore, implies the necessary existence of a world—not of *our* world, of course, and not even a world in the sense of an ordered cosmos, but simply a realm of finite existents, which can exist either in an ordered or a chaotic state.

Divine Power as Persuasive, Not Controlling

One implication of this view is that power is always shared power. If God is the supreme but never the only embodiment of creativity, then God never has a monopoly on power. Also, because the creativity embodied in finite beings is inherent to the realm of finitude—rather than freely bestowed by a creator to whom all creativity essentially belongs—it cannot be withdrawn or overridden. This rejection of the view of traditional free-will theists does not involve a rejection of the idea that human freedom is a gift from God. Although at least an iota of self-determination is inherent in finitude itself, the higher degrees of self-determining power are due to God. Our human freedom is a result of billions of years of evolution, each advance of which was divinely inspired. But because it was evoked out of the capacity for self-determination that is inherent to the world, this human freedom, now that it exists, cannot be simply withdrawn or overridden by God.

This view of shared power implies, in turn, that divine power is persuasive, not controlling. God, by hypothesis, influences every finite event, but God cannot wholly determine how any event will use its own creativity and thereby its twofold power to exert both self-determination and causal influence. This point applies all the way down: Because living cells, viruses, bacteria, macromolecules (such as DNA and RNA), ordinary molecules, atoms, subatomic particles, and quarks have the twofold power to respond with spontaneity and then to influence other things, for good or ill, we should not suppose that there is some level of the world that fully reflects the divine will—as if, for example, God for some mysterious reason wanted there to be cancer, AIDS, and genetically deformed babies. Rather, as Plato suggested, our creator would have at each level brought about the best order that was then possible.

A clarification is needed: The idea that all things have some degree of spontaneity, which has thus far been suggested, is true not of all things whatsoever, but only of all genuine individuals. This distinction, between things with and without spontaneity, reflects two basic ways in which enduring things can be organized—into "compound individuals," such as cells and animals, and into mere "aggregational entities," such as rocks and stars. In humans and other animals, the organization of the cells supports the existence of a higher-level actuality—which we call the *anima*, psyche, or soul—which exerts a dominating influence over the organism as a whole, enabling it to coordinate the spontaneities of its various members into a unified, self-determining response. Something analogous occurs, by hypothesis, in living cells and even lower-level individuals, such as atoms and electrons. Rocks and stars, by contrast, have no dominant member, so that the spontaneities of their various members cancel each other out, so that the rock or star as such is devoid of spontaneity.

Having made this clarification, I move now to an implication related to the fact that, within the hierarchy of true individuals, the power of self-determination can range from the extremely minimal to the enormous. This implication develops the basic insight of the traditional free-will theists, that there is a correlation between freedom and the higher types of value, but does so in the context of the rejection of the doctrine *creatio ex nihilo*.

Necessary Correlations between Value and Power

If that doctrine is rejected, it makes sense to suppose that there are some necessary principles, inherent in the very nature of things, about the nature of finite actualities, their relations to each other, and their relations to God. I have already suggested one such set of principles—namely, that in any world that God could create, the ultimate actual units would be events, that all such events would embody creativity, in the sense of the twofold power to exert self-determination and to influence subsequent events, and that God could influence but never interrupt or override the creatures' exercise of this twofold power. Another principle is that a positive correlation necessarily obtains among the following variables: (1) The capacity to enjoy positive value. (2) The capacity to suffer negative value (evil). (3) The power of self-determination.

(4) The power to influence others, for good or ill. To say that a positive correlation exists means that, as one variable increases, all the others increase proportionately.

It is evidently an empirical fact that the correlations obtain in our world. For example, human beings can enjoy positive values of which their pets have no inkling, but they can also suffer forms of evil from which their cats and dogs are free. We are surely right to assume that dogs enjoy more, and also suffer more, than do the fleas in their fur, which in turn must be superior to the cells of which their bodies are composed. This hierarchy of positive and negative value is also a hierarchy of power. We manifestly have far more power of self-determination, far more freedom, than dogs. We also have far more power to shape things around us for both good and ill, as illustrated by art and medicine, on the one hand, and warfare and pollution, on the other. To the extent that other types of individuals have less of this twofold power, they also seem to have less power to realize positive values and to suffer evil.

From the perspective of process theism, these correlations are not merely empirical, but reflect principles that would necessarily obtain in any world that God could create. Unlike traditional free-will theists, therefore, we need not ask why God did not create beings who could enjoy all the positive values of which we are capable but were not so subject to suffering. Such beings are, by hypothesis, metaphysically impossible. We also need not ask why God did not create beings just like us, capable of all the physical, aesthetic, and intellectual pleasures enjoyed by human beings, but with far less freedom, in the sense of the capacity to act contrary to the divine will. The same is true of the question as to why God did not create beings just like us but with far less power to be destructive of other people and the rest of life.

The idea that God could not have created such beings is, of course, a speculative hypothesis. But it is no more speculative than the contrary hypothesis, which says that God *could* have created such beings. That contrary hypothesis is, in fact, *more* speculative, because we know that a world in which these correlations obtain is a possible world, but we have no knowledge that a world in which they do not obtain is possible. The only reason for supposing that such a world is possible, in fact, is the doctrine of *creatio ex nihilo*, which we also do not know to be possible. It arose as a purely speculative hypothesis, originally suggested by a few men who, employing it polemically against an intellectual threat to faith in the goodness of our creator, evidently did not realize that their solution would pose an equal threat.

Therefore, in judging between these two hypotheses—creation out of chaos and out of nothing—we should be primarily guided not by the concern to be faithful to the (postbiblical) tradition, but by the concern to do justice, in a self-consistent, plausible way, to all the relevant considerations. One such consideration, on which this essay has concentrated, is the tension between the reality of genuine evil, and the testimony of religious experience and faith to the absolute goodness of our creator. This consideration, I have suggested, supports a contemporary version of the position shared by Plato and the Bible. Another relevant consideration is the need for an intelligible idea of how God could have created our world, which also supports a return to creation out of chaos.[65] Still another consideration, which has played a large role, is the need for a doctrine of divine power that supports an adequate eschatology, especially life after death. Since the time of Tertullian—who, May says, was "the first to adduce creation out of nothing as a proof that God had the power to awaken the dead"[66]—many Christian theologians have argued that Christian faith in resurrection requires the kind of divine power that goes with *creatio ex nihilo*.[67] As I have argued elsewhere, however, Christian hope, including hope for salvation in a life beyond death, is fully supportable in terms of persuasive divine power, so that this consideration need not block us from enjoying the benefits, for theodicy and intelligibility more generally, of returning to the biblical notion of creation out of chaos.[68]

Critique by John K. Roth

John Hick and Stephen Davis promise pie in the sky by and by. Now enter David Griffin with his God on a leash. With the exception of Griffin's, all of the theodicies in this book leave us wondering why God created the world as God did. Process theology, however, has "solved" the problem of evil. It does so by paring away God's power, but only in the most flattering ways. With metaphysically qualified omnipotence, Griffin's Greek God is a paragon of virtue. Following Plato's lead, this God never does less than the best that inherently limited power will allow. Genuine evil does abound, much of it due to freedom abused. More importantly, though, necessity creates the final solution.

Steeped in contemporary physics and a rejection of the view that "our universe was created out of nothing (*ex nihilo*)," Griffin's theory, he notes, is a speculative hypothesis, entailing that God's existence is necessarily linked to an equally necessary and uncreated "realm of finite existents." Over aeons of evolutionary time, the creative interactions of this necessary linkage have resulted in our present world, whose existence involves ongoing interaction between God's freedom and ours. This hypothesis, Griffin acknowledges, must be tested by experience and judged by its capacity to provide adequate illumination. Still, one should not be deceived. Of the options offered in this book, Griffin's is the most rationalistic, and he wants to claim that it is the one that does "justice, in a self-consistent, plausible way, to all the relevant considerations." However, if

Griffin's defense of God's "absolute goodness"—God is always doing the best God can—fits that grandiose description, the outcome is costly. It requires one to accept principles of necessity that neither should be nor are convincing. Moreover, if Griffin's theory is correct, I am persuaded that religious faith is irrelevant.

"There are," says Griffin, "some necessary principles." At the outset, Griffin assumes a great deal about the simplicity and clarity of that immensely complicated and metaphysically loaded proposition. What status, for example, does his quoted judgment possess? Is it necessarily true or is the judgment itself contingent and thus possibly false? What does it mean to say that a principle is necessary? What existence do principles have? Answers to such questions can be found, but, unless philosophy has achieved some heretofore unobtained agreement, those answers will not be completely accepted, let alone unanimously regarded as necessary. So the first problem is that Griffin's appeals to necessity overlook a basic empirical fact, namely, that few philosophical concepts rival *necessary* and *necessity* as far as unresolved ambiguity and status are concerned.

Apparently undaunted by such problems, Griffin moves ahead to state, for example, that "a positive correlation necessarily obtains among the following variables: (1) The capacity to enjoy positive value. (2) The capacity to suffer negative value (evil). (3) The power of self-determination. (4) The power to influence others, for good or evil. To say that a positive correlation exists means that, as one variable increases, all the others increase proportionally." Among other things, this necessary correlation means that each increase in the capacity to enjoy positive value entails an increase in the capacity to suffer. Such an outlook produces a crucial question: What is the evidence supporting Griffin's claim for such necessity? It is not clear that appeals to empirical facts readily provide it, for those facts are contingent. Indeed, appeals to the particularity of empirical facts would seem to provide counterexamples to Griffin's view and the sweeping metaphysical generalizations it features.

For instance, since the discovery of a polio vaccine, my capacity to suffer that disease has virtually disappeared. Thus, not only is it questionable in principle that my capacity to enjoy positive value necessitates a capacity to suffer, but also it is quite clear in fact that my immunity to polio results in a net loss where my capacity to suffer is concerned. Moreover, far from hampering my capacity to enjoy positive value, a decrease in my capacity to suffer from disease actually enhances my potential to experience what is good. A multiplication of similar cases may leave Griffin without a necessary leg to stand on, unless he can really persuade us that there is a necessity to suffer from disease in order to maximize good experience.

Another of Griffin's hypotheses about necessity affirms that "the capacity to enjoy positive value" necessarily entails higher degrees of freedom, including increased potentialities for destruction. If this theory is correct, it seems to follow that my potential to experience value is somehow dependent on my capacity to commit murder, or even to help unleash genocide. Here I think we need to ask Griffin to tell us what specific values could not be experienced if these destructive capacities were absent. I am at a loss to think of any that would be so indispensable that we could not get along quite well—maybe even better—without them. If either Griffin or God can persuade me otherwise, I will stand corrected, but I doubt that they can do so without assuming the very necessity that is in question.

Griffin's claims to the contrary notwithstanding, his doctrines of necessity are jeopardized by a lack of empirical evidence in their favor. Nevertheless, he urges that "process theism" is the best way to resolve "the tension between the reality of genuine evil, and the testimony of religious experience and faith to the absolute goodness of our Creator." Unconvinced that tensions between the reality of such evil and religious claims about God ought to be resolved, I find Griffin's theory inadequate on these terms, too, and one of the reasons is that his theodicy steals significance from faith in God.

All of Griffin's appeals to necessity intend—implicitly, if not explicitly—to buttress the claim that God is doing the best God can. If one really looks at the sorry state of the world with that proposition in mind, then it is obvious that God's best is far from enough. Thus, the problem that Griffin and his God must face is that they are badly overmatched by human recalcitrance. If the propensities for evil that lurk in human hearts and wreak their havoc everywhere were not so vast and unyielding, there might be more reason for optimism, more enthusiasm for joining hands with Griffin's weak and suffering but "perfect" God. History indicates, however, precious little moral progress resulting from God's persuasive powers. If so, it is not because God has been totally without allies. Over the centuries, many human beings have rallied nobly to their perception of God's call, and they have done so in considerable numbers, although probably not primarily because they thought the God of Alfred North Whitehead was calling them.

Beyond life in this world, God's persuasion might make things decisively better, if not well. At the end of his essay, Griffin nods toward eschatology, resurrection, and life beyond death. We receive a promissory note that these elements of theodicy are "fully supportable in terms of persuasive divine power," but even taking into account the ending note references to *Parapsychology, Philosophy, and Spirituality* and *Reenchantment without Supernaturalism*, two of Griffin's recent books, it remains a neat trick whether he can mesh those elements consistently and credibly in relation to his claims about God's weakness and unpersuasive performance in the world to date. I doubt that Griffin has performed or can perform it.

Meanwhile, Griffin's theodicy implies that when Elie Wiesel arrived at Auschwitz, the best that God could possibly do was to permit nearly ten thousand Jews a day to go up in smoke. That process had been going on for years, but remember that God really was doing all that God could do to persuade a different outcome into existence—at least according to David Griffin. A God of such weakness, no matter how much such a God tries to persuade, is rather pathetic. Good though that Platonic God may be, Griffin's God is too small. This God inspires little awe, little sense of holiness. History shows that this God's persuasive power is too scant to make a difference that is decisive enough, and unless God has the potential to act in that fashion, I think that God neither deserves nor will attract much attention.

With one hand Griffin offers the hypothesis that God lures us to realize the greatest good that is possible in our particular situations. With a leash of necessity in the other, Griffin removes virtually every good reason for religious faith in God's power to redeem and save. And so someone might inquire:

> "God, are you doing the best you can? Are you bound by necessity's chains? If so, it's sad."
>
> "Suppose I am. Can't I persuade you to help me? Together we can make everything so much better."
>
> "Really?"

CRITIQUE BY JOHN HICK

I do not pretend to have an authoritative opinion about which is the right translation of Genesis 1:1, "In the beginning, God created the heavens and the earth," or "When God began to create the heavens and the earth . . ." For all I know David Griffin may be right about this. But I doubt whether it really matters either to him or to those who developed the *creatio ex nihilo* doctrine. I doubt whether Griffin would renounce his allegiance to the Whiteheadian metaphysical system if the alternative translation was established, and I doubt whether the *creatio ex nihilo* doctrine was driven by a translation (or mistranslation) of Genesis 1:1. I think that in both cases the text is appealed to in support of a position that already stands on other foundations—in the case of Griffin, his acceptance of Whitehead's philosophy, and in the case of the *ex nihilo* doctrine, a need to affirm the sole absoluteness and ultimacy of God.

Whitehead's metaphysical system has been much more influential among theologians (particularly in the United States) than among philosophers, and Griffin is fully entitled to embrace it. However, Whitehead is not really the issue for theodicy. For the process system is only one way by which different people have come to think of God as a finite deity living in an independent environment that limits God's power and prevents God from abolishing all evil. David Hume floated the idea of a finite deity.[69] In the nineteenth century John Stuart Mill argued for the idea of a deity who is limited in power and so unable to eliminate the world's evils.[70] Edgar Brightman, of the Boston Personalist school, likewise believed that "there is something in the universe not created by God and not a result of voluntary divine self-limitation, which God finds as either obstacle or instrument to his will."[71] And many others, in various religions, have also thought in similar dualist terms. So what is important for theodicy is the idea of a benevolent God of limited power, regardless of the route by which this concept is arrived at.

Clearly the finite-God idea does not provide a solution to the traditional problem of evil, which arises from belief in an all-good and all-powerful deity, but is in effect a denial that there is properly any such problem. What is primarily of interest in Griffin's paper, then, in relation to the whole theodicy discussion, is his argument that no viable theodicy is possible given the traditional premise that, in his words, "God can unilaterally bring about any possible state of affairs, provided that such states of affairs do not contain anything self-contradictory, such as round squares, or anything that could not without self-contradiction be unilaterally brought about by God, such as the free decisions of creatures."

Griffin discusses both what he calls "traditional all-determining theism" and "traditional free-will theism." According to all-determining theism "literally every event and feature of the world—whether in the physical world or the human mind—is fully determined by God," and Griffin lists a series of great theologians who, according to him, have taught this. I doubt very much whether most of them did in fact teach this. But that historical question is not important here. I know of no one today who advocates a total divine determinism that leaves no room for any human free will—though there may be some extreme fundamentalist Calvinists of whom this is true. So for most of us, and all of us in this book, "all-determining theism" is a straw man. Griffin's other category is free-will theism, which holds that "a world with genuinely free creatures, who can freely choose the right and the good and thereby freely develop moral and religious virtues, is a better world than a world that, while sin-free, is devoid of the values made possible by genuine freedom." This is the position that most of the theodicies under discussion today adopt. Griffin offers three arguments against it.

The first is that while it may account for the existence of moral evil it does not account for the existence of natural evil—earthquakes, tornadoes, hurricanes, cancer, etc. I would accept this, but I add in my own chapter (and elsewhere[72]) that one next has to ask what kind of world would constitute an environment in which morally and spiritually immature persons can develop through their free responses to one another and to that common environment. And the answer is not a pain-free paradise, but something like our existing world. But I have developed that line of thought in my own chapter, and there is no need to repeat it here.

Griffin's second objection is that, without infringing on human free will, "God could intervene to prevent any specific instance of evil," diverting bullets, preventing sinful acts from producing their intended effects, preventing natural disasters from occurring. I have responded to this also in my own chapter. Let me add a further consideration here. Suppose that whenever a would-be murderer shot at his victim, the bullet was miraculously turned away, and if "whenever human beings use their freedom to rob, injure, rape, murder, and otherwise violate the freedom and humanity of other human beings," God intervened to frustrate the attempt. Generalizing, suppose the world was so regulated that it was impossible for anyone to harm anyone, and so for anyone to be harmed by another in any way. The choice between right and wrong actions would then cease to exist and ethical concepts would never have developed. This would not be a person-making environment.

Griffin's third argument is that God should have created us without the freedom to do wrong, although perhaps with the illusion of such freedom. We would then live happily and harmoniously and, if we add in here Griffin's previous points, that there could be no diseases or accidents or anything else to mar this paradise, except presumably death. But I believe that Griffin here misses altogether the deeper nature of love between people as a mutual bearing of one another's burdens in the vicissitudes of life. Such love expresses itself most deeply in mutual giving and helping and sacrificing in times of difficulty. And it is hard to see how this deepest dimension of human love could ever be developed except in an environment that has much in common with our familiar world. It is difficult to see how it could ever grow to any extent in a paradise that excluded all suffering. For such love presupposes a life in which there are real difficulties to be faced and overcome, real tasks to be performed and goals to be achieved, setbacks to be endured, dangers to be met; and if the world did not contain the particular problems and difficulties and challenges and dangers that it does contain, it would have to contain others instead. We do however have to accept that the sheer extent of the evils afflicting humanity remains a mystery—though I have argued that this mystery is itself a necessary aspect of the person-making character of the universe.

This line of thought is capable of much further development,[73] but in sum it does not seem to me that Griffin has shown that it is impossible rationally to retain faith in a loving Creator. We are not driven to the expedient of belief in a limited deity.

CRITIQUE BY D. Z. PHILLIPS

There are important agreements, but more important disagreements, between myself and David Ray Griffin. We agree that it is not feasible to hold that, on closer inspection, all evils turn out to be goods. Evil is a reality. We agree, too, that human beings can reject God's will. To say, with Griffin, that God's will can be frustrated is another matter, to which I shall return. Griffin is no more convinced than I am by the free-will defense and its instrumentalism, which allows God to use horrendous means to reach unspecifiable ends. Griffin's objection to the defense is that it is theologically thin compared with what he takes to be richer alternatives in process thought, but he thinks that it succeeds in showing that there is no *logical* inconsistency in believing in God's omnipotence, love, and goodness in face of evil. In my replies to the other contributors, and to Stephen T. Davis in particular, I argue that the free-will defense distorts the *logic* of moral responsibility, and the conviction that decency forbids the pursuit of any purpose, however splendid, by any and every means.

Griffin and I have different difficulties with the doctrine of creation *ex nihilo*, given that we understand it as he does. My difficulty is twofold. First, it assumes that once there was nothing. This absolute use of "nothing" is unintelligible. Griffin seems to object to it on scientific grounds, whereas my objections are logical. "Nothing" is used relative to a context, as in "Nothing in my pocket" or "Nothing on earth." One cannot say, free of any context, that there might have been nothing, or that there was nothing, as though "nothing" were a state in itself that could be said to exist. It might be said, in response, that there was always something, namely, God. This notion of God, understood as a solitary consciousness, leads to my second set of logical difficulties. Is the solitary consciousness self-identifying? What makes its thoughts the thoughts that they are? The consciousness can only be *this* one, and the thoughts can only be *these* thoughts, in a wider context in which they have their significance. But any such context has been ruled out. Such difficulties lead to the incoherencies of a logically private language.

Griffin reaches similar conclusions, but by very different routes. Our agreements may therefore be misleading. Griffin's main problem with creation *ex nihilo* is that he thinks it involves an absolute conception of God's power. He wants to insist on powers of resistance in the original chaos and in all subsequent states. Thus, for Griffin, God's power is limited, and his will is frustrated frequently. But Griffin shares a conception of God's will as sheer power with those he criticizes. He simply limits this power. But this *general* use of power is incoherent. God's power is a certain *kind* of power. If one is going to measure it against the power of malice, or the power of explosions, I ask again: what measure is one using?

Generality looms large in Griffin's attempt to combine science, philosophy, and religion in his account of reality. But important differences must be observed in each context. For example, science knows no metaphysical ultimates, no first or last things. Further questions can always be asked. That is why science does not attempt to account for "all things," unlike a confused scientism. The latter compounds difficulties in seeking universal explanations. These are supposed to cover all contexts, scientific and nonscientific. Griffin, for example, claims that all things are embodiments of creativity, differing only in degree. But an explanation of "everything" is an explanation of nothing. To be informative, there must be a limit to what an explanation explains. There is no conceptual continuum between "transfer of energy" in physics, and that transfer of energy from the worthwhile to the worthless that is a degradation of the spirit. No single account can be given of mathematical necessity, physical necessity, and moral necessity. There is a generality in science, but it is not *that*. As Rush Rhees has said, what science tells us about reality is what scientists find out.

There have been searches for generality in philosophy, too: the search for an account of "all things." It has run into difficulties ever since the Presocratics. If we say "All things are water" or "All things are atoms," what account is to be given of the reality of the water or the atoms? Plato saw that reality cannot have the unity of a *thing*. Further, how are our actual practices supposed to be derived from the alleged essence of "the real"? For example, how is one supposed to derive our actual arithmetic from Pythagorean units? It is not the units that give sense to arithmetic, but arithmetic that gives sense to the units. In that context, they are mathematical units, rather than units of some other kind.

This emphasis on practice may tempt us to trade one metaphysical ultimate for another: It may be said that what is fundamental is not a substance, but a process. Heraclitus, who has been called the first process philosopher, said, "All things are flux." He had the important insight that the identity of a "thing" depends on its relation to other "things." But in his claim that each thing is always in the process of becoming another thing, he lost the identity of things altogether. Our practices, too, depend for their sense on their relation to others, but this does not mean that "relationality" is something in itself which underlies our practices. It certainly does not mean that an account can be given of them in terms of a single process. It is no more obvious in Griffin's case than in others how our actual practices are to be derived from his meta-physical principles.

Among our practices are our religious practices. In these we hear that God created us out of nothing, and that he existed before the mountains were brought forth. This "before" is no more a temporal term than "in the beginning" and "the end of time" are references to particular times. These terms must be understood in a religious context. How can God be in our beginning and in our end when we are faced by evil and suffering? That belief is difficult to appropriate.

It does not seem to me that Griffin has to face the problem of evil, since only goodness comes from his God. Evil is the result of resistances to his will. So God does the best that he can. Who can ask for anything more? Griffin uses "good" and "evil" as correlative terms. But gratitude for existence is the ability to say "Thank God" in face of the good and the evil in life. As I have said in my previous replies, sorrow is involved in God's gift of life and compassion for human beings as creatures, subject to the inevitable vicissitudes of life. To know this compassion, in response to the victims of life, or to be a recipient of that compassion, as one of those victims, is to know God. This compassion is difficult to appropriate. If we see the sufferings of others as tests in a moral experiment designed by God, we purchase the sufferer. Human life is not *for* anything, and neither are its sufferings. Were it not so, it would not be God's free gift.

Griffin and I agree that love cannot compel. It can only persuade. We have to admit that compassion may not be forthcoming for the sufferer. The world has ample testimony to that fact. Sometimes, love and innocence simply suffer. So it was on Calvary. Love incarnate is abandoned in the sacrifice. Through its abandonment, love intercedes for us in showing what can happen to it. All subsequent and prior abandonments of the innocent intercede, in this sense, on our behalf.

Because God does not have unlimited, sheer power, Griffin has to say that his love is limited, and that his will is frustrated. Is this how we must speak of Calvary? I do not think so. We cannot understand the love there without fully accepting the fact that it is love that can be crucified. The resurrected Christ, love exalted and raised on high, still bears unhealed wounds. Theodicies should not attempt to explain this away.

CRITIQUE BY STEPHEN T. DAVIS

Let me raise five criticisms of Griffin's theodicy.

(1) First, a purely philosophical point about process ontology. Griffin claims

that the ultimate units of reality are not enduring substances but "momentary events." Let's distinguish between two metaphysical viewpoints: what I will call the Aristotelian ontology and the process ontology. The first claims that reality ultimately consists of things. A thing (or substance), let's say, is an enduring object that has properties, relations, and an identity apart from other things. The second claims that reality ultimately consists of events. An event, let's say, is a real change in a thing or a relational change between things. (These definitions reflect contemporary philosophical usage; I do not claim they capture Whitehead's definitions of these or related terms.)

Now a question: Which metaphysical viewpoint is intellectually superior as the basis of a worldview? For two reasons, I find the Aristotelian ontology superior. (I do not claim that these points constitute a refutation of the process ontology—they simply record my reasons for pitching my tent in the Aristotelian camp.)

First reason: Do the events that process philosophers consider metaphysically ultimate endure for certain finite amounts of time? If they do not, then they are merely limits or boundaries (like Euclidean points), and it is difficult to see how any sort of reality can be made of them. A set of boundaries of reality does not create or consist in any sort of reality. But if events do endure (and Whitehead holds that actual occasions have duration), they can have attributes and relations just like substances, and indeed are substances, just in virtue of being enduring property-bearers. So substances are ultimate after all.

Second reason: It is possible to explain what a thing is without mentioning or presupposing events. But it is not possible to explain what an event is without mentioning or presupposing things. That is, we can identify and individuate things by means of their properties and relations; but we can only identify and individuate events by means of the things to or about which the events occur. More simply: Things can exist without events (there are possible worlds in which only immutable things exist); events cannot exist without things. Ergo, things are more ontologically ultimate than events.[74]

(2) I have no objection to Griffin's stipulation that "genuine evil" is "anything that makes the world worse than it could have otherwise been." This does indeed imply, as Griffin argues, that those theists who hold that all evil helps lead to a greater good deny that "genuine evil" exists. They implicitly affirm that all evil is only apparent. But it is important to notice something here. It may well be true to say, of some heinous event, *both* that it "makes the world worse than it could have otherwise been" (i.e., that God will not use it causally to produce a greater good), *and* that God will in the end nevertheless produce a greater good. This, indeed, is my own view: genuine evil (as Griffin defines it) exists, but God's policy of creating a world where such events can and do occur will turn out best.

(3) Griffin denies the doctrine of creation *ex nihilo*, for it is part of his program to say that God's power is limited both by the uncreated, preexistent material out of which God fashioned the world and by the built-in power over against God that every actual thing has.

I agree that creation *ex nihilo* is not categorically taught in Genesis or anywhere else in the Bible; the biblical writers were not metaphysicians. But (a) the doctrine does seem strongly suggested in several biblical texts (e.g., John 1:3; Rom. 4:17; 11:36; Col. 1:16; Heb. 11:3). Following Gerhard May, Griffin denies that these texts imply creation out of nothing. But although I regrettably have no space to prove this point, the plain sense indicates that they do. (b) The doctrine is implied both in the biblical notion of the power of God (for whom "all things are possible" and "nothing is impossible") and in the biblical notion of the absolute lordship and sovereignty of God over the world, i.e., the absolute dependence of the world on God. (c) It is a virtually unanimous aspect of the Christian tradition from early theologians (e.g., Hermas, Theophilus of Antioch, Irenaeus, Origen) until today. (d) There is no suggestion in Genesis 1:1 (however the verb *bara* is to be interpreted) of a preexistent "stuff" that was not created by God and that God depends on. Nor is this idea taught anywhere else in the Bible. My argument from Genesis 1 does not concern lexical issues but rather the fact that God creates with a kind of effortless ease, i.e., merely by speaking the word (cf. also Psalm 33:6–9). There is no hint of any long and laborious struggle to construct a world out of resisting preexistent stuff. (e) It is possible, *pace* Griffin, rationally to believe in creation out of nothing without holding that God is the source or cause of literally everything. God was not the cause of the last sin that I committed, for example (although I could not have committed it without God's permission). So possibly the anti-Marcionite theologians whose intellectual equipment Griffin impugns at this point were not quite so obtuse after all.

(4) I consider omnipotence essential to Christianity. The God of traditional Christianity can create the stars, part the waters of the sea, heal people of disease, and even raise people from the dead. But the God of process cannot heal people of cancer or deflect moving rocks, bullets, or automobiles from their paths. In fact, says Griffin, God cannot directly influence inanimate objects at all. While I do not recommend the worship of power per se (an omnipotent scoundrel would not be worthy of worship), I believe Griffin's God is nowhere near powerful enough to merit worship. Could a sick person rationally pray to such a being for healing?

In addition, I am dubious about Griffin's claim that every actual thing must have power of its own over against God. Griffin makes clear that this is only a hypothesis—one that he thinks fits the facts and helps solve the problem of evil. But even if the hypothesis is true it does not entail the much stronger claim that God cannot directly deflect a moving automobile. And even as a hypothesis it is dubious. It seems entirely possible that God has all the power there is. Perhaps God has the power totally to control all events and things but does not use it. This is my own view (and the view of many other Christians): God is fully sovereign and omnipotent, but voluntarily shares some of the divine power with the creatures.

Griffin solves the theodicy problem by making God weaker than classic Christian thinking does. But such a move will only suffice if God is so weak as to be unable to destroy any truly wayward worlds, or at least quietly put them out of their misery. (Otherwise, obviously, God would be indictable for not so dealing with such worlds.) But if God does not possess the ability to do so, God is hardly worthy of worship.

(5) Unlike Hick's theodicy and mine, Griffin's is not strongly eschatological. And I do not believe the problem of evil can be solved without crucial reference to the future. Thus in response to Griffin's view that God aims, intends, seeks, works, and tries to overcome evil, we must ask: does God have the power, influence, or persuasive ability to make the divine intentions succeed? If God might not succeed (and this is what process thinkers must say; they cannot be sure but can only hope that God will emerge victorious), then, again, God is not worthy of worship. God is a good being who works hard: we can sympathize with and perhaps even pity God. Some of us will choose to fight on God's side in the battle against evil, and we can all hope God will win. But I see no reason to worship such a being.

God obviously ran a great risk in creating this sort of world. But was the risk worth taking? Most Christians believe it was. They believe God foresees the future of the world, i.e., the coming kingdom of God, and they believe God has revealed that the risk was worth taking. But on process thought we do not know whether the risk was worth taking, for we do not know how the world turns out, and neither does God.

Griffin hints that he believes in eternal life, but clearly eschatological concerns play little role in his theodicy. He says he cannot imagine that present and future evil is so bad as to make it better that human life had never been created. Is Griffin saying that the intrinsic goods that now exist are so great that they outweigh any evil events that might occur in the future? It would seem an exercise in pollyanna optimism if so. What if ten years from now all human beings die, cursing God, after years of horrible physical and mental suffering? Will God's great adventure have turned out worthwhile? I hardly think so. At this point orthodox Christianity seems far more realistic. Good events do indeed occur—so it declares—but the power of evil is pervasive. The world is not worthwhile as it stands: it needs to be redeemed.

So even if we grant Griffin his view of omnipotence (which I am unwilling to do), it still follows that God is indictable for creating the world if in the end evil outweighs good. The God of process reminds me of a mad scientist who fashions a monster whom the scientist hopes will behave but whom he cannot control. If the monster runs amok the scientist's decision to make the monster will turn out to have been terribly wrong. The scientist will be indictable.

REJOINDER

The main criticisms of my position involve the interrelated issues of *creatio ex nihilo*, divine power, and worshipfulness. I will begin by responding to this cluster of criticisms.

Creatio ex Nihilo

Thinking I object to this doctrine on the wrong grounds, Phillips says that whereas his grounds are philosophical ("logical"), mine are scientific. I do not know why he thinks this. Somewhat contradictorily, he then mentions that "Griffin's main problem with creation *ex nihilo* is that he thinks it involves an absolute conception of God's power," but Phillips claims that "Griffin shares a conception of God's will as sheer power with those he criticizes." Again, I cannot imagine where he got that idea. Phillips next says that "God's power is a certain *kind* of power," as if this were not my contention. But it is, as statements below will illustrate.

Hick begins by suggesting that my argument was merely about the proper translation of Genesis 1:1, whereas my point is that *creatio ex nihilo* is not biblical at all. Hick's response, in any case, is to say that I may be right but he doubts "whether it really matters." This is noteworthy. One of the chief criticisms of process theology has always been that, by virtue of its rejection of *creatio ex nihilo*, it could be ignored in Christian discussions of theodicy. Hick himself said: "To solve the problem of evil by means of the theory . . . of a finite deity who does the best he can with a material, intractable, and coeternal with himself, is to have abandoned the basic premise of Hebrew-Christian monotheism."[75] In making such claims, Hick was echoing the dominant consensus, a crucial factor in which was the conviction that *creatio ex nihilo* is the biblical view. But now that it appears not to be, Hick claims that it does not matter, that the real foundation of the doctrine is "a need to affirm the sole absoluteness and ultimacy of God"—which supports John Stuart Mill's judgment that this doctrine is the product of a wish.

Whether the doctrine is biblical does, in any case, matter to Davis. He admits that it is not explicitly taught but thinks that it is "strongly suggested" by those New Testament texts that May, himself a believer in *creatio ex nihilo*, says do *not* support it. Against the weight of May's scholarship, Davis places his own judgment that "the plain sense indicates that they do." But Davis does not mention the crucial point in May's argument—that the traditional appeal to those passages had falsely assumed that *creatio ex nihilo* had been taught in 2 Maccabees and therefore could have been presupposed by early Christian writers. Davis also argues that neither in Genesis 1:1 nor "anywhere else in the Bible" is there any suggestion "of a preexistent 'stuff' that was not created by God," but here Davis goes against the majority opinion of Hebrew Bible scholars. Davis rightly says that in Genesis 1 "God creates with a kind of effortless ease," but this picture stands in contrast with other passages, in which a real battle with chaos is reflected (Ps. 74:12–17; Isa. 51:9–11), and even in Genesis 1 neither the waters nor the darkness are said to be created.[76]

Omnipotence and Worshipfulness

The main charge from Davis, Roth, and (by implication) Hick is that the God portrayed by process theism is not worthy of worship. I addressed this issue in "Worshipfulness and the Omnipotence Fallacy" (in *God, Power, and Evil*), in which I argued that what people consider worshipful is partly a matter of cultural conditioning. Having come to associate worship with a God possessing coercive omnipotence, Western thinkers are—I cited Terence Penelhum as saying—"merely bored" by any solutions to the problem of evil that solve the problem in terms of a God without that kind of power. As a result, I suggested,

> [although most theologians] would agree that a worshipful being must be perfect only in the sense of being the "greatest conceivable" . . . , they do not carefully consider the arguments of the so-called "finitists" that only their revised view of God, not the traditional one, really meets this criterion. Rather, they are so "bored" with the "finite" God that they curtly dismiss it with mockery and name-calling. (258)

Insofar as this was a prediction of future responses, Roth fulfilled it, beginning his critique by speaking of my "God on a leash" and closing it by describing this God as "too small" and "rather pathetic." Davis, while not resorting to name-calling, holds essentially the same view, saying that "Griffin's God is nowhere near powerful enough to merit worship." This same charge is implicit in Hick's characterization of this God as a "finite deity," a "benevolent God of limited power," belief in which Hick considers a mere "expedient."

All these charges imply that the traditional doctrine of omnipotence, according to which all power essentially belongs to God alone, makes sense. Process theists argue that it does not. Accordingly, although process theists

Creation and the Problem of Evil   139

agree that God, to be worshipful, must have perfect power, with "perfect" defined as the "greatest conceivable," we do not find traditional theism's idea of omnipotence consistently conceivable, so we do not find that it provides a standard in terms of which to say that the power of process theism's God is imperfect, finite, or limited.

These critics also speak as if we agree with them about the *kind* of power God has while suggesting that God has less of it than they think. But our point is that, in light of both Christian faith and good philosophy, divine power should be thought of not as coercive power, but as persuasive power, the power of love.

One dimension of the philosophical argument is that traditional theism, in attributing coercive power to God, implicitly treats God as a finite being with a body. As pure mind or soul, I would have only persuasive power. I have coercive power by virtue of my body, especially my hands, through which I can "manipulate" things. But, theologians have always said, God is pure spirit, having "no hands but our hands." And yet traditional theism attributed to God the kind of power that could intelligibly be attributed to God only if there were a divine body between the divine spirit and us. On this basis, I have argued that "coercive power, far from being a necessary attribute of a universal, omnipresent being, is, like a voice, a beard, and a hand, an attribute that can characterize only a finite, localized being."[77]

The argument from Christian faith, along with the way in which its significance has been distorted by traditional theism, was addressed in my chapter in *Evil Revisited* on "Worship and Theodicy," from which I now beg the reader's permission to quote at some length.

> The question of what idea or image of God in fact evokes a religious response from us is largely a question of the image or concept of God we have been conditioned by our social upbringing to associate with religious feelings. Because the dominant religion of Western culture has been Christianity, the crucial question for most of those in this culture is what notion of deity has been portrayed by Christianity. . . .
>
> The central theological tragedy of Christianity is that, having originated with events that radically challenged the prevailing notion of divine power as controlling, unilateral, overwhelming force, it soon returned to and even intensified this notion.
>
> Christianity takes as the supreme incarnation and revelation of God a man who taught love of enemies, forgiveness, and nonretaliation, and who died on a cross as the victim of the powers of this world. Christianity even adopted the cross of Jesus as its chief symbol, thereby suggesting that salvation comes through God's suffering love. The idea that God's agent of deliverance from evil would be one who was the victim, rather than the conqueror, of the coercive powers of this world stood in strong tension with the idea of God as the one

whose "mighty hand" controls all earthly forces, including the coercive power of an imperialistic state. . . .

But from the outset this radically different understanding of divine
power (which had roots within the Hebrew Bible and analogues in
other traditions, such as Platonism) had to contend with tendencies to
dilute it, and even to absorb it within the prevailing view of divine
omnipotence. Already within the New Testament we see the attempt
to say that Jesus' death was the fulfillment of the divine plan, which
means that God was in complete control all along. The fact that Jesus
did not fit the preconception of a messianic warrior-king was handled
by distinguishing between the first and the second comings. As Burton Cooper critically summarizes this rationalization: "in the first
coming, Christ comes as the vulnerable one, the one who suffers for
us, but in the second coming, Christ will show himself as the monar-
chial Christ, the one who comes with coercive power." The result of
this rationalization is that the revolutionary implication of taking a
"suffering servant" as the chief incarnation and revelation of God is
muted. . . .

This tendency was reinforced by several theological developments.
. . . [To the ones I mentioned I should have added the development of
the doctrine of *creatio ex nihilo*.] . . .

Although the two ideas of divine power have coexisted side by side,
the idea of coercive omnipotence has been dominant. Persons in our
culture have thereby been taught, in countless ways, to equate divine
power, and thereby real power, with the power to control, the power
to coerce, the power to destroy. . . . Given these images and feelings
embedded deep in our psyches, it is very difficult to feel that some
other kind of power—in particular, the power of suffering, persuasive
love—is real power, divine power, power worthy of worship.

[T]he idea of God suggested by process theism can solve the problem of evil, is intellectually satisfying in many other respects, and
would have many beneficial psychological and social effects. . . . And
yet it is widely perceived to be religiously inadequate, because it does
not portray God as having the kind of power with which religious awe
has been associated from childhood on. (209–11)

An exemplification of the final point is provided by Roth, who says that
"[t]his God inspires little awe, little sense of holiness"—attitudes that *are*
evoked in Roth, evidently, by a God who, while lacking in goodness, possesses
overwhelming power. Roth mockingly says, in reference to Auschwitz, that
"the best [Griffin's] God could possibly do was to permit nearly ten thousand
Jews a day to go up in smoke." Roth prefers a God who had the power to prevent this Holocaust but did not do it.

Roth also supports his point by referring to the history of the world. Saying that the God of persuasion I portray has not been effective enough in the
world to inspire awe and worship, Roth speaks of God's "unpersuasive perfor-

mance in the world to date." Personally, when I contemplate the creation as a whole, I am overwhelmed. When I view the heavens and the beauty of our planet, when I reflect upon the fact that creatures as wondrously complex as dolphins and ourselves were brought into being out of tiny trajectories of energy such as protons and electrons, I stand in awe before the Powerful Wisdom that could produce such results out of partially self-determining entities. But perhaps Roth is more difficult to impress than I am.

Or perhaps Roth simply takes all of this for granted. In saying that there has been little progress, he speaks only of *moral* progress; in speaking of resistance, he speaks only of *human* resistance. I agree that resistance has been far greater at the human level; the purpose of my variables of power and value is to show why the human capacity for resistance is necessarily so great. I also agree that moral progress has been ambiguous, with gains balanced by losses. The work in progress to which I referred in my critique of Roth's essay seeks to explain why, due to civilizational anarchy, such ambiguity has been inevitable and also how we, through global democracy, could overcome it. The claim implicit in my title—"The Divine Cry of Our Time"—is that this is the goal toward which God is now calling us. In any case, I turn now to a number of other criticisms.

Response to Hick

Dismissing my Whiteheadian theodicy as unimportant because it simply presents one more version of "a finite deity," Hick declares that "[w]hat is primarily of interest" in my essay is my argument that, given the traditional idea of God, "no viable theodicy is possible." Hick, accordingly, devotes most of his "critique" of my theodicy to one more defense of his own. But he does introduce this defense with a criticism. After quoting my statement that according to all-determining theism "literally every event and feature of the world . . . is fully determined by God" and then mentioning that I had named several great theologians who had taught this, Hick says: "I doubt very much whether most of them did in fact teach this." I can only hope that Hick does not intend this as an example of "philosophical criticism" for young aspiring philosophers to emulate. I had devoted an entire chapter of *God, Power, and Evil* to each of the theologians I had named. Is it now acceptable to cast aspersions on a colleague's scholarship without citing a single example of misinterpretation?

Response to Phillips

Because Phillips has a distaste for metaphysics (except for his own, which he does not acknowledge), it is not surprising that his main criticism of my position is directed at the fact that it *is* metaphysical. I frankly cannot see how most of his argument, which summarizes his standard, one-size-fits-all criticism of metaphysics, is relevant. His one reference to my position in particular is that I claim "that all things are embodiments of creativity, differing only in degree." But creativity is embodied only in *actual individuals*, and they constitute only one of Whitehead's eight categories of existence. Although I did, in the passage Phillips draws on, speak loosely of "all things," the examples— electrons, living cells, and human beings—show that I was speaking of enduring individuals. And the fact that not all things differ "only in degree" is shown by my distinction between "compound individuals" and "aggregational societies," which differ in kind. These points are relevant to Phillips's criticism that "an explanation of 'everything' is an explanation of nothing," which he illustrates by saying that no single account can be given of mathematical, physical, and moral necessity. That is precisely why Whitehead's metaphysics, unlike the materialistic metaphysics presupposed in the scientism Phillips rightly opposes, has not just one but eight categories of existence, including eternal objects of the objective species (mathematical forms) and the subjective species (such as moral norms). Phillips also complains that he cannot see "how our actual practices are to be derived from [Griffin's] metaphysical principles." But who would suppose that they should be? One can never derive the specific from the generic.

Response to Roth

Roth raises questions about my judgment that there are "some necessary principles." His first question is what status this judgment has. As I said, the whole position—that our world was created out of chaos so there are some necessary (metaphysical) principles—is a speculative hypothesis. (Roth had, in fact, acknowledged this in his previous paragraph.) Roth then asks whether my judgment is "necessarily true or . . . possibly false?" The latter, of course, which is why I call it a speculative hypothesis, not an a priori truth. (Perhaps Roth, who issues a warning about confusions surrounding the concept of necessity, has himself succumbed to the confusion that if a judgment is *about* necessity it must itself claim to *be* necessary.) He then asks "What does it mean to say that a principle is necessary?" As I explained, it would mean that this principle would obtain in any world God could create. He then asks, "What existence do principles have?" At the outset of my final section, I had said: "Although the brief account provided here will necessarily leave many questions unanswered, the interested reader can consult the more extensive accounts that I have provided elsewhere," followed by a reference to the relevant writings. Had Roth been such a reader, he could have learned that I affirm Hartshorne's position that they belong to the eternal essence of God.[78] Roth would evidently find all these answers irrelevant, however, because he says that, because of the lack of agreement among philosophers, whatever answers I give "will not be completely accepted." Does Roth hold his own speculations to this impossibly high standard?

In any case, Roth turns next to my discussion of four variables of power and value. With reference to my suggestion that the positive correlations obtaining among them in our world are necessary correlations, which would hold in any world God could create, Roth asks: "what is the evidence supporting Griffin's claim for such necessity?" Again, as I said, this is a speculative hypothesis—although more grounded speculation, I pointed out, than Roth's supposition that they would *not* necessarily obtain in every possible world.

Roth then challenges, by means of "counterexamples," the idea that these correlations hold even in *our* world. Against the principle that the capacities to enjoy positive value and to suffer rise together, he points out that a decrease in his capacity to suffer from disease does not decrease his capacity to experience positive values. But my principle involves, as I said, "types of individuals," which I illustrated in terms of humans, cats and dogs, fleas, and cells. More relevantly, to rebut the correlation between the capacity to enjoy value and the capacity to be destructive, Roth says that this would mean that his "potential to experience value is somehow dependent on [his capacity] to help unleash genocide." Exactly. No dogs, even no chimpanzees, could unleash genocide. The human capacity for symbolism—the same capacity that allows us to enjoy literature, mathematics, science, philosophy, and all other distinctively human pursuits—gives us the capacity to formulate and carry out genocidal plans.

Response to Davis

One of Davis's questions about my position involves its Whiteheadian view that the most fundamental units of the world are momentary events rather than enduring substances. His main argument in favor of the priority of substances is that Whitehead's events ("actual occasions") either have duration or they do not, and if they do, which he correctly sees to be Whitehead's view, then "substances are ultimate after all." That is fine. Whitehead's complaint about the traditional view of substances was not "the employment of the word 'substance'" but "the notion of an actual entity which . . . remains numerically one amidst the changes of accidental relations."[79] The fact that Whitehead's "substances," being momentary actual occasions, overcome this notion is important for several reasons, one of which is that it allows us to conceptualize the interweaving of efficient causation and final causation (self-determination), which we in practice presuppose all the time (as I have explained in chapter 3 of *Reenchantment without Supernaturalism*).

Another question from Davis is whether my idea that "every actual thing must have power of its own over against God" really entails that "God cannot directly deflect a moving automobile." Yes it does, partly because this power is (by hypothesis) nonoverridable and partly because of the distinction between aggregational societies, such as automobiles, and compound individuals, such as human beings. God can "deflect" my body—albeit not unilaterally—because I have a dominant member, my mind or soul, which God can persuade and which can then cause my body to change course. But an aggregational society by definition has no dominant member, so there is no locus in it through which God can influence the spatiotemporal trajectory of the society as a whole.

Davis also argues against me, he thinks, by saying that it is possible "to believe in creation out of nothing without holding that God is the source or cause of literally everything," such as Davis's most recent sin. Of course it is. Having defined traditional theism in terms of acceptance of *creatio ex nihilo*, I described two versions of it, the all-determining and the free-will versions.

Davis, finally, thinks that my theodicy is not strongly eschatological. I think that, when he reads some of my later writings, he will be surprised.

5

Theism without Theodicy

D. Z. Phillips

Theodicy Rejected, Not Revised

"Theism" is the belief that the world has been created by one God. In contemporary Anglo-American analytic philosophy of religion, "theodicy" is used "broadly to cover any theistic response to questions about how theism can be true in view of the existence of evils."[1] Thus, at a stroke, theism is taken to entail theodicy. On this view, anyone denying theodicy will be taken to be denying theism. That is how John Hick takes my denial: "his fundamental objections to theodicies is the radical and wholesale objection that since there is no *theos* there can be no theodicy."[2] Hick acknowledges, however, that I disagree with him, and many other philosophers, over what it means to speak of the reality of God. Exegetical accuracy should have led Hick to say that, in my opinion, theism does not entail theodicy—the exact opposite of the view he attributes to me. Why is my view so difficult even to recognize, whether one agrees with it or not?

Theodicy offers a kind of language in which to reflect on the reality of God, the divine attributes, and their relation to human suffering. We can be lulled into a complacent acceptance of its parameters. But what if the confusion is in this very language? Again and again in the history of philosophy, problems can only be dealt with by rejecting the language in which they are posed. Other possibilities will not be recognized. Instead, they will be thought of as defective forms of the same kind of argument, or even as a failure to argue at all. Swinburne complains: "I do not share Phillips's conviction that evil is pointless, and I do not find enough *argument* in Phillips's paper to show that it is."[3] Hick characterizes my opposition to theodicies as a failure to recognize "that the serious and honest theist must face the challenge which the fact of evil, and above all the fact of undeserved suffering, pose to his faith in God."[4] I am asking, however, whether the challenge Hick mentions, which I do not deny, is distorted by theodicy. I am not an antitheist, like J. L. Mackie, whose opposition is expressed within a theodicist framework.[5] I want to probe the character of that framework.

The language of theodicy has a philosophical history. "It is certainly no exaggeration to say that virtually every contemporary discussion of the theodicy-question is premised, implicitly or explicitly, on an understanding of God overwhelmingly constrained by the principles of seventeenth- and eighteenth-century philosophical deism."[6] Philosophers question God within parameters set by Hume's *Dialogues Concerning Natural Religion*: "Is he willing to prevent evil, but not able? then he is impotent. Is he able, but not willing? then he is malevolent. Is he both able and willing? whence then is evil?"[7]

In Hume's *Dialogues*, these questions are asked of the God of Cleanthes: an anthropomorphic God. By contrast, we find Job saying of God:

> For he is not a mortal, as I am, that I might answer him,
> that we should come to trial together
>
> (9:32)

Cleanthes, on the other hand, says it is clear that "if we abandon all human analogy . . . I am afraid we abandon all religion, and retain no conception of the great object of our adoration."[8] For him, an anthropomorphic God is the only logically possible conception of God. Philo wonders how Cleanthes "can still persevere in [his] anthropomorphism, and assert the moral attributes of the Deity, his justice, benevolence, mercy and rectitude to be of the same nature with these virtues in human creatures,"[9] and thinks that "so long as there is any vice at all in the universe, it will very much puzzle you anthropomorphites, how to account for it."[10]

Are there alternatives to anthropomorphism in the *Dialogues*? I want to explore two suggestions made by Philo which, given Hume's assumptions, he cannot develop in any promising direction. Philo says that someone could advance an *a priori* conception of God's goodness. Because he still thinks of God's goodness as "a goodness like the human,"[11] he thinks such a suggestion is the high road to ignorance. More interestingly, he also says that someone might have an *antecedent* belief in God's goodness. Though human misery would disappoint such a person, "he would never retract his former belief"[12] in face of it. By "former" belief, Philo means a belief held prior to acquaintance with the world. The person holding such a belief he describes as a person of low intelligence. This is not our actual situation. We *are* in the world. Therefore, along with fellow theodicists, Philo says that we must argue inductively to God from known phenomena.

Philo's conclusion is premature. An antecedent belief need not be an *a priori* one. We are taught conceptions of God in scripture, catechisms, stories, etc. These conceptions have not been arrived at inductively. In that sense one might call them antecedent. But the point of these conceptions is to give us a way of understanding human life. This leads Simone Weil to say that what we have here is an experiential ontological argument: "The Gospel contains a conception of human life, not a theology. If I light an electric torch at night out of doors I don't judge its power by looking at the bulb, but by seeing how many objects it lights up. The brightness of a source of light is appreciated by the illumination it projects upon non-luminous objects. The value of a religious or, more generally, a spiritual way of life is appreciated by the amount of illumination thrown upon the things of the world."[13]

My argument is that theodicy fails to do justice to the things of the world. In the Christian tradition, God is said to be Spirit. Our question then becomes: How does this notion of spirit illuminate the problem of evil, while remaining true to the facts of human suffering? This question will be addressed in the fourth section of the paper.

Theodicy's Bee Stings

Referring to what I have called antecedent beliefs in religion, Wittgenstein says: "Religion says: *Do this!—Think like that!*—but it cannot justify it, and, if it tries to, it becomes repellent, because for every reason it offers there is a valid counter reason." With theodicists, for example, the impression is created that counter-reasons are suppressed and not given the attention they deserve. Then, as in Wittgenstein's case, "you feel you were being cheated, that someone was trying to convince you by trickery." Wittgenstein is not saying that a theodicist sets out deliberately to deceive anyone. The theodicist is the victim of the deception. The deception and dishonesty are in the thoughts that hold him or her captive. But when someone is offered these thoughts in defense of a theodicy, they strike the person as thoughts of that kind; thoughts that have not given suffering the attention it deserves. This happens because an anthropomorphite does exactly what, according to Wittgenstein, should not be done: "Someone can be told for instance: 'Thank God for the good you receive,'" but not in such a way that you would also "complain about the evil, as you would of course do if a human being were to do you good and evil by turns." If one ignores this advice, one seems committed to showing, somehow, that the evil is not what it seems to be. That is what Wittgenstein, and many others, find repellent. The embarrassing result is that what seems like a sensitive account of suffering to the theodicist will strike others as almost a paradigm of insensitivity.[14] This comes as an understandable shock to the theodicist.

Theodicy, which is supposed to explain evil, is said, at its worst, to contribute to it.

Wittgenstein makes his point in terms of an allegory of the bees: "I can say: 'Thank these bees for their honey, as though they were kind people who have prepared it for you;' that is *intelligible* and describes how I should like you to conduct yourself. But I cannot say: 'Thank them because, look, how kind they are!'—since the next moment they may sting you."[15] I want to look at some of the bee stings that, I shall argue, theodicy suffers.[16]

The first bee sting results from the following argument: Suffering prompts moral responsibility. That people are morally responsible is a good thing. Therefore, this justifies the suffering. The argument leads to a grotesque inversion of moral relations to the sufferings of others. Instead of our concern being directed towards the suffering, the suffering is said to have its point in the concern. It would have the Good Samaritan saying, "Thank you, God, for another opportunity for my moral development." Surely, when not philosophizing, the theodicist does not regard people's sufferings, in an instrumental way, as being *for* anything. As Somerset Maugham says: "It may be that courage and sympathy are excellent and that they could not come into existence without danger and suffering. It is hard to see how the Victoria Cross that records the soldier who has risked his life to save a blinded man is going to solace *him* for the loss of his sight. To give alms shows charity, and charity is a virtue, but does *that* good compensate for the evil of the cripple whose poverty has called it forth?"[17]

It is important to appreciate the conceptual character of the criticism. Brian Davies asks, "Is Phillips wrong in taking the line that he does? It is very hard to see how we are to settle the question, for what is now at stake is a fundamental *moral* option. . . . One side is saying that the whole attempt to justify God in terms of consequences is simply intolerable. . . . The other side holds that it is not intolerable."[18] But what is at issue is not a moral dispute, but whether conceptual justice has been done to the notion of moral responsibility.

Theodicy incurs a second bee sting in trying to avoid the first. The purpose of suffering is now said to be in the sufferer. The theodicist tells us that God has created human beings immature, so that they may develop morally in the course of their lives. One way we develop morally is by coping with suffering and that, it is said, is why God allows it.

This second argument does not, in fact, avoid the first bee sting. The suffering we experience may be caused by what happens to loved ones. A mother may show great strength of character in coping with the death of her child. But does that strength justify the death? Is that something a theodicist would actually say to a mother: "God allowed the death of your child so that you might develop strength of character"?[19]

The third bee sting is caused by the general claim that, of necessity, theodicy has to make: that suffering is always beneficial to the sufferer. When theodicists are not philosophizing, they know this is not true. Do they really need reminders such as this: "I set down in my notebooks, not once or twice, but in a dozen places, the facts that I had seen. I knew that suffering did not enoble; it degraded. It made men selfish, mean, petty, and suspicious. It absorbed them in small things. It did not make them more than men; it made them less than men; and I wrote ferociously that we learn resignation not by our own suffering, but by the suffering of others"?[20]

If we try to maintain the generality of the theodicist's claim, hard questions must not be avoided: "What is the value of suffering like that in *King Lear*? What was the value of the *degradation* that belonged to the sufferings in the concentration camps? When, for instance, a man is going to pieces morally and knows it. 'Joyful acceptance'???"[21] Rhees adds: "If I could put my questions more strongly, I should do so. For I think that religious apologists have generally been irresponsible and frivolous in writing about this matter. They have deceived both themselves and others by such phrases as 'suffering for Christ,' 'joyful sacrifice,' etc."[22]

The fourth bee sting comes from trying to explain hard cases where the disastrous effects of suffering are all too obvious. The apologetic takes the form of moving the culpability from God to the victims of suffering. Swinburne asks us to at least keep open the possibility that such people have "given in to forces which [they] could have resisted" [because] "that's just what we don't know until philosophers and scientists together have solved the free will problem."[23] Even if this recourse to philosophical and scientific ignorance were unproblematic, it should at least dent the confidence of any general theodicist claim in this context. It cannot be said that every time a person is crushed by circumstances, that person had the resources to resist. If that were claimed, Rhees has an apt reply: "'They could have refused.' Could they? ('We who have not fallen'—the fall that there is in *that*. Circumstances by which people are defeated.)"[24]

The fifth bee sting comes from the fact that Swinburne's recourse to ignorance concerning free will is not unproblematic. Swinburne sublimes the judgement, "We don't know whether so-and-so could have resisted the circumstances which crushed her" and gives it a metaphysical status. Its actual home is as a specific judgment, alongside other judgments we make in this respect: "She could have resisted that" or "She didn't stand a chance." These judgments derive their sense from the concrete circumstances that occasion them, not from philosophy or science. Why should they be reduced to the one Swinburne favors? To do so is to suppress the variety of moral judgments we actually make.

The sixth bee sting comes from the attempt to deny the judgment that gives theodicy most trouble, if we think of life as God's finishing school, in which immature beginners are supposed to become mature adults. This is the judgment that people are sometimes defeated by circumstances. To deny, with Swinburne, that we can ever be certain of this is also to deny the appropriateness of that compassion that this certainty can occasion.

Consider the following example: "For six years the captured Gallic general Vercengetorix was kept shackled, solitary, in total darkness, expect on one day of each year when he was brought out in his chains and exhibited for the scorn of the Roman mob. Do you honestly think that *anybody* would be ennobled by that? Or: if he 'joyfully accepted it' how long could he keep this up—remember that he never spoke to anyone from one year's end to the other. Take any saint you like and try to imagine it."[25]

What can a theodicist say to such things? There are times when Swinburne appeals, not to our philosophical and scientific ignorance concerning free will, but to an ignorance he alleges we have in such situations, compared with God's greater knowledge. For example, when God hears the screams of human beings, Swinburne says that God "may know that the suffering A will cause B is not nearly as great as B's screams might suggest to us and will provide (unknown to us) an opportunity to C to help B recover and will thus give C a deep responsibility which he would not otherwise have. God may well have reason for allowing particular evils which it is our bounden duty to stop at all costs simply because he knows so much more about them than we do."[26] Alvin Plantinga also appeals to our ignorance, adding that "it is only *hubris* which would tempt us to think that we could so much as grasp God's plans here, even if he proposed to divulge them to us."[27] One difference between Swinburne and Plantinga is that the latter admits "that most of the attempts to explain why God permits evil—*theodicies*, as we might call them—seem to me shallow, tepid, and ultimately frivolous."[28] But even in the appeal to our ignorance and God's unknown purposes, the instrumental view of human suffering, which we have already criticized, is reintroduced.

The appeal to our ignorance in face of horrendous evils has far-reaching consequences, since it involves the thought that these evils may not be so horrendous after all. Swinburne urges us not to be too hasty in our judgments. For example, "if we saw a man sawing off another's leg . . . our initial moral indignations might have been quite misplaced—maybe the man was doing his utmost to save another's life, removing a wounded leg in the absence of anaesthetics."[29] Notice the introduction of unfavorable circumstances on which Swinburne's necessary skepticism depends. This skepticism depends on a contrast with certainty—the certainty that the doctor was trying to save his patient. How, then, can Swinburne rule out, as he must, the possibility of examples going in the opposite direction? Our initial moral admiration of the fact that prisoners are being treated medically might have been quite misplaced—the prisoners were being mutilated by their racist captors. Theodicy cannot accommodate a counterexample simply by invoking an example favorable to its case. How are the racist atrocities countered by invoking the doctor trying to save a patient's life by amputation in the absence of anesthetics?[30] Theodicy cannot depend on a one-sided diet of examples.

The seventh bee sting comes from the consequentialist suppression of the absolute moral condemnation of atrocities. Swinburne suggests that, in philosophy, we must be open-minded about every situation. In the busyness of life, we are sometimes forced to act before all the implications of a situation can be explored. But with respect to his symposium with me, Swinburne says, things are different: "We are not delaying essential action by insisting on moral theorizing. We are doing philosophy. And when we are doing philosophy . . . it is *never* a 'sign of a corrupt mind' to be open-minded about things."[31] But Swinburne is not being philosophically open-minded about the moral judgments we make. If he were, he would recognize that faced by atrocities it is possible *not* to think that there can be any further interests that would justify them. If in some situations we are morally over-hasty, in others we are not. Sometimes, initial moral judgments are not vindicated. At other times, they are. Emphasizing certainty in one context, Swinburne rules out its logical possibility in another.

The eighth bee sting involves the way in which the logic of anthropomorphism pursues the God of the unknown plans. A God, so conceived, must be judged by moral standards already available to us. If we are certain of an atrocity, we are equally certain of our judgment in very many cases. Hence the justice of the following criticism: "And neither shall we tolerate that swindle which the believers are guilty of when they call an act 'a most shameful crime,' 'a most irreparable infamy,' as long as it is done by a man, but an 'act of inscrutable love' if God is its author. Either one or the other: the same law and the same sentence, but not the same law and different sentences."[32] Anthropomorphism can demand no less. Nor can we justify God by appeal to different standards, since, within anthropomorphism, they must be assessed in relation to our own. The results are of no use to the apologist, since outside all our standards of decency is the place we reserve either for the monstrous, or for something not even worthy of moral judgment. In the first case, we end up with a really malignant demon, unlike Descartes's; in the second case, we are confronted by "a ruler of grotesque primitivity, a cosmic cave dweller, a braggart and a rumble-dumble, almost congenial in his complete ignorance about spiritual refinement."[33]

The ninth bee sting is not often recognized: The anthropomorphite abandons anthropomorphism when the going gets tough. The appeal to God's unknown plans is such an abandonment. Cleanthes, at least, is consistent, and will have none of it: "No! . . . No! These arbitrary suppositions can never be admitted, contrary to matter of fact, visible and uncontroverted. Whence can any cause be known but from its human effects? Whence can any hypothesis be proved but from the apparent phenomena? To establish one hypothesis upon another is building entirely in the air."[34] Swinburne pursues Cleanthes-like strategies in most of his arguments, but what he meets in human life forces him to abandon them, and to take refuge in ignorance: philosophical and scientific ignorance about free will, or human ignorance about God's plans.

A tenth bee sting must be mentioned before I leave the concerns of this section of my paper. Swinburne claims that God cannot send unlimited suffering to anyone, since there is a limit to what anyone can stand: "persons only live in our world so many years and the amount which they can suffer at any given time . . . is limited by their physiology."[35]

The bee sting in the argument is the suppressed confusion between conceptual and actual limits that it relies on. The infinite series, 2, 4, 6, 8 . . . is limitless, because it makes no sense to speak of the last number in the series. In people's actual sufferings, "unlimited" refers to that which is extravagantly beyond what a person can stand. If a person dies of his wounds, or is crushed by his troubles, would it not be grotesque to number the wounds or troubles, and claim that that number cannot be unlimited, because the rule "plus two" can be continued to infinity?

I have selected ten bee stings to comment on in this section. I believe their effect is such that what we need to do is not to revise theodicy, but to reject it.

God and Grammar

In the previous section, I have deliberately ignored the theodicist's main response when faced by the problem of evil: the free-will defense. Human life, it is said, cannot be what it is without freedom. That freedom involves the risk of all the evils I have mentioned. Whatever we think of these evils, human life is worth it. In reply to this defense, it has been suggested that God could have seen to it that human beings freely always make the right decisions, so avoiding the evils they perpetrate. Unlike Swinburne, who argued that for good reasons God has chosen not to do this, I argued that the very suggestion contains a metaphysical notion of "seeing to it" that is unintelligible.[36] Hick sees this as a backhanded support for theodicy, and says that my logical objections make theodicy even stronger.[37] This reaction is natural for a theodicist, as long as we fail to recognize the sense in which the free-will defense is both profoundly right and profoundly wrong.

The free-will defense is profoundly right in thinking that we could not have anything recognizable as human life without the freedoms and their attendant risks that we have mentioned. It is also profoundly right in thinking that a religious response to life involves, in some sense, being grateful for it. On the other hand, the free will defense is profoundly wrong in thinking that since human life is God's gift, the gift must be *for* something. By thinking that the gift must be for something, the relation between God and the world becomes an anthropomorphic one, and human beings, as we have seen, become the objects of God's moral experiment.

The gift of life is said to come from God who dwells outside the world. I am taking it for granted that no one wants to argue that God's dwelling place is one which could be located empirically, or that God could be empirically located as the object that dwells there. Anthropomorphism turns God into an invisible man. Thus, Swinburne thinks of God as a person without a body,[38] because of his Cartesian assumption that a human being is a person with one. On this view, the essence of a person—human or divine—is consciousness. This confusion has many implications, but one example must suffice here.

If there is no necessary connection between consciousness and a body, it ought to be possible for consciousness to inhabit a radically different body without loss of identity. Wittgenstein asks us to imagine consciousness addressing us out of the mouth of a lion. He says that we would not understand him.[39] The words are physical sounds, of course, but let that pass. The words do not say anything in the mouth of a lion, because the lion does not participate in that form of life in which "saying this" has its sense. Sever that connection and what we have is not "pure consciousness," but nothing at all.

Things grow conceptually worse if we eliminate the physical words of the voice of consciousness and imagine consciousness simply in dialogue with itself. We run into all the logical difficulties concerning a logically private language, rules that are supposed to generate their own application, and ideas that are supposed to generate their own meanings. In short, we end up with what Wittgenstein called a magical conception of language, rules, and ideas. Hick thinks of God as a "consciousness," because he thinks of human beings as "consciousness," too. But talk of "consciousness" in both contexts is problematic. Because he does not realize this, he becomes impatient with me for not giving a direct answer to the question of whether "in addition to all human consciousness there is another consciousness which is the consciousness of God."[40] I can only reply, with Charles Hartshorne, in words that could have come equally from Wittgenstein: "Confusion in the posing of a question generates confusion in the answering of it."[41] In speaking of "consciousness" in the way he does, Hick not only reifies an idea, an accusation Feuerbach might have made of him, but reifies a confused idea. So I do not deny it; it is not intelligible enough to deny.

Although Hick claims that God is a "consciousness," he also says that God is "beyond the scope of human conceptuality."[42] I think this confuses "religious mystery" with "epistemological mystery," but I cannot explore it further here.[43] We do speak of God in our language. This may puzzle us. In that case, it awaits analysis. In that sense, "God" is as humble a word as "chair" or "table."

What is the grammar of "God"? A Hindu saying that fascinates Hick can help us: "Thou art formless: thy only form is our knowledge of thee."[44] How is this to be read? I suggest the following: "'God' is formless" means that it does not refer to a quasi-empirical object; it is not a "something," as Wittgenstein might say. In the same way, Aquinas insisted, God is not a substance, nor a member of any species or genus.[45] But, Wittgenstein would say, "God" is not a "nothing" either. If we want to understand the sense in which God is said to be real, the divine's "only form," we must look to see what is meant by knowledge of the divine.

The very language regarding the divine may suggest that it is epistemically out of reach. Is not God's dwelling place said to be outside the world? Aren't we tempted to say, for skeptical or Spinozistic reasons, that that is no place at all?

Peter Winch invites us to consider a similar skepticism applied to geometry. We are told that parallel lines meet at infinity. If we ignore the geometry and simply ask, "Do parallel lines meet?" the answer will be, "No." So why not say that "at infinity" is no place at all? But the notion that "parallel lines meet at infinity" does have an application, but not one that can be inferred from the phenomenon of parallel lines. That application is to be found in the proofs and constructions that surround it, and which it illuminates.

If we ignore religious contexts, and ask where "outside the world" is, the answer will be, "No place at all." But the notion does have an application. It is not inferred, however, from the mixed character of human life (Cleanthes's anthropomorphism). "God dwelling outside the world" derives its sense from the illumination that it makes possible for the mixed life which surrounds it.[46]

God's gift of life is a gift from "outside the world." Obviously, the analogy of one person handing over a gift to another will not do here. The gift of a day, not to mention the gift of life, cannot be thought of as being "handed over." The nearest analogy to the religious conception of such gifts we have, in a human context, is our talk of a gifted child, or of a gifted artist. The emphasis is on the sheer givenness of the gifts. Anthropomorphism has no place in the conception of such gifts as God-given. But why should the gifts be said to come from "outside the world"?

All parties are agreed on one feature of the gift of life: the gift is imperfect. Perfection, absolute purity, and pure holiness are absent from the gift. We come to know these things through their absence, and through our longing for them. In this way, God becomes *present* to us through this form of absence.

God, in the form of these perfections, is *other than* our imperfect world. The "otherness" is a *spiritual* relation.

In Christianity, the notion of creation can be understood in terms of this "otherness." Creation is understood, not as an assertion of power, but as a withdrawal. Perfection allows something other than itself to exist. This "allowing" is seen as a grace, or as an expression of love.

At this point, it is grammatically tempting to ask: To whom do this grace and love belong? We begin to think of an individual to whom they are contingently related. This individual is thought of as having power which, at times, is expressed in love or grace. But who or what is the "it" that exercises this power?

Feuerbach has shown what happens when we separate love and grace from God in this way: love "shrinks out of observation as a collateral, an accident; at one moment it presents itself to me as something essential, at another, it vanishes again. God appears to me in another form besides that of love; in the form of omnipotence, of a severe power not bound by love; a power in which, though in a smaller degree, the devils participate."[47] On this view, God's power can be exercised in any number of directions. As Swinburne says, "I accept that an omnipotent being can prevent any evil he chooses."[48] This, as we have seen, leads to all the questions as to why he does not do so.

Feuerbach's analysis should lead us to think again about the divine attributes. In "God is love," is the "is" one of predication as in "Tony Blair is Prime Minister"? In the latter case, I can refer to Tony Blair without knowing that fact. He is that person over there who has arms, legs, a face, and so on. But when I say "God is love," or "God is gracious," what is the "it" to which the love or grace are attributed? There is none. That is "the metaphysical subject" which, as Feuerbach says, is an illusion. Feuerbach's mistake is to think that this forces us to think of "love" and "grace" as *human* predicates. He does not see that "God is love" and "God is gracious" are rules for the use of "God". To that extent, he is still in the grip of the metaphysics from which he thought he was free. Further, the pure love, grace, and holiness we speak of are unrealizable in this life and are, in that sense, "outside the world." It is said that we could not look fully at such perfections, the face of God, and live.

Acceptance of Life as God's Gift

We have presented for consideration a view of creation, not as an assertion of power, but as a withdrawal, so that human life may exist. Simone Weil suggests that creation, so conceived, involves both love and suffering. Love is involved because the gift of human life is given without reason. Human beings eat of the tree of the knowledge of good and evil, but, *contra* theodicy, this is not a moral experiment on God's part. Creation is an expression of free grace, but the gift also involves suffering for God and man. On the divine side, imperfection is allowed to exist with all that condition entails. Divine compassion is in response to the fact that human life, to be human, must be like that. On the human side are the sufferings that imperfections bring, and the longing for a perfection that can never be realized. Again, *contra* theodicy, human beings, in this view, do not see themselves as growing more mature daily under divine supervision, but as sinners who stand in daily need of grace.[49] Both the divine and the human recognize with Hamm in Beckett's *Endgame*, "You're on earth; there's no cure for that."

This view could be confused with fatalism if we simply emphasized God's absence. It is essential to recognize that this aspect is linked to the sense in which the divine can be present in the world—*present* in the form of absence. This point leads to our central question: How can a believer accept the gift of life, make it his or her own, while realizing that it is said to be a gift of love that also involves untold sufferings? Simone Weil's elucidation of a Christian conception of creation leads, not to fatalism, but to the problem of evil: What does it mean to accept God's gift in a suffering world?

I said that the free-will defense is profoundly right in recognizing that the religious response to life is one that involves, in some sense, being grateful for it. We are now in a position to see that that gratitude is for life as a whole; it is a way of accepting the gift. It is not arrived at by calculating whether the good things in life outweigh the bad things, and being grateful for that reason—"As though it were our experience of God's goodness that led us to love God. No, unless we know the love of God— . . . unless we could say 'Thank God'—we should not know even what was meant by God's goodness."[50] The problem of evil then becomes the issue of how we can say "Thank God" in this way, accept the gift, faced by the sufferings of human life.

Why this torment? That question is asked in a wide range of circumstances. Many of these involve the inhumanity that people have shown to others. Acceptance of life as God's gift involves opposing this inhumanity. If life is thanked for, and seen as a grace, we do not see things as ours by right. Those things include other people whose existences are also graces. Simone Weil sees a parallel between divine withdrawal in creation, letting human life be itself, and the withdrawal from the assertive, powerful self that we are called upon to make, allowing freedom for the other person. It is important to emphasize this constant call to die to the assertive self in relation to others, a call that has an imperative in personal and political contexts, to counter any suggestion that gratitude for life as such leads to quietism concerning human suffering. Gratitude for life entails compassion for others, but neither come easily to us: "It is not surprising that a man who has bread should give a piece to someone who is starving. What is surprising is that he should be capable of doing so with so different a gesture from that with which we buy an object. Almsgiving when it is not supernatural is like a sort of purchase. It buys the sufferer."[51] Is not that a common reaction to the God of theodicy who plans an obstacle course for our moral development? *That God buys the sufferer.*

Why this torment? This cry, from the midst of affliction, is not always answered, not even in a way that purchases the sufferer. What then? Can God be said to be present in that suffering? I offer no universal panacea. I am talking of what does occur in religion, not of what must occur there or elsewhere. Sometimes the cry, from the midst of affliction, when that cry goes unanswered by others, still does not plunge the sufferer into despair. The miracle of grace comes in an ability still to see a point in life *through that which is being violated.* Love need not seem pointless when ignored and violated by others. This approach is what prevents the sufferer from falling apart. The presence of this realization in the sufferer that love cannot compel, that sometimes it simply suffers, is the presence of divine compassion. It is not a compassion that changes the situation in relieving the distress. In that sense, the compassion does not try to do something, since it realizes that nothing can be done. When nothing can be done, people who refuse to recognize that fact purchase the sufferer. They refuse to recognize the plight of the sufferer. When some people are in this situation, they have been known to speak of a fellowship of suffering, in which, for them, what is being violated is not rendered pointless by its violation. They do not reject the gift of life. They may die, but in the case I have in mind, they do not curse God and die. A person deserted in affliction, if he or she does not lose hold of the point of what is violated, is not alone. In that sense, God or love remembers the sufferer and is in the suffering.

John Hick has accused these remarks of being highly elitist, something of which their proponents, he claims, are unaware. He thinks that the religious response I have talked of is only possible for "the fortunate ones who are not chronically undernourished, and living in fear of starvation, not trapped in abject poverty and desperately anxious for our own and our family's and community's short-term future. . . . But to think that *all* men and women are free to join in this positive response would be like saying that the desperately poor and starving . . . are free to rise into inner serenity and peace. This would be true only in a cruelly ironic sense. In principle they can do so, but not in reality."[52]

I am so astonished by Hick's reaction that I feel I must have misunderstood him. I said nothing of all people being free to respond in the way I spoke of. I simply said that some do. Also, Hick caricatures the response. I did not speak of the inner serenity and peace Hick attributes to me. I am speaking of those, in the conditions he describes, who have not cursed God, but who have found

God to be with them in their suffering. Perhaps Hick thinks I mean that this entails the "joyful acceptance" I criticized in the second section of the paper. I hope so, since otherwise Hick is making the claim that no one below a certain level of economic subsistence can experience God as present with them in their suffering. Think of the condescension in *that*. Perhaps Hick thinks I regard the suffering *as a means* to the experience of God, which is the justification of it. That would indeed be cruelly ironic. Perhaps what leads Hick to think in this way is his own theodicy, in which suffering is treated as a means for moral development. The extreme suffering he talks of reduces that theodicy to silence in this life, and forces him to say that the development must await a life to come. When the afflicted are abandoned by those concerned with their moral development (which I would regard as an unqualified good fortune, were it not for the bread they might bring), Hick seems committed to saying that, of necessity, God abandons them at the same time, and will get around to them later, after death.

Hick speaks as though I am advocating the fellowship of suffering as (what it would have to be on his view) a *beneficial* spiritual exercise. I repeat: suffering is not for anything. This assumption seduces theodicy. In fact, seeking suffering has been condemned. On the other hand, some saints, and they are few, have prayed for it if it be God's will. Peter Claver prayed to become a leper so that he might share the sufferings of lepers as one of them. I believe it was at Ravensbruck that a piece of paper was found on which a prayer, scribbled by one of its victims, ended with the words, "And may the love that we have found be their forgiveness." It would be crazy to say that *anyone* in these circumstances can pray that prayer. Think of that to which the stories of Elie Wiesel bear witness. All I am saying—and I wonder at the fact—is that *someone* did. Peter was a poor fisherman, perhaps below Hick's level of economic subsistence, but it is said of him that he requested to be crucified upside down because he was unworthy to die in the same way as his Lord.

Why this torment? So far I have referred to suffering, even extreme suffering, where the suffering is still informed by a conception of a divine love. It still speaks to the sufferer. But what of suffering in which the connection is broken, where the speech is silenced? In the case of suffering children, it hardly makes sense to speak of that connection being present in the first place: "No statement, theological or otherwise, should be made that would not be credible in the presence of burning children."[53] Here, it makes little sense to speak of an informed death.

Socrates dies an informed death, but does Jesus? When he asks that, if possible, the cup be taken from him, the heavens are silent. In the worst of all afflictions, those that arise from injustice, he dies with spittle on his face. In his agony on the Cross, he cries out, "My God, My God, why have you forsaken me?" The children do not cry out in this way; they are silent. Faced with examples such as these, what is there to say?

Innocence and love do not triumph when they are the extreme victims of evil: they suffer. They offer no explanations, no end to which evil is the means. They are dumb. We who witness this may see how love cannot compel, how it can be rejected.[54] But it is seen via a Crucified One in Christianity, where the price of the revelation is the abandonment of the victim. The extremity of love is shown in its suffering this end. Isaiah warns us not to falsify such possibilities, not to turn them into something attractive: "when we shall see him, there is no beauty that we should desire him" (53:2). In fact, our natural reactions are the opposite: "He is despised and rejected; a man of sorrows, and acquainted with grief: and we hid our faces from him; he was despised, and we esteemed him not" (53:3). As for attempts to show that this suffering is a means to a good that justifies it: "He was oppressed, and he was afflicted, yet he opened not his mouth: he is brought as a lamb to the slaughter, and as a sheep before her shearers is dumb, so he opened not his mouth" (53:7). Faced by such examples, would that theodicists did the same.

There is welcome evidence that theologians, including process theologies, have been more sensitive in their discussion of human suffering than contemporary theodicists in the analytic tradition.[55] Yet, there has been a tendency to think that to say that God's love cannot compel, that it can even be crucified, implies a divine limitation in God. Maurice Wiles says: "God's creation of our world necessarily implies a divine self-limitation in relation to traditional understandings of omnipotence and omniscience."[56] But Hartshorne says, correctly in my view, that "to speak of limiting a concept seems to imply that the concept without limitation makes sense."[57] In talking of the love of God in relation to suffering, I am not limiting the concept of God, but trying to bring out *the kind* of love that concept involves. After all, is it not part of the claim of process theologians that their "Galilean perspective" does more justice to biblical concepts than do the theodicies they criticize? I cannot discuss that matter. I shall simply ask whether the rejection of divine immutability and simplicity by them is not a premature resignation to the fact that those terms must be understood in the ways their opponents suggest? Could not Simone Weil have embraced them? What is more, if, with Hartshorne, we think of divine power as the "general providential tendency favoring the good and able to guarantee it a minimum of persistence through all time," are we not back with the *a priori* optimism of the theodicies I have been criticizing? I am simply asking the question: Does this come from making God's love an element in a process, instead of being the constant light that illuminates our world?

Why this torment? How is gratitude for life shown in relation to the evil in others? I do not mean the evil they suffer, but the evil in them. Christians are told to hate the sin and love the sinner. What does this mean? One may keep a friend although he has done shabby things, but how far can this be taken? What does it mean to say that we must hate what Charles Manson has done, but love Charles Manson? Rhees says that one feels like asking, "Well, then, who *is* Charles Manson?"[58] Yet, he goes on to say, the Christian command does have sense. It means that the evildoer is seen in *hope.* This hope is not based on any evidence that the evildoer will change. Indeed, one may be quite pessimistic about that. But the Christian does not give up on him. This is another way of saying that God's mercy in relation to human beings is never misplaced.

Why this torment? How is gratitude for life related to the evil for which one is responsible? Rhees replies: "Gratitude makes it possible to accept even one's passions and one's own vileness. I do not mean discounting them as faults, or thinking that what I am is really not so vile after all. I mean recognizing my vileness for what it is—and in some way being grateful nevertheless. I do not say I can manage this, but I think it does happen. And then a man may recognize the foul way he has acted, and still look beyond, instead of being ridden by it."[59]

What does Rhees mean by "looking beyond" the evil in one's life? How can this mortal put on immortality? Rhees replies, with Simone Weil: by the right use of death as a gift. When he looks back over his life he sees that the record is not good. There is little point in saying, "Try to do better." This is the result of trying to do better. Contrast this with theodicy's conception of life as God's moral development project. Rhees finds hope in the Christian notion of death, but not the hope of development the theodicist finds there. What he finds is the hope of judgment or, better, the hope *in* judgment.

Death is not a state of a person like being unconscious. In death we cease to exist. That is why it is religiously important not to use it as an easy way out, not even as a way of bringing the evils one has done to an end. There would be no "Thy will be done" in that. In relation to himself, for Rhees, God's love and mercy is the undeserved grace of being able to see his life, with all its weaknesses, as part of the majesty of God's will.

> What I wish came more deeply from my heart were a thanks for this life of innocent defilement and degradation: since otherwise the majesty of death—*lachrysmosa, dies illa*—would have no meaning. My tendency to write *melius fuerit non vivere* is an expression of the same *unwillingness to know*—which—if it masters me—will keep me from seeing death as the sole beauty and majesty; as the centre of "Thy will be done." To look on death if this means looking away from the world—is again a form of deception: a *failure* to see death as the word of God . . . (Is this the tendency which finds its most vulgar expression in "That will be glory for me"?).[60]

Concluding Remarks

Writing about suffering is extremely demanding. One feels the necessity of drawing back from generalities that play around with what people go through. Faced by the deeper discussions of Simone Weil and Søren Kierkegaard, I feel that I have only scratched the surface of things. But I do hope to have shaken the philosophical complacency of those who take the appropriateness of the language of theodicies for granted. I have not done so by replacing one theodicy by another, but by reminding ourselves of other possibilities.

I am extremely conscious of themes I have not touched, themes that are rarely discussed in arguments concerning the problem of evil. I have said nothing of the suffering that love itself causes in intimate relationships between men and women, between parents and children, between friends, where they drag each other down, not through lack of love, but because of it. I have said nothing of the sufferings of the wicked, where the sufferings are unrelated to their wickedness. Moreover, I have not discussed the sense in which there is suffering *in* evil. The suffering of Judas is not a common topic in the problem of evil. Kierkegaard is one of the few to discuss such suffering in what he has to say about despair. Finally, I have not discussed different moralities and religions, those of warriors, for example, where we find very different conceptions of suffering and different attitudes towards it. Philosophically, we often assume a homogeneity where none exists.

I am not a theologian, and I have made no effort to produce a systematic apologia. As a philosopher, I have to leave things ragged if they are ragged. If I were a theologian, I might be tempted by the thought that an unsystematic, rather than a systematic, theology, might do greater conceptual justice to the tangled web we weave. In that tangled web I never cease to marvel at a miracle: that theism survives theodicies.

CRITIQUE BY JOHN HICK

In his chapter Dewi Phillips selects two writers on theodicy as the targets to focus his arguments, Richard Swinburne and myself. I do not see us occupying the same position. Swinburne, in his recent book *Providence and the Problem of Evil*,[61] makes God responsible for every individual evil (or, as he prefers to say, "bad state") that occurs, by either specifically causing or allowing it, though always for a good reason. Thus God ought not to eliminate any evils. Swinburne takes this so far as to say that, "Each bad state or possible bad state removed takes away *one* actual good. Each small addition to the number of actual or possible bad states makes a small addition to the number of actual or possible good states."[62] Most of Phillips's "bee stings" are directed against this theodicy; and I have also criticized it for much the same reasons.[63] In doing so I also agree with Phillips in rejecting Swinburne's concept of God as, in my own formulation, "that of the human person magnified to infinity in some of his attributes (such as omnipotence and omniscience), but on the same level as us in that there are things which he is not permitted to do, others that it is his duty to do, and also in his having human-like anxieties and desires. Further, he has a hands-on control of the universe such that he is specifically responsible for either enacting or allowing each individual bad state."[64] With Phillips, I do not accept this anthropomorphic conception of God.

Phillips's other target is myself, his source for my ideas on theodicy being my chairman's "Remarks" at a Swinburne-Phillips symposium in 1977. But despite this rather narrow base, he is right in identifying the central issue between us as the concept of God, or the meaning that we give to "God." Many subsidiary issues arise, but there is only space here to concentrate on that one central issue.

Phillips's concept of God is such that the traditional theodicy problem does not arise. But I am by no means the only person to find Phillips obscure, and indeed evasive, on whether or not he is advocating a religious nonrealism. At first sight he seems to think of God in a way very like Swinburne's. Thus he follows Wittgenstein in using the example of "a man who always thinks of events which happen to him as rewards or punishments. When something good happens to him he thinks in terms of a blessing and a reward from God. When he is ill he wonders what he has done to deserve the illness, or if he does something wrong he is convinced that he will be punished for it."[65] But it quickly becomes evident that Phillips does not think that there is a God as thus conceived, although the idea of such a God is at work in this man's life and is expressed in his religious use of language. I understand Phillips as saying, or rather implying, that the concept, or idea, or picture of an objectively real God is a very powerful concept which, although uninstantiated, is nevertheless central to a whole coherent way of thinking, imagining, and living, which is the religious form of life. I take him to imply that this concept of God does not answer to any reality beyond human language and human forms of life. One can further clarify this reading of Phillips by noting its implication that before there were any humans there was no God, for God exists only as a factor in our religious language and behavior. On this understanding Phillips is in the same camp as such avowedly nonrealist theologians as Don Cupitt, and this is a subset of the larger naturalistic camp. If this is not Phillips's position, he has never made the difference clear to me, or to many others of his readers or fellow conference discussants. He and his followers customarily say that the question whether God exists independently of our believing that God exists is a wrong question; but they never make clear why.

Phillips's religious nonrealism tends to be concealed, possibly even from himself, by certain related positions which I, for one, also hold: (1) God is not an object in the sense of being one item among others in the universe. (To exist objectively, as distinguished from subjectively, is not the same as being an object in this sense.) (2) The reality of God cannot be established, or even shown to be more probable than not, by philosophical arguments, whether the traditional "theistic proofs" or the current anthropic principle argument or Swinburne's use of Bayes's probability theorem. (3) The meaning of God's reality to individuals and faith communities is shown in the way in which they live, hope, fear, feel, worship, react to the events of their lives, treat their neighbor, and indeed in the manner of their lives as a whole. But is it not evident that none of this entails that God does not exist objectively, in the sense of existing independently of human belief, language, and behavior? Whether God exists is not a grammatical question but a question of fact.

In another paper of mine from which Phillips quotes, in which I criticize naturalism, including nonrealist versions of religion, I point out that the kind of religion that Phillips preaches, in which we are exhorted to respond to life's hardships—not only the relatively petty ones that everyone knows, but real tragedies and disasters, the premature death of loved ones, starvation, slavery, genocide, Holocaust—with faith in God's goodness and love, is highly ironic if he believes that there is in fact no good and loving God. I said that "in the light of the massive reality of evil—that is, pain, suffering, and deprivation caused both by fellow humans and by the environment—a naturalistic philosophy can only be accepted with equanimity by a privileged elite. For humanity as a whole naturalism is very bad news. It means not only that evil has always been a massive reality, but that past evil is irreparable, in that those who have suffered from it have ceased to exist; and it must be expected that this will be true also of present and future evil. There can be no question of the universe being, as the religions teach, such that good is ultimately brought out of evil. . . .[66] True, some saintly people can rise to a religious acceptance of whatever tragedies engulf themselves and their loved ones as being mysteriously within God's ultimate all-embracing love and providence. But is Phillips really suggesting that such people are using this language, referring to a divine love and providence that eternally enfolds them and their loved ones, in a nonrealist sense, believing that in fact there is no loving God who exists outside their own religious language and "form of life"?

If all this is a misunderstanding on my part, as Phillips suggests in his paper, and as I must hope, does he in the end affirm the reality of God as transcending the human, and as holding men and women in being to an ultimate good fulfillment for all, and not only for those who arrive at an unshakable love of and trust in God in the course of this present life?

I must add a brief postscript. In my "Remarks" at the Swinburne-Phillips symposium, and in *Evil and the God of Love*, and in my chapter in the present book, I am engaging in the specifically Christian theodicy project. I do not go beyond that to consider a religiously pluralist understanding of evil. This is the next big issue to be faced, but it is not within the remit of the present book.

CRITIQUE BY DAVID RAY GRIFFIN

Phillips affirms theism but rejects theodicy. I will begin by exploring why he rejects theodicy, then ask in what sense he affirms theism. My approach is to build on his recognition that his position and mine have much in common, especially the insistence that nothing should be allowed to dilute the affirmation that God is love.

I found reading Phillips's reasons for rejecting theodicy to be a strange experience. In *God, Power, and Evil* and *Evil Revisited*, I developed, as the subtitle of the former book indicates, "A Process Theodicy." But the objections that Phillips raises to theodicies as such—that they treat suffering instrumentally, deny that it is ever unbearable, implicitly portray God as a monster or at least less moral than the average parent, and deny that any of the evils of our world are genuine or at least horrendous evils—are objections that I raised against *traditional* theodicies, in which God is assumed to have coercive omnipotence.

The explanation for this strangeness is that Phillips, who had worked out his attitude toward theodicy in relation to the type presented by traditional theists such as Swinburne and Hick, throughout most of his essay simply equates theodicy with that traditional type. In his note on the book edited by Adams and Adams, however, he cites their recognition of a radically different theodicy, which says that God has "an extensive power to 'persuade' but no power at all to compel." Phillips henceforth indicates that his criticisms have been directed at "theodicies in the analytic tradition." Agreeing with Surin's statement about the rootage of this type of theodicy in the seventeenth and eighteenth centuries, he withholds the term "traditional" from it. But I, having pointed out that the crucial assumption, *creatio ex nihilo*, goes back to the second century, stand by that term. In any case, Phillips's favorable reference to the alternative conception of divine power—according to which "God's only omnipotence is the omnipotence of love"—suggests that he might not be opposed to a theodicy based on process theism.

That conclusion could seem contradicted by the fact that his objections to theodicies are often phrased in terms of their "anthropomorphic God," defined as one that can be understood by analogy with human beings. Given that meaning, the God of process theology—who is the chief exemplification of, rather than an exception to, the categories applying to all other actualities—is even more anthropomorphic than the God of traditional theism. But there is a meaning of "anthropomorphism" that corresponds with the fact that Phillips's criticism of it has less to do with analogical language than with coercive power. Given this alternative meaning, the deity of traditional theism is implicitly anthropomorphic precisely by virtue of having the power to control worldly events. That is, we as human beings have coercive power by virtue of our bodies, especially our hands, through we which can "manipulate" other things. Although traditional theologies called God incorporeal, they assigned to God the kind of power that would make sense only if God had hands with which to manipulate the world—hence Philo's query as to how Cleanthes' anthropomorphic deity can be considered moral. Because process theism is *not* anthropomorphic in this sense, the next question is whether Phillips has other reasons, independent of the problem of evil, for rejecting it. I will explore this question by examining his theism.

Against critics who have interpreted him otherwise, Phillips insists that he *affirms* the reality of God, that the issue is only what it *means* to make this affirmation. On the basis of earlier writings, I had concluded that although Phillips disclaimed theological "realism" as he defines it, some of his God-affirmations *are* realistic in the more standard meaning of intending to refer to something that exists independently of our perceptions and conceptions, such as the Christian conception. Phillips, at least at times (especially in "On Not Understanding God" in *Wittgenstein in Religion*), seemed to think of the word "God" not as defined by Christian usage but as referring to "sheer power"—the power embodied in conquest and despotism, in treason and transitoriness, in the limitations of time and place, in the blind forces of nature (which bring the sun and rain on the just and unjust alike)—in short, in the "contingencies" and "vicissitudes" of human life. As such, the word "God" would refer to Tillich's "being itself" or "power itself," Whitehead's "creativity," or Nietzsche's "vitality," which is "beyond good and evil." Thus understood, it is true that "the Lord giveth, and the Lord taketh away." Given this understanding of reality, one can respond either by seeing this very mixed world as absurd, with at best a "god of blind caprice," or by seeing life as a gift, to be accepted with gratitude, thereby speaking of a "God of grace." Phillips himself has affirmed the latter option while recognizing with Wittgenstein (in the present essay) that reality or power as such, like the bee who gives you honey one minute and stings you the next, is not kind.

In the present essay, however, the word "God" seems to have a different referent. Rather than being beyond good and evil, God is "perfection, absolute purity, and pure holiness." Rather than being sheer power, "God is love" and therefore "cannot compel." Although some of Phillips's statements now seem to deny power to God altogether, some of them recognize that love *is* a power, albeit different in kind from worldly power, because it can empower us—to accept life as a gift, to oppose inhumanity, and to refuse to give up on people, including ourselves, in spite of their evil. Although Phillips at points suggests that, unlike process theologians, he is speaking of God's love only as a light, *not* as "an element in a process," and of God's presence in the world only in the form of absence, he also refers to "the presence of divine compassion" and, in *Wittgenstein and Religion*, says that "the central religious conviction [is] that God is at work in people's lives."[67] His view that God is both present in the world and yet, as perfect, "*other than* our imperfect world" is fully compatible with Whitehead's view that God's "primordial nature," with its envisagement of divine values, enters into the world and yet transcends it (but without transcending as did the God of traditional theism and deism, being instead the Soul or Spirit of the world).

What I am suggesting is that one could read the present essay as indicative of a turn in what I am taking to be the realistic side of Phillips's thought, a turn parallel to one that occurred in Whitehead's thought. While writing the Lowell Lectures on which *Science and the Modern World* was based, Whitehead had understood Ultimate Reality in a Spinozistic way, as sheer energy or creativity (then called "substantial activity"). Before publication, however, he introduced God as a "principle of limitation" that divided, among other things, "the Good from the Evil." Still later, Whitehead came to see God as not a mere principle but a full-fledged actuality who, besides persuading the world toward truth, beauty, and goodness, is the "great companion" and "fellow sufferer." In this later position, creativity, which as such is beyond good and evil, is still that twofold power of spontaneity and efficient causation that is embodied in every event, so that contingency, as Phillips sees, characterizes the world through and through. But the word "God" refers not to this sheer power but to a bias influencing this power, which we may experience as a "still small voice" calling us to use our power to promote truth, justice, and beauty. Although speaking of this kind of divine providence provides a basis for hope, it does not reintroduce the complacent optimism that Phillips rightly fears.

Speaking of this kind of divine providence, furthermore, is justified by the criterion that Phillips, following Weil, suggests: "the amount of illumination thrown upon things of the world." Phillips has said that his "contemplative" philosophy seeks "an understanding of the possibility of discourse."[68] To understand this possibility, however, involves understanding how our universe, in some 15 billion years, brought forth creatures capable of discourse; neo-Darwinian orthodoxy, in spite of the bravado by some of its spokespersons, does not provide this understanding (as I argue in *Religion and Scientific Naturalism*).

What I am doing is reading Phillips as thinking of God as persuasive and suffering love in a way that is open to having these notions ontologized. Given this ontologizing, his affirmation of theism, defined in his opening statement as "the belief that the world has been created by one God," would mean that the universe emerged from the (supposed) Big Bang to us through a systematic bias exerted on the evolutionary process by the Divine Love. Some of Phillips's statements, to be sure, seem to reject that possibility. He says that when he says "God is love," there is no "it" to which the love is attributed, that the "metaphysical subject" is an illusion. But we would need to explore what exactly is being thereby rejected, because Whitehead himself rejected the "metaphysical subject" as traditionally understood, namely, as an underlying substance existing prior to one's moment-by-moment relations and responses. More generally, Phillips has rejected "metaphysics," but this term is also open to multiple interpretations. For example, Hilary Putnam has recently explained that by rejecting "first philosophy" he rejects any view holding that the ideas we inevitably presuppose in life are not necessarily valid in philosophy. But that rejection would not rule out what Whitehead means by metaphysics, which is simply the attempt to show how we can coherently affirm all the ideas we inevitably presuppose in practice—including our *moral* ideas.

This ontologizing of his God-talk would overcome what is arguably the weakest feature of Phillips's philosophy of religion as previously enunciated. That is, Phillips had claimed that he was simply describing how religious language is actually used by believers. But then, on the basis of his own rejection of theological realism, he made completely implausible claims about this, such as his claim that when religious assertions about God refer to a time before human beings existed, they do "not mean that God existed before men in the sense in which mountains, rainbows, or rivers did."[69] By becoming explicitly ontological, Phillips could also overcome the inconsistencies produced by the fact that, although he has strong opinions about what should not be believed (such as any traditional theodicy), he constantly denies that his philosophy leads to "substantive results" about "what we should believe."[70] Likewise, by explicitly recognizing that he has substantive beliefs that provide a basis for ethical norms, he could more consistently recognize that his writings propose substantive conclusions as to "how we ought to live," such as his beliefs that we ought to reduce the oppression and suffering in the world.

CRITIQUE BY STEPHEN T. DAVIS

Phillips is never an easy thinker to understand. I have tried, on other occasions, to come to grips with and react to his overall Wittgensteinian stance in the philosophy of religion (see, for example, chapter 3 of my *God, Reason, and*

Theistic Proofs [Edinburgh University Press, 1997]). I mention this point because my deepest difficulties with Phillips have to do with what might be called his apparent religious nonrealism (see point [1], below).

Let me make five points about Phillips's essay.

(1) "The consciousness of God." In this book, the five of us are discussing the problem of evil, not the metaphysics or (as Phillips might prefer) grammar of God. Still, there are places in "Theism without Theodicy" where Phillips's views on this other topic peek out at us from under the covers, and I need to record my disagreement. I will just mention one.

Trying to pin Phillips down at a point where many philosophers find him unclear, Hick asks Phillips whether in his (Phillips's) view there is "in addition to all human consciousness . . . another consciousness which is the consciousness of God." Phillips somewhat petulantly replies that the statement that there is such a consciousness "is not intelligible enough to deny." Now my point here is not to deny that there are conceptual problems with the statement that "There is a consciousness that is the consciousness of God." Phillips is correct that there are (whether these problems can be solved is another matter). I simply want to insist that Phillips knows good and well what Hick was driving at—as I do and as everybody else does—and that Hick's question deserves a straight answer.

(2) "Evil is not what it seems to be." Phillips thinks most theodicies entail this statement, and he finds it morally repellent. The person who makes it, he says, has not given suffering the attention it deserves. Now I agree that in some sense theodicists are committed to the notion that evil is not, or at least is not entirely, what it seems to be. What sense is this? Well, it is certainly not the sense that theodicists must belittle human suffering, pretend that it is really not so bad, pooh-pooh it (so to speak). I will never agree that theodicies inevitably do that.

In what sense, then, do theodicists affirm that "evil is not what it seems to be"? Just in the sense that they (or at least theodicists like me) affirm that

- the problem of evil has a solution;
- a good and all-powerful God exists, after all;
- evil is not the whole story; and
- suffering will one day come to an end.

Now here is the crucial question: Is it (as Phillips charges) morally insensitive for theodicists to make these sorts of statements to people who suffer? Well, if the statements are false, yes. In that case, Phillips would be quite correct. But if the statements are true, it is not only not morally insensitive for theodicists to explain their theodicy to people who suffer—it would be morally wrong for them not to do so. Indeed, these statements would constitute the best possible news that sufferers could hear.

Accordingly, Phillips's charge that the whole enterprise of theodicy is morally insensitive is a weird case of question-begging. He must be assuming ahead of time that all theodicies are false.

(3) The Bee Stings. My heart was strangely unwarmed by Phillips's ten bee stings. Most of them sound like powerful arguments against somebody (maybe Hick or Swinburne), but not me. I don't justify suffering by claiming that it prompts moral responsibility (although suffering sometimes does that). I don't say that all suffering has a purpose (although some of it certainly does); so far as I can tell, some suffering serves no good purpose at all. I do not claim that all suffering is in the interest of the sufferer (although some of it can be, and has been in my own life), and I reject Phillips's claim that all theodicies have to say that suffering is beneficial to the sufferer. I don't deny that people are sometimes defeated by circumstances. I don't claim that every time sufferers are crushed by circumstances, they had the resources to resist (depending on what "resist" means). I don't claim that God's morality is totally different from ours. Finally, I don't think God's plans for the future are unknown (not at least in general terms); I believe they have been revealed to us.

I suppose I am guilty of admitting my ignorance in places and of trying to justify God on consequentialist grounds. But, on the first point, I deny Phillips's charge that appealing to ignorance involves the thought that "evils may not be so horrendous after all." No, I'm convinced they're just as hor-rendous as Phillips thinks they are. It's just that I think they will be overcome. On the second point, I see nothing logically or morally untoward in arguing that God's policy, in creating this sort of world, will turn out best in the long run. And I confess I just do not grasp Phillips's claim that a conceptual diffi-culty exists in so arguing. Suppose it could convincingly be argued that God's policy will not turn out well, that ten years from now all living things will die, kicking and screaming, in agonizing pain, and that there will be no afterlife. Many antitheodicists would fasten on that fact—so I suspect—in order to craft a consequentialist atheistic argument. And why on earth Phillips thinks con-sequentialist reasoning in defense of God entails suppression of "the absolute moral condemnation of atrocities" is, well, quite beyond my ken. It only does so if atrocities are said to be disguised goods, and it is no part of my theodicy to say that they are.

(4) Life as a gift. Phillips labors mightily to deny the idea that the gift of life is for something. Some of what he says makes good sense to me. But is the upshot a denial that God could have had a purpose in mind in creating life? If that is the proper reading of Phillips at this point, no wonder he opposes the whole project of theodicy. There is no theodicy problem apart from belief in

a morally good God who has certain desires or hopes or intentions as to how the world should turn out, i.e., who in creating life had certain aims in mind.

(5) Blaming the victim. In my opinion, Phillips's own rejection of theodicy is itself morally insensitive, or at least can be. I agree with him that the true home of the problem of suffering is not the philosophy of religion classroom but the actual experience of sufferers. I happen to know from my experience as a pastor that many sufferers desperately want to know whether their suffering has any meaning, whether it will be overcome, whether a better world awaits them, whether an all-powerful and loving God will save them. If any answers to those questions are available, the people who suffer have the right to know them. To deny them that right, to reject the program of theodicy wholesale, is in my opinion a species of "blaming the victim."[71]

Fortunately, however, my colleague Phillips is a morally sensitive person. In places in his essay (especially in its last half), his better nature takes over. He stops condemning the very project of theodicy and he offers something at least in its neighborhood. That life is a gift for which we can be grateful despite suffering, that we sinners need grace and that grace is a miracle, that a point in life can be discerned even in the midst of suffering, and that true gratitude for life entails compassion for others—these are themes I heartily endorse.

Critique by John K. Roth

D. Z. Phillips's mantra is *Why this torment?* The repetition is as good as the question. Both show that no theodicy puts the question *Why?* to rest. As this book attests, theodicy's "answers" and "solutions" for "the problem of evil" settle scarcely anything. Albeit unintentionally, they prevent closure as they provoke questions instead. *Why this torment?* persists among them.

Phillips intends his mantra to support the view that "theism does not entail theodicy." Moreover, he wants to reject theodicy, not revise it, because "theodicy fails to do justice to the things of the world." Theodicy, he thinks, does more harm than good, because it typically urges people to endorse problematic arguments. Under the subheading "Theodicy's Bee Stings," Phillips identifies ten that, in his judgment, divert attention from the best religious insights. Nevertheless, Phillips thinks that "theism survives theodicies," and his essay aims to support that survival. His effort is more instructive than successful.

Phillips has not rejected theodicy but disguised it. This disguised theodicy is embedded in his Wittgenstein-inspired insistence that he understands the relation between "God and grammar" in ways that eliminate confusions that have given rise to the project of theodicy. Following Wittgenstein, Phillips thinks that if we understand—which means accepting Phillips's understanding—how God-language works religiously, then people will not be tempted to write theodicies anymore. Ironically, however, Phillips takes his mantra—*Why this torment?*—less seriously than he should, and the result is not theodicy rejected but theodicy disguised. Headed in the right direction, Phillips's understanding of God-language lures him back into theodicy's snares.

To amplify this analysis, consider that Theo Richmond, a Jewish journalist and scholar, spent years studying the history of Konin, the Polish town from which his parents had emigrated to England just before World War I. Many of Richmond's relatives were not so lucky. Among the approximately three thousand Jews in Konin's population of some thirteen thousand, they witnessed the German occupation of the town—it stands 120 miles west of Warsaw—on September 14, 1939. Richmond's research revealed that perhaps two hundred of Konin's Jews survived the Holocaust. The degradation, torture, and death that befell them belong in the category of horrendous evil, or there can be no such thing.

It came to Richmond's attention that a postwar trial in Konin included the deposition of a Polish Catholic who had been imprisoned by the Gestapo. Early one mid-November morning in 1941, F. Z. (as Richmond identifies him) was removed from his cell, driven to a forest clearing, and, along with about thirty other Poles, ordered to collect clothing, shoes, and valuables from Jews who were stripped before they entered two killing pits that would become their mass, unmarked graves. Specifically, F. Z. remembered the following episode: A layer of quick lime covered the larger of the two pits. Naked Jews—children, women, men—were forced into that pit until it was full. "Two Gestapo men," F. Z. continued, "began to pour some liquid, like water, on the Jews. But I am not sure what that liquid was. . . . Apparently, because of the slaking of the lime, people in the pit were boiling alive. The cries were so terrible that we who were sitting by the piles of clothing began to tear pieces off the stuff to stop our ears. The crying of those boiling in the pit was joined by the wailing and lamentation of the Jews waiting for their perdition. All this lasted perhaps two hours, perhaps longer."[72]

Why this torment? Phillips's question, which seethes through the particularity of F. Z.'s testimony, arouses many responses. Phillips inclines to agree with me that none of them could be completely satisfactory, but he does not leave it at that, which a thoroughgoing rejection of theodicy—or what I would call *antitheodicy*—enjoins. Instead, under the guise of eliminating linguistic confusion, Phillips's self-proclaimed clarity about what he calls "the grammar of 'God'" spins off a theodicy in disguise.

Phillips's grammar lesson inveighs against anthropomorphism and the metaphysics it invites. When we say "God is love," for example, or "God is gracious," we are ill-advised to envision a "metaphysical subject" called God "to which the love or grace are attributed." Favoring language in which "God is said to be Spirit," Phillips contends that expressions such as "'God is love' and 'God is gracious' are rules for the use of 'God.'" Phillips's employment of these rules results in a view of creation that contains his disguised and problematic theodicy.

Phillips's religious grammar leads him to construe divine creation "not as an assertion of power, but as a withdrawal, so that human life may exist." This divine withdrawal brings about the gift of life, which is not, Phillips insists, "*for* something" but instead "an expression of free grace." Now, the clarity of this religious grammar lesson is already less than Phillips claims, because we have not a clue about what it means to say that creation is "a withdrawal," but very rapidly the puzzle that Phillips has created in the name of clarity grows still more complicated and confusing. The gift of life, Phillips goes on to say, is imperfect, which means that it "involves suffering for God and man." Nobody is likely to quarrel with that, but then Phillips adds that "divine compassion is in response to the fact that human life, to be human, must be like that."

Here, Phillips may be the one who needs, more than he provides, a grammar lesson. What is the grammar of *must* that operates in his claims? Do its rules encompass Konin? Next, what about the grammar of *compassion*? How do its rules—especially when one says "God is love"—apply to the pit of lime-boiled Jews witnessed by F. Z. on that November morning in 1941? And what about the grammar of *gift*, which figures so prominently in Phillips's perspective?

"The gift of life," suggests Phillips, is "a gift of love which also involves untold sufferings." Life as a *gift* of *love* that involves *untold sufferings*? What is God thinking or doing if that is not just Phillips's grammar but also God's? Of course, Phillips will protest that such questioning violates his supposedly clear rules of grammar, because anthropomorphism has crept in. How any religious language—Phillips's included—can avoid anthropomorphism is a problem in its own right, but here the salient point is that Phillips's religious grammar, because it cannot allow a question of the kind just raised, gets reduced to silence that is softer on evil—and on God—than I think it ought to be.

The extent of Phillips's silence is unfortunate for two reasons. First, a more limited role for silence has its place in a true rejection of theodicy. Phillips is correct: sometimes there is nothing one can say without courting banality or justified outrage. F. Z. would understand that position. One reads his testimony—it contains so much heavy silence—and there are no words that can do justice to what he described. Silence alone, however, will not suffice,. F. Z. testifies. In addition, the judicial setting of his testimony involves protest: what happened was wrong; it ought not to have been.

Phillips quotes the words ascribed to the crucified Jesus—"My God, my

God, why have you forsaken me?"—but, unlike Jesus (unless *his* grammar is confused), Phillips's religious grammar seems unable to allow words like those to be directed explicitly to God. Yes, Jesus' words could express his agony, but it is unclear how Phillips could allow them to be directed explicitly to God, for Phillips's God is not likely to be One to whom they could be directed. However, if such words cannot be directed explicitly to God, then Phillips has not rejected theodicy but disguised it. The disguise is this: Phillips's rules of religious grammar endorse views of creation epitomized by his phrase that "human life, to be human, must be like that." The grammar of the little word *that* does not clearly and explicitly exclude Konin's killing pits. So, how does Phillips's religious grammar rule when it comes to the relation between Konin and God? It is not clear what Phillips wants to say, or even can say, about God at this point, but his grammar rules about "God" tend to enforce silence that gives evil privileges it does not deserve.

Second, Phillips knows some of the right grammar needed to break unwarranted silence, but his disguised theodicy too much strikes him dumb. Phillips makes good moves when he urges that "suffering is not *for* anything," when he stresses that "acceptance of life as God's gift involves opposing . . . inhumanity," and when he writes that "gratitude for life entails compassion for others." He is right again when he stresses that "innocence and love do not triumph when they are the extreme victims of evil: they suffer. They offer no explanations, no end to which evil is the means. They are dumb."

Phillips underscores some of the ingredients in what I call a theodicy of protest or an antitheodicy, but he does not—indeed, I think, cannot—capitalize on them. He has no God on whom they could be brought to bear. Phillips's God-as-Spirit gives life by creation through withdrawal. This God's love does not compel, but, Phillips offers, God's love is "the constant light which illuminates our world." And then there is death itself, which, Phillips indicates, can be seen "as part of the majesty of God's will." This may sound good, but still one wonders how the grammar of "the majesty of God's will" is to be understood in relation to the terrible cries of the dying against which F. Z. tried to stop his ears at Konin.

Early on, Phillips suggested that he wanted "to do justice to the things of the world." His essay does so in part, but only in part because it also takes the sting out of his mantra *Why this torment?* Unfortunately, at the end of Phillips's day, that question is not what it seemed to be. For according to his grammar rules, either *Why this torment?* cannot be directed explicitly to God or it receives the response of Phillips's disguised theodicy, which basically says, "Creation is understood, not as an assertion of power, but as a withdrawal. Perfection allows something other than itself to exist. This 'allowing' is seen as a grace, or as an expression of love."

Once more, I think of F. Z.'s deposition about Konin. It contains no words like those—and rightly so.

REJOINDER

In *Philosophy's Cool Place*, I argue that philosophy has the contemplative task of doing conceptual justice to the world in all its variety. I discussed the temptation to go beyond this task in claiming that philosophy can tell us what to believe, or how to behave. Due to a merging of philosophical and theological interests, my critics are not free of that temptation. In the first section of my reply, my aim is to show, by reference to their own words, that my emphasis on conceptual issues is not as puzzling to them as they sometimes suggest, and that they also are engaged with these issues. In the second section of my reply, I engage what I take to be their confusions about central concepts relating to the problem of evil.

I

Davis has been known to say, "Since Phillips came to Claremont, the word 'confusion' is heard more often than it used to be." That may well be true, but confusions concerning logic and reality, and language and reality, are as old as philosophy itself. They are to be found in the Presocratics, in their assumptions concerning the kind of account they thought philosophy could give of reality. In this respect, Socrates tried to bring people to admit that they did not know what they claimed to know. I have argued that we should renounce the knowledge theodicies claim to give us. With respect to it, we should say, as Berkeley did of other problems, we first throw up a dust and then complain we cannot see. But Wittgenstein, more than any other in the history of philosophy, gives center stage to issues concerning conceptual clarification and elucidation. His aim is to rescue our world from what so many philosophers have made of it. My aim was to rescue the reality of suffering from the treatment of it in theodicies.

When Wittgenstein speaks of relieving the mental cramp of others, showing the fly the way out of the bottle, and so on, he gives the impression that he is free of the confusions he finds in others. That does not do justice to his philosophical practice. The voices he wrestles with, in his *Philosophical Investigations*, are voices in himself. That is why he described philosophy as working on oneself. The obstacles to be overcome are not only obstacles of the intellect, but obstacles of the will. We resist giving up certain ways of thinking; we think we must cling to them. This approach is illustrated by Davis's response to my view that theodicies belittle human suffering: "I will never agree that theodicies inevitably do that." He finds the same resistance of the will, with respect to theodicies, in me: "a weird case of question-begging" that comes from "assuming ahead of time that all theodicies are false."

Questions of meaning precede questions of truth and falsity. If something is conceptually confused, questions as to its truth or falsity do not even get off the ground. In this respect, my critics, to different degrees, accept that my ten bee stings reveal confusion. Each thinks that someone is confused, but not himself. Roth embraces all the criticisms of theodicies, and identifies them with his own: "Phillips inclines to agree with me that none of them could be satisfactory." Griffin accepts all the criticisms, too, but exempts a process theodicy from them. Davis is unharmed by my bee stings, because he believes they sting others: "Most of them sound like powerful arguments against somebody (maybe Hick or Swinburne), but not me." Hick identifies that "somebody" with Swinburne, but absolves himself: "Most of Phillips's bee stings are directed against this theodicy; and I have also criticized it for much the same reasons. In doing so I also agree with Phillips in rejecting Swinburne's concept of God."

The centrality of issues concerning conceptual confusion is shown also in the extent to which my critics claim to find it in my work. Davis's opening sentence is, "Phillips is never easy to understand," and he says of my claim that consequentialism is incompatible with absolute moral judgments of atrocities, that it "is, well, quite beyond my ken." Roth says of the concept of creation as divine withdrawal: "we have not a clue about what it means." With respect to an alleged religious nonrealism, Hick finds me "obscure, and indeed evasive." Griffin finds my claim that God cannot be said to exist before man, in the sense that this can be said of mountains, rainbows, or rivers, "completely implausible." The problem, in replying, is that the critics do not tell me why they reach these conclusions. We have reactions without many reasons.

Perhaps some of my critics think that detailed reasoning is unnecessary because, as they suggest, they have the majority on their side. That consideration would not have impressed Socrates, Schleiermacher, Kierkegaard, or Wittgenstein, who, in different ways, took themselves to be reminding a majority of their conceptual forgetfulness. When Polus boasted that the whole of Athens agreed with him (and perhaps it did), Socrates replied that he was not talking to them. He wanted only Polus's vote, the vote of the one he was discussing with. Each individual must come to an understanding for himself in philosophy. Thus, it is odd when Roth says, "Phillips thinks that if we understand—which means accepting Phillips's understanding," as though, when Roth disagrees it is not his disagreement. One does not understand because one calls it understanding. What is being understood, or misunderstood, is the matter being discussed. So I, and my critics, have no option but to keep discussing. Theirs is the only vote I want, no matter how pessimistic I may be about receiving it.

II

Conceptual confusions are different from mistakes. The latter are intelligible, but false, whereas the former lack sense. Hick is right "in identifying the central issue between us as the concept of God, or the meaning that we give to 'God.'" He agrees that "God is not an object in the sense of being one item among others in the universe." He rejects, with me, an "anthropomorphic conception of God." What is his alternative? Davis says that Hick has asked me to give a straight answer to whether there is "in addition to all human consciousness . . . another consciousness which is the consciousness of God." After all, he says, "Phillips knows good and well what Hick was driving at—as I do and as everybody else does." Really? I do not think Hick can say what he means. And how can Davis, since he does not "deny that there are conceptual problems" with talk of the consciousness of God. Conceptual problems are problems of intelligibility. Davis says that I say "somewhat petulantly that [Hick's] statement 'is not intelligible enough to deny.'" But that statement is the conclusion to arguments. Davis ignores them, so here are some reminders.

   What makes the words or thoughts of "consciousness" the words or thoughts they are? Cut off from wider surroundings, they are robbed of sense. In matters of meaning, as in matters of fact, thinking does not make it so. There must be a distinction between my thinking, and whether that thinking makes sense. But, confined to consciousness, there is no such distinction; no distinction between "thinking I've got it right" and "getting it right." The thought is treated as a "super-sample," required to do the logically impossible, namely, to generate its own use. The notion of "pure consciousness," whether it be God's or anyone else's, inherits all the difficulties of a logically private language. Furthermore, "consciousness" cannot tell me who I am, since it is neighborless. Whose consciousness is it? One might reply, "*This* one." But *this* one as distinct from which? In the sense of "awareness of there being a world" we have no acquaintance with a number of consciousnesses. But in "there being a world," "I" has no special status. That is why solipsism collapses into realism. Not even God's "consciousness" could tell him who he is. The problems come from too restricted a range of categories, from the thought that if "God" does not refer to a body, it must refer to a consciousness.

   Hick agrees with me that we must look for the meaning of "God" in those religious contexts in which it has its sense. In my case, however, he thinks this results in an identification of "God" with language. This odd claim is of long-standing. Peter Winch, in *Trying to Make Sense*, and myself, on numerous occasions, have tried to show that Hick's claim comes from confusing the grammar of a concept with what we actually say. But let me try again.

If I say, "The tablecloth is red," I am not saying anything about the meaning of "red." I am not talking about meaning. I am describing the table. But when I say, pointing to a color chart, "This is red," I am not describing anything. I am giving a rule for the use of "red." The rule does not refer to some realm of existence independent of our actual color judgments. When I say, "God is love" I am expressing religious gratitude. I am not speaking of "meaning." But when I say that the "is" in "God is love" is not an "is" of predication, I am not describing anything, but elucidating a rule for the use of "God." The contact with reality, in the first context, is given in "The tablecloth is red," and, in the latter context, in "God is love." Hick confuses the two contexts when he says that, according to me, "God is a very powerful concept which [is] uninstantiated." But what the concept does is to determine what "instantation" comes to. Hick says: "Whether God exists is not a grammatical question but a question of fact." But what does saying this amount to? Hick does not think that the grammar of "fact" corresponds to that of "empirical object." I have argued that Hick's use of "consciousness" has no grammar, being the product of confusion. To where should we turn?

Roth describes me as "Favoring language in which 'God' is said to be Spirit." But why "favoring"? Am I not simply turning to biblical usage, which is distorted by talk of 'God' as "a person without a body"? If God is said to be "real," can anything other be meant than "a spiritual reality"? Strip away the love, grace, mercy, etc., that believers refer to, and there is no further "it" to which they refer. In that sense, God has no biography. That is why Feuerbach came so close to the matter in his denial of "the metaphysical subject." "God" is the light, the element, the spirit in which, for the believer, all things are seen. Were I to accept Griffin's invitation to ontologize these notions, I should be guilty of a confusion akin to Hegel's reification of "thinking."

We are still faced with the issue of the sense in which God is said to be independent of us, other than the world. With Winch's help, I tried to show that these are themselves spiritual relations. So Hick is wrong in thinking that I deny that there is any notion of "independence" involved in belief in God. Love, grace and mercy are independent of us, in the sense that we are answerable to them and can be deluded about them. They are "other than" the world in two senses. First, they are other than the things of the world. Second, they can never be realized, in their purity, in the world. This is the sense of "the absence" Roth finds difficult. For this reason, some have said that God's reality is not a matter of "existence" at all, and have spoken of "necessary existence." It is an attempt to do justice to "God" as "the eternal" to which we are answerable. "The eternal" is personal, in that "answerability" must be mediated in the personal details of our lives. It is not a theoretical matter. Rather than repeat my comments on these issues, I'll quote some comments by Rush Rhees and relate them to my critics, in the hope that his words will fare better than mine. Rhees's comments come from a hitherto unpublished book on *Plato and Dialectic*, but I also refer the reader to his *On Religion and Philosophy*.[73]

"The relation of eternal life is not the relation of an incorruptible substance to what is corruptible. (Hick and Davis?) That is not the point at all. That will not tell what the importance is which the eternal life might have for the soul. *In particular: it will not tell you what it is to aspire towards eternal life.* . . . Then someone may say: 'Although he has come to the end of his life on earth, it is not the end.' Our question is how we are to understand that statement. The main point is that it is not like any statement or question about the body. That is why speculation as to whether it is something immaterial . . . is so wholly besides the point. . . . The question, 'Is there something which does not perish?' has nothing to do with it. . . . 'The temporal depends on the eternal.' . . . 'These things will pass. There is only one thing that will not pass, and that is what happens to your soul.' . . . Why do people feel that if all strivings are to be entirely forgotten, as if they had never been, then they are futile?" (Some of Hick's and Davis's worries about "what is going to happen" seem to harbor this assumption.)

Rhees is saying that what is important is not the durability of the soul, but its answerability: what it aspires to become. Belief in immortality is belief in what has unchanging importance, such that talk of it perishing after death has no application, which is to say that it makes little sense to speak of it perishing, as it does to speak of it not perishing.

Rhees says: "Through misunderstanding, it seems to me, it has been taken to be the idea 'What can I hope for?—hoping for a life beyond the grave.' (An assumption central in Hick's and Davis's thought.) Whereas the Christian hope is hardly distinguishable from faith and from charity, as opposed to despair, and so is the Christian belief in eternal life."

If Rhees is right about the confusions he refers to, and which I have discussed, this could not be, as Davis fears, a case of "blaming the victim." It would be a case, philosophically, of liberation, and of pointing enquirers in the direction of Christian concepts and beliefs, not with a view to advocating them, but with a view to doing conceptual justice to them, whether one can embrace them personally or not. In my ten bee stings, my claim is that this is what theodicies fail to do.

These conclusions apply to Davis's contention that consequentialism is compatible with absolute moral judgments about atrocities. By such absolute judgments, I mean the refusal to contemplate anything as an instrumental justification of such atrocities. But Davis's consequentialism, in terms of the unknown details of God's plan, is precisely a readiness to entertain such a justification. Hence the contradiction. I noted how an instrumentalism runs through the views of Davis and Hick, and is not entirely absent in Roth.

I have referred to faith in "eternal things," but what does this amount to when the world can inflict horrendous evils on human beings? Roth, as we have seen, is as opposed to the answers theodicies give to these situations as I am. He says that in witnessing the silence to which sufferers are often reduced, our response should be one of unending protest. Roth thinks I want to go further, and to offer what he thinks is a disguised theodicy. Perhaps Roth is in the grip of the assumption that any response, other than the one he advocates, must take the form of a theodicy. I showed, in "On Not Understanding God," that this is not so.

On the other hand, Roth may think I am offering a theodicy, because certain of my remarks may have misled him. Referring to the atrocities that occur, I said that human life must be like that. Roth takes me to be saying that particular atrocities had to happen. Understandably, he asks where that "must" comes from. What I meant, however, is that one cannot think of what we call human life as something in which such atrocities could not occur. As Beckett's character says: "We're on earth. There's no cure for that." To avoid confusion, however, it would have been better had I said, not, "That's what human life must be like," but "That's what human life is like." People protest when atrocities occur, but no technique or explanation could ensure that they do not. Perhaps Roth would agree that this is why Elie Wiesel is skeptical of sociological or psychological explanations that promise to make the sources of evil manageable.

Once this misunderstanding is clarified, we are still faced with Roth's claim that silence and protest are the only proper responses to the atrocities to which he refers. If that is his personal moral or religious response, I have no wish to rob him of it. But if he says, as a philosopher, that it is the only *possible* moral and religious response, that general thesis cannot be maintained. It may be that the only response he finds possible for himself makes it difficult to see the possibility of others. It is important to remember that, in the fourth part of my paper, I am considering different cases, not offering a general view.

Roth and I recognize that in some cases the innocent go like lambs dumb to the slaughter. What has happened robs them of a language that informs their fate. Their cries are cries of abandonment. I do not deny that some respond to these cries with protest—Wiesel and Albert Camus, for example. But there are other responses in which the silent sufferings become, for others, intercessions for humankind, in the sense that, in showing what can happen to love, they show, at the same time, what love is. This would be misunderstood grotesquely, if it were said that these sufferings happen *in order that* we may be shown that, or that what is shown justifies the sufferings. That reasoning would deserve all my bee stings, and bring back, in a particularly horrendous way, the instrumentalist treatment of suffering that Roth and I deplore. Nevertheless, there is a sense in which, in Christianity, Christ's sufferings are said to be for us. Although he, too, went like a lamb to the slaughter, and cried out in abandonment on the Cross, that very act is central in the Eucharist because of what it shows us: something we are invited to regard as food for our souls. That is not the same as the response of which Roth speaks. I mention it, not in advocacy of it, but in order to leave a conceptual space for it in the discussion of the problem of evil. It is part of philosophy's contemplative task that I mentioned at the outset: the task of doing conceptual justice to the world.

The Problem of Evil
and the Task of Ministry

John B. Cobb Jr.

The reality of evil confronts everyone. For most people in Christendom and many people in other places, the reality—or problem—of
evil also calls for an explanation. The problem of evil faces pastors in
two ways: in their own lives and in their thought. They are also called
to minister to other people at points in their lives when they experience evil with peculiar poignancy.

I

An all-too-common experience for pastors is ministering to parishioners who
have terminal cancer. The parishioner, in our day, rarely turns to the pastor
for healing from the disease, although a renewed interest in the relation of faith
and healing is underway. The parishioner turns to the pastor more often with
the question of why. For thousands of years, religion has been associated with
the explanation of evil and—consciously or unconsciously, whether encouraged by the express theology of the pastor or not—persons in their suffering
turn to representatives of religion for answers.

Many responses are possible. In our psychological age many pastors have
decided not to try to give any answer at all. The pastor's task is to be present
with and to "hear" the sufferer, to let the parishioner know that expressing fear,
anger, and loneliness is acceptable. I do not dispute the validity of this
approach, which in many cases is no doubt the best one possible.

The question of why can be appropriately understood and dealt with psychologically, but to treat it only that way fails to take the questioner with full
seriousness as a human being. A pastor who has not reflected about the question, who has nothing to say, has a truncated ministry.

One important type of answer is scientific, discussing what is known of the causes of cancer and seeking to understand how they have operated in this case. Many people can benefit emotionally and spiritually, as well as intellectually, from understanding better what is going on, evil though it may be. But the parishioner turns to the pastor for a different kind of answer.

A second type of answer comes from India under the label of *karma*. Everything that happens has a reason as well as a cause. In this sense, our universe is rational. Good things happen to us because we have acted so as to deserve them, either in this life or in an earlier one. The same is true with respect to evil things. At first blush, speaking of cancer patients in relation to such a moral law seems extremely cruel, but the situation is more complex. Many people can deal better with evil when they understand that it is just, rather than seeming wholly irrational. In the Indian setting, one knows that to experience this evil now meant that some of the accumulated bad karma was working its way out, and that less need exists to suffer in the future. Bearing the present evil well builds good karma.

These ideas have been less explicitly developed in the West, but they have their appeal. We expect to reap what we sow. Also, parallel currents of thought run today. The pastor may be persuaded, for example, about a connection between the personality, emotional temperament, and past behavior of the parishioner and the onset of cancer. In some sense, the cancer is the wages of sin. If so, instead of railing against fate or God, recognizing one's own responsibility for what happens in the body may be healthier. Indeed, the body may be able to resist the cancer better and the spirit may be more serene, if, even at this difficult point in life, there is repentance.

But most pastors do not think primarily in this way. In the Christian context, the pastor is expected to be one who can speak rightly of God. The thought of God has always been bound up with the experience of evil, but the relation, even among Christians, has been multifarious, as has been well illustrated in the preceding essays.

In the theistic context, one explanation of evil that has been prominent in the past, although absent from this book, is that it comes as punishment. Among those who ask why, many suspect that they are being punished; many pastors over many centuries have encouraged that suspicion. For the theist, the relation between sin and suffering did not work its way out in karmic fashion, but was mediated by the all-knowing and all-just God. Thinking in this way could add intensity to feelings of responsibility and urgency to the importance of repentance. Such an approach could also give the sufferer some sense of meaning in the suffering and also the hope that paying this price now could reduce the likelihood of future punishment. Providing a

Person as the source of the suffering opened the way to the possibility that by penitence, prayer, and good works, the sufferer could persuade God to mitigate the suffering.

Perhaps some of the essayists would allow for this viewpoint as an explanation in some contexts, but clearly all of them agree that there is much suffering that is not punishment. One may contract cancer because of genetic predisposition or because of environmental conditions over which one has no control, while the polluters go scot-free. Hence these essays direct us to other explanations.

In John Hick's essay, we have a modern formulation of another major theme in Christian reflection about God and evil. We may understand evil as a necessary part of God's plan for soul-making. The pastor who thinks in these terms will look on this illness as an occasion for spiritual growth both in the patient and in the family, as well as in the pastor. The explanation will not be that God has singled out this person for cancer so that spiritual growth can occur. The question of *Why me?* cannot be given a theological answer, but the pastor can explain why cancer is in the world and how God intends that we respond to it. Happiness and enjoyment are not the aim of life. Spiritual growth is. Hence, what appears at first glance as unmitigated evil *can* be the occasion for the most important good. Even if, in this particular case, we cannot believe that any good will come of it, we can nevertheless believe in the goodness and mercy of God. We can believe that the death that this cancer will bring is not the end of life but the transition to other lives, and that eventually we will all be perfected. The pastor who can communicate this conviction effectively to the sufferer will make an important difference in the dying experience.

Other pastors may be dissatisfied with Hick's response. True, much evil can prompt growth, but much does not. Like Stephen Davis, they see no signs that the course of history on this planet expresses the sort of spiritual advance of which Hick speaks. The hypothesis that this growth occurs in other worlds after death is too ad hoc. In any case Hick's position has no biblical warrant. Like Hick, the Bible is committed to a final salvation, but the Bible does not present this occurence as the outcome of millennia of spiritual growth through many worlds. Instead, in the twinkling of an eye, the kingdom of God will come, and everything will be changed. Furthermore, Hick's expectation that all will ultimately be brought to fulfillment conflicts with biblical teaching that some people choose to reject God forever. The pastor cannot simply reassure people that all will be well for everyone in the end. The most important matter always, but especially as a parishioner approaches death, is to call for the faith through which one's ultimate destiny is assured. Should the suffering raise doubts about the goodness and power of God, the pastor can show that these Christian affirmations are not contradicted by the evil in the world, even by the murderous cancer. Some evil is understood simply in terms of the out-working of natural law. Much evil is the result of the sinful expression of the freedom God has given to human beings. God has allowed this sin because only through free creatures can the good that God desires be achieved. Some of the resulting evil works for spiritual maturation in the present, and all is overcome in the kingdom of God. Therefore we can have faith in God and assurance of God's ultimate victory, even when in our present experience evil seems triumphant. We can also know that God is with us in our present suffering.

But not all pastors agree with either of these accounts. Some pastors believe that not only is this cancer an unjust and unmitigated evil that will conduce to no one's good, but much senseless evil of this sort cannot be explained as necessary for, or the result of, creaturely misuse of freedom. As noted in the introduction of this book, the Holocaust has become the sym-bol of such evil. Of course, a few people may have grown spiritually or oth-erwise profited because of the Holocaust. Perhaps, for example, many people outgrew immature forms of faith. But the Holocaust was far from "cost effi-cient," as our writers like to say. Pastors who agree with Roth cannot assure the parishioner about any positive meaning in cancer or that its evil will finally be overcome. Instead they will side with another aspect of the parish-ioner's feelings: anger. The parishioner is likely to feel guilty for this anger, especially when directed against God. These pastors will encourage the expression of this anger and share in it. God deserves our rage. Nothing God will ever do will justify this pointless evil, this waste of a human life. Never-theless, the pastor will have another message as well. Despite God's respon-sibility for evil—God's guilt—we can believe that God is also a God of love. This world of unjust suffering does not have the last word. The sufferer's hopes for a new life beyond the grave are safely grounded in the resurrec-tion of Jesus Christ. These pastors will not try to soften the paradox of con-demning God's injustice here and the confidence of God's graciousness beyond. Both elements are part of the Christian's faith and experience. Nei-ther should be softened. Our task is not to achieve a smooth harmony of these conflicting beliefs but rather to let both have their full expression in faithfulness to what we see and believe.

Still other pastors may agree that the fact of cancer and its unredeemable evil must be taken with utmost seriousness, but they discount any reason to attribute evil to God. On the contrary, the reality of morally unjustifiable evil should lead us to rethink the role of God in determining what happens in the world. If we begin with the idea that God is the all-determining power, avoiding the conclusion that God is not wholly good is difficult indeed. But is that what is revealed in the cross of Christ? The power of that cross has been the power to draw people to it, not the power of compulsion. The power of the cross does not prevent suffering and death or hostile rejection, but neither is it the power that causes these evils. Even in the midst of these evils, the power works for good. The pastor who believes this may follow Griffin's thinking and encourage the sufferer to take with utmost seriousness all that can be learned about cancer cells and their perverse behavior, as well as all the human sins, including but not limited to the patient's, that have contributed to the cancer. But God's work and presence are not to be found in this type of education. Instead, God is to be found in the life forces within the body that struggle against the cancer, even though they are losing. More importantly, God is to be found in the sick person's own experience, sharing the agony, struggling against despair, guiding toward serenity in the face of death, and finding opportunities to express love even in these terrible circumstances. God is suffering with the sufferer, not causing the suffering. God is in those who watch helplessly as the sufferer dies, trying to transform their impotent rage into constructive determination to do what they can to reduce the suffering of others. The parishioner who experiences God in this way can die with the knowledge of God's presence and love.

Finally, some pastors agree with Griffin that God does not act externally by compulsion, but they think that even Griffin's view is too anthropomorphic. God is radically unlike creatures and cannot be thought of in the same way as the entities of ordinary experience. God is not an explanatory factor in the human situation. Our thought of God is inseparable from our experience of grace and our gratitude for it. We cannot abstract from the grace we find in life and seek its external cause in an entity we then call "God." Since God is not an efficient cause of any particular event in the world, issues of theodicy do not arise. As Roth emphasizes, trying to explain evil as contributing to a greater good or assuring people that evil is finally overcome is pointless and worse. On the other hand, railing against God because of the evil in the world is simply to misunderstand how the word "God" should function in the Christian's vocabulary. A pastor who thinks in this way can follow Phillips's lead. In doing so, the pastor will not have any one response to make to the parishioner's suffering. The question is what the dying parishioner is actually experiencing. Perhaps the parishioner, despite suffering, shows compassion and concern for others and remains grateful to God. The pastor will celebrate the grace that such actions manifest. But if the suffering is simply degrading and dehumanizing, the pastor will not deny that reality or look for some redeeming feature. The pastor will acknowledge and support the reality of the parishioner's experience. If prayer and the reading of scripture mediate grace to the sufferer, the pastor will certainly rejoice in the ability to be of help. If simply being there and listening bring any measure of comfort, the pastor will be present.

This review of the five positions taken in this book is intended to show that, indeed, what we believe about God and evil does matter. But this review also shows the burden placed upon the pastor in a time when authors on the subject diverge so much from one another. By what criterion should we decide what to say to a person who is dying of cancer?

One possibility is to return to the psychological criterion with which we began. What will be psychologically most beneficial to the sufferer? The tone of these essays indicates how much nonphilosophical factors shape the positions of the philosophers. All write as Christian believers. Their differences emerge more from what they understand to be the requirements of Christian faith or what they find personally religiously satisfying than from strictly philosophical considerations. For example, the rejection of Griffin's position by Davis and Roth is much more an expression of their need to believe in an all-powerful God than any inconsistency or distortion of the facts that they discern in his writings. If religious satisfaction is so important to the philosophers, the pastor may judge that what is needed in relation to the sufferer is a word that will satisfy. Of course, speaking words that one does not find persuasive oneself simply because of what one judges the other to need is not wise. A dying person wants honesty of communication. The decision as to what is satisfying to the pastor is as important as the judgment of what the cancer patient needs to hear.

Still, the question of what is satisfying is not merely psychological. Satisfaction does not come from beliefs that do not ring true to us, and many factors influence what "rings true." Familiarity and compatibility with other beliefs are two. Logical consistency and consistency with facts are others. All of these factors are operative in these essays, and are important to pastors.

II

Finding in one academic community five philosophers of religion who have devoted extended attention to the problems of theodicy is striking. I suspect that they have jointly written more on this topic in recent decades than the whole community of North American theologians. At first glance this statistic seems odd. We are accustomed to thinking that theodicy is a theological question. Why is it discussed primarily by philosophers?

The answer, I think, is found in Davis's introduction, where he points out that theodicy as a problem is dependent on theism as a belief. He then proceeds to define "theism" as the belief that the world was created by an omnipotent and perfectly good moral being. Even in this book, given Davis's definition, only two theodicies—his own and Hick's—are presented. Roth, Griffin, and Phillips are not theists as Davis defines the term. Nevertheless, Roth and Griffin take their bearings from the traditional discussion and then reject particular premises: in Roth's case, the pure goodness of God; in Griffin's case, God's omnipotence. Only Phillips turns his back on this whole way of approaching questions.

In this respect the contemporary theological community in general is more like Phillips. As in Phillips, the issue of religious language and how it is to be understood is often central. Attention is focused much more on issues of anthropology and Christology than on theology proper. Even when God is treated thematically, little discussion takes place about God's ontological or metaphysical character and of problems following upon that. Where such reflection has occurred, God is viewed in categories that do not give rise to theodicy. Tillich is the most important example here. The nature of the power of Being Itself is so different from that of particular beings that asking why God causes or allows evil is meaningless. In Germany, most theologians reject the "theist" label.

Of course, I am exaggerating the difference between theologians and philosophers. Even among German theologians who reject the label "theist," some have held all the tenets required by Davis. Karl Barth, for example, was forced by his understanding of God to deal with the question of evil. Emil Brunner was even more clearly qualified as a theist by Davis's definition, and he could not avoid theodicy.

I am not here supporting the dominant theological community against the philosophers. I believe, with the theologians, that the power of Christian faith is mediated chiefly through its symbols and images, and that these symbols be so shaped and formed as to mediate truly good news rather than oppression and repression is immensely important. But I believe that the power of these symbols depends on their being received as expressive of the nature of a reality to which they point, a reality that has ontological or metaphysical status. Of course, believers may be wrong about the referential element in symbols, but that stance does not make the question unimportant. I am grateful that among philosophers some continue to treat this issue as of central importance. On the other hand, I regret that more of the philosophical discussion is not informed by theological developments of the past two centuries. Philosophers seem more confident in the capacity of reason to settle questions about God than are theologians. I am grateful to Phillips for noting the great divide. We process theologians would like to be a bridge, but we have but a tenuous foothold in either conversation.

III

The problem of evil in Western society arises for many people out of shock at the contrast of what they feel should be the situation and what they discover actually occurs. That shock is not felt in the same way in India. Buddhist cultures assume the universality of evil in the world and have taken this as the starting point of reflection. Given this reality, they ask, how can we attain a state of blessedness? We must overcome the delusions of ordinary experience that bind us to the world of suffering. The contrast of the world of evil and suffering is not with the just and righteous world that *should* be but with the experience that can be attained when we see through the ordinary reality to what really is. Evil is not a challenge to belief in the goodness of God but a call to begin the process of overcoming the delusions that bind us to the ordinary world.

My intent is to reinforce that point made by Davis in the introduction. What we call the problem of evil is a function of our theism. Belief that the world is created by a good God arouses expectations. Life does not correspond with these expectations. When the discordance is extreme, we are shocked and outraged. Although this response is not the major theme of the Bible, the shock and outrage gain expression there, too. Within Christendom, even people who are not believers in God often begin with an expectation that is thwarted by historical experience and share in the outrage.

Outrage can be valuable, evoking action to mitigate evil and giving intensity and meaning to life. Outrage breaks up the stultifying complacency of too much religious life and forces attention again and again to the facts, stimulating fresh thinking and exposing the deadness of many of the inherited solutions to our intellectual problems.

However, another direction is now possible for us. In recent centuries we have begun with theism. We have tried to reconcile the facts of the world to the doctrine with which we have begun. The facts have forced the promoters of the doctrine on the defensive. The strongest defense now possible of an entirely traditional theism is that it is not logically impossible. Davis does not claim that his position is plausible to anyone who is not already convinced, on quite other grounds, that theism is true.

Perhaps the time has come to try a different strategy. Perhaps we need to look at the world without the optimistic expectations generated by the theistic hypothesis. Let us see how in the whole evolutionary process, advance in the overall complexity and richness of the biosphere has been purchased at the expense of the early and often painful death of the great majority of sentient creatures. Individual animals are not prized or treated "justly" in the process. Many patterns of mutual cooperation have developed within the evolutionary process, but their function is to enable one group to survive at the expense of others.

The emergence of human life did not change this situation. Within tribes and, later, villages, cities, and nations, cooperative behavior has been an asset, although as the group has grown larger, these positive relations have more often been within smaller subgroups. Both in the larger group and in the more intense subgroups, such as clans or classes, much of the value of cooperation has been in enabling that group to compete more effectively, and more destructively, with other groups. Our virtues have contributed to our destructiveness with respect to others. The Holocaust is more an illustration than an exception to this characteristic of human life on the planet, the slaughterhouse that has been human history.

When we view the world through expectations established by theism, we are outraged by what we see. The world does not have the goodness or express the justice we seem to have the right to expect. But when we look at the world through expectations established by the Holocaust, we also find much to astonish us. In spite of everything, in most times and places, the majority of people enjoy life and find it good. The mutual support that has developed out of the social need to survive often goes beyond generosity and occasional sacrificial service. Sometimes human concern extends beyond one's own community to others, even to competitors. Some people are self-critical and change their views when confronted by evidence. Beauty is prized for its own sake. One man voluntarily took hemlock rather than betray his convictions about obedience to law. Others spoke truth to power at great risk and often at great cost. One taught inclusive love and accepted crucifixion out of his own embodiment of that love. Many others, inspired by him, have tried to make justice and righteousness effective in human society. What can all this mean? Must not something be at work other than narrow self-interest and absolutization of one's own group? Can we not call that God? Can we not find in events of this kind a clue to the nature and reality of that God?

Perhaps if we begin here, we will gain more credibility in a world that has grown weary of the defenders of theism. Perhaps we would ourselves have more confidence in our own affirmations. Of course, that approach will only be a beginning. By itself this worldview will not tell us much about the nature of God's activity or how powerful God is, but it will offer a solid basis for theological reflection. Perhaps we could learn once again to praise God out of our own real experience of God and vital historical memories—a refreshing change from defending doubtful dogmas.

Afterword

Marilyn McCord Adams

The Dissonance of Double Encounters

"But what do *you* think, what is *your* answer to the problem of evil?" my teaching assistant protested, after we had chewed our way through classic sources and contemporary treatments, matching objections with replies, weighing each and finding all somehow wanting. My own encounters with evil had been non-negligible, but they were spiritually unresolved enough that I didn't know what to say.

My tongue was not loosened until a decade later, when I was working at a Hollywood parish during the AIDS epidemic, and spiritually desperate gays and lesbians started walking through our sanctuary doors. Many were "church-damaged." Early in their lives, they had "connected" with God, even experienced calls to various sorts of Christian leadership. Later on, confident preachers and congregations had consigned them to outer darkness, with the strident conviction that embracing same-gendered lovers was an abomination to the Lord! Thus exiled from the church, most had sought out gay and lesbian sub-cultures, which furnished whole spectra of mentors to help in their struggle to define authentic homosexual identities for themselves. Now, in their twenties and thirties and early forties, they faced death in their partners, in whole circles of friends, and often in themselves. Their questions were non-academic and urgent. What did the God of their early encounters have to do with the sudden plague that threatened to annihilate their whole social world, dissolving them with it? They were tormented by their need to know, what did either have to do with being lesbian or gay?

With this congregation, passive listening, silently sitting *shiva*, were insufficient, although there were eventually many hours and days and nights for

191

that. Before they got too sick to think, in the midst of their mourning others, they wanted help in trying to understand how to put their fragmented worlds together. Sunday mornings, when I looked out on the congregation, into their faces gray-green from doses of AZT, I could feel their demand: "It's now or never. We'll be dead in six weeks. For God's sake, think of a way to show us how—despite this present ruin—God loves us, is loving us even now. Isn't there, surely there must be, a good word for us from the Lord?"

So I felt forced, even divinely pressured, into an assignment it would have been foolhardy to volunteer for, arguably blasphemous to assume. The congregation's demand was complex. They were "in my face" with how bad AIDS was. No use speaking, no credibility in talking if I were unwilling to peel my eyes to probe the perversity of a disease that not only dealt untimely death, but first brought stepwise degradation—blindness, deafness, dementia, and incontinence before suffocation and kidney failure. I had to take in how contagion produced social alienation, sometimes abandonment and betrayal by friends and lovers, estrangement from family; how uninfected society distanced itself by "blaming the victim," the better to reassure ourselves that because I am not one of *them*, this could not happen to me! I had to be realistic: for thousands, AIDS was (at least *ante mortem*) no edifying spiritual exercise. How often it made them and those around them morally the worse, left them bitter and confused, and seemingly separated from God. Job-style prayers of protest had to be my first words, through tears and LA traffic to and from homes and hospitals: "I don't understand why *?\#! You're so powerful, what's Your excuse? How can You love us and still do things this way?"

Nevertheless, I would not merely have disappointed, I would have broken faith with the experience of many including my own, had I stood up to say, "Sorry, God isn't as good as you thought. God doesn't love you as much as you hoped." What made their (and for that matter, my own) spiritual struggle so intense was not merely the terror of their encounter with degrading suffering and death, but the fact that they (we) had also tasted and seen the goodness of the Lord. They expected me to scour the resources of our experience, of scripture and the Christian tradition to find some way to put the puzzle together, to sketch some soteriological strategy to explain how both things could be so. They also required me to be the stand-in target for their protests and objections to any proposed answers, and all the while to continue to drop hints that might eventually enable them to make the plot resolve. And so, ironically, it was the AIDS epidemic that drove me, eventually enabled me to say something about God and evil that I and many (though not everyone) in my congregation could believe in, something that I could stand in some pulpits and honestly say.

The Importance of Conceptual Framing

My Hollywood experience showed me how theoretical and practical—pastoral, existential, evangelistic—problems of evil can, do, and should inform one another. Practical encounters challenge "arm-chair" "short ways" by forcing one to "get real" on a daily, even hourly basis. In turn, theoretical reflections underlie the pastoral process of helping those who encounter evil—not least, by ruling out stock explanations (such as those delivered by individual and collective versions of the Act-Consequence Principle—good for good, evil for evil), and eventually by suggesting more subtle and sensitive interpretations. My own encounters with people with AIDS also confirmed what Job and his friends have learned over the centuries: that where God and evil are concerned, much depends on how the issues are conceptually framed.

Problems of Evil

Thus, even at the theoretical level, it is important to recognize and distinguish the multiple problems that evils raise. Like many other writers, Stephen Davis seems to take the so-called logical problem of evil to be that of whether the existence of God is logically compossible with the existence of any evil at all (e.g., with a one-hour toothache), and the *evidential* problem to be that of whether evils in the actual world count as evidence against the existence of God. Again, in treating the latter, Davis seems at first to see the contrast in terms of *amounts* of evil: God could coexist with some evils, but the actual world contains too much. In fact, however, one can raise the question of logical compossibility with respect to any and all packages of evil a possible world may contain. I prefer to distinguish between *abstract* and *concrete logical* problems of evil (whether the existence of God is compossible with any evil at all vs. with evils such as the actual world contains). Moreover, as Davis's reflections on moral monsters and their deeds acknowledge, even if our probability calculi furnish no conceptual machinery with which to assess whether actual *amounts* of evil render the existence of God unlikely, the *kinds* and possibly distribution of actual evils do raise further compossibility problems. My own focus, therefore, has been on *the concrete logical problem* of whether the existence of God is logically consistent with evils in the amounts, and of the kinds, and with the distribution found in the actual world. In my judgment, excessive focus on the abstract logical problem has combined with the tendency to construe the difference between logical and evidential problems in terms of amounts, to distract philosophers from engaging the problems raised by evils of the very worst types. (Davis's evolving reflections seem to bear the marks of this tendncy: major wrestling with the morally monstrous comes last, and the appeals to ignorance and eschatology seem less than fully integrated with his free will approach to the [abstract] logical problem.)

Definitional Difficulties

Coming from another angle, discussions can be shaped and distorted by our definitions of "evil." Within the present volume, David Griffin stipulates that genuine evil is that which—all things considered—makes the world worse than it would otherwise be. It follows that genuine evil is non-defeasible by cosmic considerations (it is, in Davis's language, *gratuitous*). Thus, no matter how monstrous they may seem, any event, action, or state of affairs that contributes to a higher value in the world as a whole (e.g., that is a necessary constituent in the best of all possible worlds, or a world with the best balance of moral good over moral evil that God could get) is not a genuine but only a *prima facie* evil. In my judgment, this choice is rhetorically unfortunate because it misfits our ordinary usage where the worst evils are concerned. Sometimes we do speak of small or medium scale set-backs as not really evil because of the lessons we have learned or worse ills avoided or relationships fostered. But most (Roth and I included) would rightly recoil from the suggestion that the Holocaust and the AIDS epidemic were only *prima facie* and not *genuinely* evil. I suspect that this is part (though not the whole) of what lies behind Roth's adamant insistence that, where the Holocaust is concerned, it would be morally insensitive to suppose that God could do anything to set things right: for on Griffin's definition, that would be to admit that the Holocaust was not genuinely evil after all. Roth presses his protest that to take seriously the worst that befalls us, the truth that it *was* genuinely evil has to ring out forever! Responding to this, Griffin himself agrees that it would be morally insensitive to deny that there are genuine evils, and then accounts for their occurrence in terms of a metaphysics of Divine persuasive power that cannot guarantee their prevention. Likewise, Davis feels the pressure of Roth's case and finds himself morally compelled to admit that gratuitous evils occur, and that the free will defense alone cannot explain why God permits them.

In my judgment, Griffin's definition, and Davis's identical definition of "gratuitous evil," are further problematic because of their cosmic focus. In assessing an event, action, or state of affairs, their question is whether it makes *the world as a whole* better. Certainly, I would agree with Griffin and Davis (for that matter with Leibniz) that the God of biblical religion has cosmic aims and interests. Genesis 1 records the Divine self-evaluation, that God has done a very good job in making the world. In Job 39–40, YHWH scolds human fault-finding with the reminder that Divine interests are not utterly anthropocentric. Nevertheless, what suffering people are worried about in the first instance is not Divine competence in world-making, but rather whether their plight shows that God does not care about, is not interested in being good to them. At some stage they may or may not be *de facto* consoled either by Griffin's counsel that perfect power cannot prevent their misery, or by classical assurances that Divine omnipotence limits chaos, that God maintains the world as a stable frame within which they unravel according to natural laws. But what makes the worst we experience so spiritually pernicious is its power to call into question Divine goodness to created persons, and more broadly to furnish *prima facie* reason to doubt whether life can be worth living after all.

For these reasons, I have preferred to focus on the category of *horrendous evils*, which I define as "evils participation in which (either as a victim or as a perpetrator) constitutes *prima facie* reason to doubt whether the participant's life could—give such participation—be a great good to the participant on the whole." In most (if not all cases), the destructive force of horrors extends beyond their concrete disvalue (such as pain and material deprivation) to invade the deep structure of the person's frameworks of meaning-making and seemingly defeat the individual's value as a person. Thus, paradigm horrors—such as Nazi doctors pouring phosphorus on or vivisecting their patients; the violent man first raping a woman and then axing off her arms; the skeletal AIDS patient, blinded and vomiting blood, unable to put two thoughts together—degrade the victim and the perpetrator (if any) as well.

My definition satisfies Roth's demand that the Holocaust and the AIDS epidemic remain horrendous eternally, insofar as they did and do constitute *prima facie* reason to doubt whether the participants' lives could—given their participation—be great goods to them on the whole. Yet, it makes room for the possibility that Roth does not countenance: viz., that what is and always will be a *prima facie* reason, might not be an *all-things-considered* reason to deny overall positive meaning to the individual participants' lives, and so not an all-things-considered reason to deny that God has been good to them.

Justification or Defeat?

Another obstacle to meeting my parishioners' demand—that I take seriously both the depth of their suffering and the goodness of God—has been the focus on theodicy, taken etymologically for the project of *justifying* the ways of God to human beings. Roth and Davis fall in line with contemporary discussions that understand justification in terms of morally sufficient reasons why God would permit and not prevent evils. Such reasons usually take the form of identifying some Divine purpose (e.g., creating the best of all possible worlds, or a world with as favorable a balance of moral good over moral evil as God can get, or a state of affairs in which all souls are—through a process involving their free participation—"made" fit for and come into eventual union with God) for which evils are constitutive means or side effects of policies instrumental to or constitutive of Divine purpose. Theodicies contend that the good end of realized Divine purpose is the reason-why that justifies the (constituent or instrumental) means and side effects involved. Hegel is notorious for his thesis that the whole slaughter-bench of history is justified because it is necessary (as a constitutive means) for the self-development of Absolute Spirit.

Roth protests that there could not be an end that would *justify* the slaughter-bench of history in general or the Holocaust in particular. In Roth's estimation, free-will defenders—Davis included—vastly over-estimate the competence and the dignity of human agency, when they reckon that its worth and the overall value of a world including its possible or actual performances to be an end that could justify the history of human ruin. Here I heartily concur, and would further press the point that human agency is too immature and flimsy in relation to the Divine for classical free will strategies—of shifting primary responsibility for evil onto created free agents—to work. Whether one believes in Adam's fall or credits evolution, God is the One Who set us up in an environment in which we are radically vulnerable to participation in horrors. Primary responsibility for their occurrence must rest with God!

Moreover, I agree with Roth and Phillips that it is indecent to think of God as choosing (what I conceive of as) horrors in advance as instrumental or constitutive means to some greater good. Moreover, I take it to be an epistemic measure of how bad horrors are that we can think of no plausible candidate sufficient reason why God would permit them. But on my view—*pace* Phillips—this is not because God is not a purposive agent or that God has no goals for creation. I am even willing to allow that God has reasons for creating a world with horrendous side effects, and that these may include a love for material creation, a desire for a harmonious cosmos, and the will to give created agency scope. But the attempt to turn these considerations into so-called morally sufficient reasons why God has permitted horrors worsens the problem of Divine goodness to horror participants by suggesting that God cares more about such cosmic considerations than about human beings.

In my experience, the why-question is *spiritually* fruitful when pressed with God—after all, it won Job a face-to-face encounter with the Maker of all things—but *theoretically* intractable. For that reason, I find it preferable to frame the search for a solution to incompossibility problems a different way: in terms of whether there is any way for God to make good on horrors, not just within the context of the world as a whole, but within the parameters of the individual horror participant's life. Here I draw on Roderick Chisholm's contrast between balancing off (in which value-parts bear a merely additive relation to each other and to the value of their resultant whole) and defeat (in which the negative or positive value of the part contributes to a greater positive or negative value in the whole by virtue of a relation of organic unity that the former bears to the latter).[1] My contention is that God can be shown to be good to created persons if and only if God guarantees to each a life that is a great good to him/her on the whole and one in which any participation in horrors (whether as victim or perpetrator) is not merely balanced off but defeated within the context of the individual horror participant's life. Once again, to say that horrors are defeated is not to say they were not genuinely horrendous; nor is it to claim with Davis that they will pale into insignificance (presumably by being over-balanced by the goods of Kingdom come). After all, even where horrors are defeated, participation in them remains *prima facie* ruinous to the positive meaning of the participant's life. Rather, horror-defeat means that their negative value has been overcome by weaving them into a larger meaning-making framework of positive significance for the individual in question.

Appeals to Eschatology

In human beings, the survival instinct normally manifests itself in a persistent hope that pragmatically presupposes that human life is worth living. Thus, even Roth, who is "in our face" with the depth of Holocaust horrors, holds out the eschatological hope that human protest might produce a Divine change of heart and a willingness to treat us better. Recognizing that the life stories of many do not resolve into *ante-mortem* happy endings, Griffin refers us to (but unhappily does not summarize) his recent book, which argues that process theology can still leave room for eschatological hope. Hick's soul-making theodicy puts heavy weight on *post-mortem* careers and future spiritual development culminating in mystical union with the Real for everyone.

By its very nature, hope outruns present certainties. Yet contributors to this volume challenge each other as to whether such hopes are reasonable even in the weak sense of being consistent with the other assumptions underlying the approach to evil in question. Roth reconciles actual evils with the existence of God by denying perfect goodness; Griffin, by denying classical interpretations of omnipotence and creation *ex nihilo*. In consequence, Griffin sees no reason to believe Roth's partly evil God would be moved to repentance by our protests, while Roth finds it incredible that Griffin's God has the right kind of power to make good on the worst evils that have already befallen us. When Davis speaks of an eschatological redemption, overcoming, or transcending of evil, Roth counters that—in view of Davis's admission that there are gratuitous (Griffin's genuine) evils—such overcoming cannot be complete or perfect. Against Hick, Roth protests that Hick does not explain *how* evils that cannot be undone are erased by the ultimate progress and perfection of all.

I think that these disagreements are more easily sorted out if we subsume the worse life has to offer under my alternative rubric of horrendous evil. Davis's characterization of the morally monstrous as gratuitous evils, encourages him to conceive of the eschatological resolution in terms of Chisholmian balancing off.[2] Roth, in turn, senses that mere balancing off would not fully resolve the plot, because it would leave the worst aspects of human experience surd, meaningless, because undefeated. It trivializes the Holocaust to suppose that it will (like adolescent embarrassment at wearing unfashionable clothing) pale in insignificance, or (in the manner of apocalyptic theology) fade from memory in the blaze of Divine glory that awaits the blessed. Where the Holocaust is concerned, neither we nor God should ever forget! Because Roth takes Griffin's definition for granted—that genuine evils are indefeasible—he in effect charges that the most that Hick's eschatological scenario can provide is a way to balance off.

In forwarding the category of the horrendous, I mean to be agreeing with Roth, not only that the very worst aspects of human life are eternally horrendous, but also that mere balancing off will not do. For horrors eat into the meaning-making structures of individual persons in such a way as *prima facie* to deprive their lives of the possibility of positive significance. Divine goodness to created *persons* requires that God not leave our meaning-making endeavors eternally frustrated where horrors are concerned. Rather to be good to created horror participants, God would have to endow any horror participation with a positive aspect by integrating it into a wider framework of positive meaning for that individual person's life.[3]

While it is possible to read Hick as holding that this-worldly participation in dysteleological evils (horrors included) is merely balanced off for each individual soul by *post-mortem* progress and ultimate union with God, his account of soul-making furnishes materials for a kind of defeat as well. For according to Hick, soul-making progresses from self-centeredness to other-centeredness or Reality-centeredness. If horror-participation defeated the positive significance of a given career for an individual, it would nevertheless contribute to the mystery of the world and hence to a favorable educational environment for others. When, in later careers, the horror-participant has made progress in altruism, he or she might look back and be glad to have been of service to others in this way, and thereby regard his or her horror participation as defeated by integration into his or her altruistic values and projects.

Like Davis, I find much to sympathize with in Hick's soul-making approach. Nevertheless, I agree with what I take to be the spirit of Roth's protest, that Hick's confident optimism that "all's well that ends well" doesn't take the *ante-mortem* damage to the individual (and perhaps our this-worldly careers generally) seriously enough. Horror-participation merely for the sake of others would be too much for God Who is good to created persons to ask of the as-yet morally immature, whose moral progress in this career is thereby forfeited. At the very least, the materials needed to endow horror-participation with some positive significance for the horror-participant must be planted in the *ante-mortem* career.

My own view is that horrors can be defeated within the context of the individual horror-participant's life, if and only if horror participation can be integrated into the horror-participant's intimate personal relationship with God. I understand the latter to be a necessary condition because in my estimation no package of merely created goods could balance off or defeat horrors' ruinous power. I regard it as sufficient because I hold that God is Goodness Itself and so a good incommensurate with any package of merely created goods or evils, and because I take it that everlasting beatific intimacy with God is incommensurately good for individual created persons. The basis for integrating horror-participation in the horror-participant's relationship with God can be laid down in the here and now (in our present careers) if God identifies with our participation in horrors in such a way as to turn such occasions into points of (often unwitting) intimate contact with Godself. The Christian tradition holds that God did just that through Incarnation and death on the cross. This is the first step.

For horror-participation to be fully defeated within the context of the individual participant's life, however, he or she would have to recognize and appropriate some of the positive meanings God has conferred on our horror-participation by identifying with us in it. And this would require God to heal the psycho-spiritual trauma caused by horror-participation, and to coach, teach, and collaborate with us in learning to make some positive sense of our lives. My notion is that without taking away their *prima facie* life-ruining power, organic connection to the participant's relationship with God would confer on horror-participation a good aspect, which—when recognized and appropriated—would leave horror-victims retrospectively—from the vantage point of heavenly beatitude—unwilling to wish them away from their life histories. On the Christian scenario, God also casts God's lot with horror-perpetrators by dying a ritually cursed death—a fact which, when recognized and appropriated, can enable human horror-perpetrators to accept and forgive themselves. Retrospectively, perpetrators would recognize that these acts did not separate them from the love of God who identified with them on the cross. They would be reassured by the knowledge that God has compensated their victims (via Divine identification and beatific relationship). They would also be amazed at Divine resourcefulness in forcing horrors to make positive contributions to God's redemptive plan (cf. Synoptic Gospel passion narratives). This would be the second step in horror-defeat.

To make the plot fully resolve, however, God would have to end our vulnerability to horrors by transforming our environment and/or our relationship to it. This would be the third step. Incidentally, it is because I have not been able to see how the perfect persuasive power of Griffin's God would be sufficient to accomplish these last two steps that I retain the classical conception of Divine omnipotence. But I have not seen the new book to which Griffin alludes or examined its arguments.

My claim is that these three steps together explain how God could be good to horror-participants by guaranteeing them a life that is a great good to them on the whole and one in which any horror-participation is defeated. For Chalcedonian Christians, the first point would be a matter of faith. But because it is obvious (as Hick notes) that millions of horror-participants have died without recognizing God present with them, *a fortiori* without having been in a position to appropriate the positive meaning it restores to their lives, my second two points would be matters for eschatological hope. And although these are matters of speculative theology and nowhere defined as dogma, they are consistent with the Apostles' and Nicene Creeds and the determinations of the ecumenical councils.

Method and Metaphysics

Since I follow Hick in endorsing universal salvation, Davis would protest that my approach is therefore inconsistent with scripture. Davis complains that his interlocutors in this volume do not seem to feel a strong need to be normed by scripture and Christian tradition, and wonders what their methodological assumptions are.

Hick responds that "the theodicy project" is an exercise in "metaphysical thinking," which "consists in the formation and criticism of large-scale hypotheses concerning the nature and process of the universe." Hick recognizes two demands: that the theodicy hypothesis be internally coherent, and that it be consistent with the data of the religious tradition on which it is based, and of the world. Hick's proposal is remarkably congruent with medieval guidelines for theory-building, which direct attention to the data of reason, experience, and authority (scripture and religious tradition).

The idea is that Truth is one, so that the truths of theology must be consistent with the veridical deliverances of science and human experience, as well as philosophy and other things reason finds obvious. Where the "data" sets are plentiful and pull in different directions, the interests of consistency and coherence drive theory-makers to privilege some and marginalize others. In patristic and medieval philosophical theology, philosophical convictions about the immutability and impassibility of the first cause drove thinkers to embrace a flexible hermeneutic that explained away biblical references to Divine emotions and changes of mind. Apparently, Davis's own sensibilities about what Divine Goodness would do lead him to construe biblical talk of hell fire as metaphorical. Here less entrenched data have to give way to more firmly rooted convictions in the interests of preserving consistency, coherence, and explanatory power.

Griffin's contribution admirably illustrates the balancing act in which a Christian philosophical theologian is engaged. Philosophical reflection so convinces Griffin that perfect power is by nature not coercive but persuasive, that this thesis is—for him—non-negotiable. Wishing to stand within the Christian circle, he then tries to rebut the charge that scripture and tradition set up a strong presumption in favor of creation *ex nihilo*, by arguing that this is not the doctrine of most relevant biblical passages and that it was a relative late-comer within the theological tradition. What divides Davis from some other Christian philosophical theologians—Griffin and the early Hick included—is not that he takes scripture and tradition as normative while others do not, but rather issues about what it means to take them as norms, about whether and to what degree and under what interpretations the deliverances of scripture and tradition may be regarded as defeasible. Hick reads the Bible and sees an evolving God-consciousness, whose different stages forward a variety of contrasting theological pictures. Griffin seems to agree, and so do I. Where problems of evil are concerned, the Bible both advances Act-Consequence Principle explanations (in the psalms and proverbs where individual prosperity and suffering are concerned; in Deuteronomy and various prophetic passages where collective weal and woe are at stake) and subjects them to devastating critique (in the book of Job) and contradiction (in the Servant Songs of Isaiah). The Holiness Code puts the burden on us to become holy as God is Holy, while the passion narratives show Christ becoming curse for us by dying on a cross. Experience of the horrendous convinces me that it would be blasphemous to suppose that God visits horrors on anyone (individuals or groups) as punishment for anything—blasphemous to suppose that the second destruction of Jerusalem (an earlier holocaust) was (as Luke's Gospel suggests) Divine judgment on the Jews for rejecting the Messiah, blasphemous to declare that the AIDS epidemic was Divine judgment on the abomination of homosexual lifestyles. But privileging such conclusions from experience forces one to understand the authority of scripture and/or its interpretation in different ways from those that Davis probably prefers. Put otherwise, Davis, (at least early) Hick, Griffin, and I share the same norms, but we assign them different patterns and degrees of entrenchment.

Not everyone agrees that Truth is one, however. In his early work *The Concept of Prayer*, D.Z. Phillips offers a remarkably clear statement of one sort of Wittgensteinian approach: many language games are played; the criteria of reality are internal to each language game, so that there can be no such thing as Reality with a capital "R" over and against which various language games can be measured for veridicality. Thus, it is as much a conceptual confusion to attempt a theoretical integration of the truths of science or history with those of myth or religion, as it would be to try to offer a theoretical justification of why one language game should be played in preference to another. Moreover, the various language games themselves are not theories but complex social practices. For Phillips, metaphysics or the variety of metaphysical systems do not number among the language games he countenances, but represent the philosophically confused project of trying to give theoretical explanations of everything.

In fact, the later Hick (of *The Interpretation of Religion*) seems to stand somewhere in between the methodology he proposes in the above quotes and Phillips's Wittgensteinian position. In that notable work, Hick's focus is on complex religious practices associated with the world's great religions. There he seems to hold that there is such a thing as Reality with a capital "R," which human beings encounter and in response to which they come up with the variety of narratives and philosophical conceptualities that such traditions contain. Nevertheless, the metaphysical size-gap between human beings (our cognitive capacities included) and the Real is too great for any of these conceptual systems to *correspond* with Reality and so count as *literally* true. At best, narrative and metaphysical claims may be *mythologically* true, insofar as the religious practices of which they are a part meet the pragmatic soteriological criterion of being efficacious in transforming members from self-centeredness towards other- or Reality-centeredness.

If Phillips's position in *The Concept of Prayer* seems straight forwardly anti-realist (in the sense of not believing there is any language-game-independent Reality to which language games correspond or fail to correspond), the later Hick might be said to be an anti-realist where religious discourse is concerned, insofar as the criteria for its evaluation are pragmatic rather than theoretical after all. Because the religious traditions thus evaluated contain philosophical discourse, he does not mind recommending his Irenaean theodicy again here, as a piece of explanation internal to the Christian tradition and mythologically true. Phillips is rightly puzzled over Hick's continued rejection of the doctrine of the fall, on the ground that it conflicts with *historical* and/or *scientific*— tradition independent, or tradition shared?—facts. Does he think, then, that some theological theories are literally and not just mythologically false? Further clarification would be helpful as to how religious language relates to other sorts of discourse, and why religious truth is mythological and scientific truth literal, when—from a broadly Kantian point of view—both systems operate within the phenomenal realm.

For my part, I take my stand with Davis and Griffin and perhaps Roth in embracing a metaphysical realist position, according to which there is a Reality with a capital "R" to which our philosophical and theological theories aim to correspond. But these issues are as philosophically fundamental as problems of evil are religiously basic. I close by thanking the contributors for weaving a rich tapestry of overlapping and contrasting reflections, and leave fuller discussion of realism and anti-realism controversies for another day!

A Divine Response

"Now Hear This"
Frederick Sontag

It is we, always and only we, who speak for God. I know of no one, in his or her right mind, who claims that any Divine Being always speaks to us in clear, authenticated ways. True, the Mormons had golden plates given to Joseph Smith with an engraved message, and many have always claimed to "hear God's voice" in their particular scriptures, Christian, Jewish, or otherwise. The religious literature of the world is full of powerful passages that, over the ages, have been inspirational to millions. But no one I know has claimed that "a divinity on high" issues heavenly certified messages designed to eliminate all obscurity so as to be accepted as such by all—not even all believers in a particular religion.

Given what has been written by the authors of this book—both about God's views and their own—it seems to me that God needs a defense attorney. Almost everything in the authors' various assertions and denials depends greatly upon their correctly defining the Divine mind and its intentions. Someone needs to form "a divine response," particularly since so much in the authors' statements, both pro and con, depends upon fathoming the Divine master plan. So let the ship's loudspeaker system blare out, "Now hear this."

Most of what every author says and claims depends on "omnipotence," "wholly good," plus—almost the most important question—the divine "eschatological" intentions. In other words, they are moving beyond the present time and our own duration. So this subject needs projection, or perhaps a defining revelation. In any case, no answer is deducible simply from the present state of the world. So, what might God say about these human, all too human, conjectures?

A: "Peace, gentlemen," our Divine respondent might begin by saying. "There is no use in attacking one another, or prejudging the God you communicate with, since no certainty will be obtained until the projected Day of Last Judgment. Philosophers, scientists, and politicians have sought certainty for centuries. For a time, modern scientists too thought that providing certainty might be within their grasp. And much advancement was accomplished by science. But now, finally, our hope to produce final theoretical certainty seems to be 'gone with the wind.' Governments' projected utopias were also built on this hope to revolutionize human nature by modern technologies, e.g., Freud or Marx. But at the close of the twentieth century, ladies and gentlemen, human followers of any of a variety of religious views should have no doubt about the impossibility of establishing utopian societies or revolutionizing human nature on their own. Shall we dub the twentieth century 'the human holocaust century?'

"This brings us primarily to our authors' fascination with their projection of 'omnipotence' as the key Divine attribute, which no God ever asserted in the absolute way on which they seemed fixed. 'Omnipotence' means many things, never only one. 'All powerful,' perhaps, but you also seem to take it to mean completely fixed and determined, whereas I thought the years before the close of the twentieth century should have made it clear that any powerful divinity can now easily decide to live with our human uncertainty, and that I must have originally put indeterminacy into the human evolutionary plan intentionally. This has just recently become the way a twenty-first century divinity now must accept its ability to live with constant uncertainty. Any worthy divinity now needs to possess the power to maintain its life through uncertainty, whereas we always used to eliminate uncertainty in trying to establish the divine life as our desired model.

"Only the weak always need to try to achieve certainty. To be 'omnipotent' means to be all-powerful and so to be able to sustain life through chaos and every threatened destruction, whether now by intervention or in the future by divine revolution. Most authors seem fixed on certain knowledge because of their weakness. Gods do not demand it (except when it is projected onto them by humans seeking certainty), just because their power is so immense that it makes them confident of their ability to live through the challenges brought on by our human uncertainties. Jesus knew that he could not sustain himself through death's threat, but he trusted in God's unlimited power to renew his life, even if once lost.

"'All-good' is an attribute many of our authors use in ways that also seem to come more from your human structure than from the life of divine Gods. God 'never promised us a rose garden,' and Eden certainly was not one. Job was challenged when his God thundered, 'were you there when I laid the foundations of the world?' The one who created the world and humans never intended, so the history of the world seems to indicate, for us to have 'the best of all possible worlds.' That was for philosophers, in an optimistic modern world, to speculate about. No religious leader who understands his or her people's relationship to the God who chose them can ever think that their relationship to divinity's plan entails an easy life for them. I never said that I am all-good. In fact, I could not be, given the world created by my evolutionary commands. However, my power did allow me to ordain a good and bad world as your proving grounds.

"Now let's turn to the myriad speculations about what I intend and project to happen beyond time's extent. It seems that there was time before the evolutionary development of your world and that humans in their terror-filled development came from something proceeding that rather than from nothing, even if it all came first from God's own nature by Divine creative power. We gave up, centuries ago, thinking about the natural order as being fixed from the beginning. We see so much and expect so much from continued creative development, and not from fixity, as we begin the twenty-first century. There is no longer any reason to combine Divinity's nature with fixity. That seems to have evolved beyond fixity too, given the way humans describe their gods so variously.

"Your evolutionary divinity, now emerging after centuries of humans trying to restrict divine power to one certain channel, exposes itself by ordaining and accepting the massive agonies encountered along an elected evolutionary trail that also involves massive uncertainties. Such a twenty-first century divinity need not reject uncertainty or perplexity even concerning the losses en route. 'All-powerful' no longer need imply fixity. 'All-good' no longer need mean ignorance of the faults built into the system that an infinite power elected as the path to your development. Since 'time before time' has meaning again in our evolutionary universe, so does 'time after time.' That is a divinely established point when decisive decisions might again yield dramatically different contexts for human life. Such radical transformation becomes perfectly conceivable today, although not certain to happen in any particular way.

"Yet, just as the universe before evolution's start cannot be visualized except by imagination (compare this with Hollywood's and Silicon Valley's successful business ventures!), so the many religious projections of life-after-the-end-of-this-time cannot be seen now. This fits the definition of faith in Hebrews as 'belief in things unseen' (Heb. 11:1). Given the uncertainties in our own world at present, evidently we must learn to live with even more uncertainty as the twenty-first century of uncertainty takes over. Yet, we still cannot be prevented from projecting new forms of life after this present time cycle comes to a halt. We can believe in things unseen, empiricism too having 'gone with the wind,' along with The Old South. But this depends on faith, never on things seen with certainty.

"Your editors," our Divine respondent might want to warn us, "set out five facets of theistic belief, as if to give a fixity to their attempts to deal with evil, which could just as easily be said to be simply the theistic belief of one time: (1) One God, (2) Who created the world, (3) Omnipotent, (4) Personal, and (5) a perfect God. Yet, maybe these are all far from fixed in meaning and in fact are the main questions that have brought out hundreds of responses and definitions, not one fixed agreement. The divine nature may not be such as to be easily bought into words, in spite of Wittgenstein's hope. There is the possibility, now being more widely accepted, that the important truths, such as what to be 'divine' means concerning my nature, are such that story and symbol are 'more appropriate, rather than definite words, to convey religious truth.'"

B: In fact, this Theology of Divine Protest may actually end on a note of hope, which "protest" might not seem to allow. Roth says, "A God encountered in Jewish and Christian experience makes possible an option that keeps hope from dying." In spite of holocausts, some of our American Midwestern Protestant optimism about the future and our "Progress" can return. This can be held onto by faith, "a belief in things unseen," but there certainly are no longer any reasons to believe in Progress of any radical kind, as the twentieth century adds up its sorry tales. Can God's promises for a remade future be relied upon? Roth at least certainly does not find the closing century's record of destruction any reason to deny that "God's good promises can be more real than they have been."

Of course, Steve Davis wants to help Roth by saying that God's will is wholly good *and* that God can and therefore will one day redeem all evil. The question is: Why should one believe that, given our world to date? How can all the evil that has destroyed so much ever be "redeemed"? All past evils pale in significance to the twentieth century record. "Redeemed" is a beautiful word, but has any God actually made such a promise? Davis "will only worship and trust a being whom I believe is wholly good." But again, where has divinity made any public claim for such purity of nature? Of course, David Griffin reclaims all the past centuries' lost optimism in progress by claiming that God is calling us [him?] to form a global order leading to a global democracy. So Hegel and Marx's belief in history's ultimate progress returns!

C: Some Divine Conclusions: "Now hear this."

(1) "You too often take 'omnipotence' to mean to provide security and certainty for you, much as you wish for it to solve the security worries of all finite beings. True, some in the ancient tradition took this divine 'power attribute' to mean the fixity of all contingencies, whether humans could foreknow these or not. In actuality, with this full and unrestricted power range, an infinite power can just as well enable any divinity to deal with and to accept uncertainty. The divinity has open options for dealing with the uncertainties, now so evident in the evolutionary descent of animals and plants and humans, without worry of failure—ultimately. 'Divine knowledge' no longer need mean a fixity of events in the twenty-first century, but rather the power to accept uncertainty.

(2) "This, of course, also extends to 'limitless goodness,' so much prized by certain theologians. Dealing with the mixtures of good and evil that are in human and in Nature's behavior all the time, such a monotone deity has often been attractive to uncertain humans. But as my divine words projected in the Old Testament proclaim, 'I create weal, I create woe' (Isaiah 45:7). Unlimited power gives me the ability to accept evil into the natural and human orders I produced. But it does not threaten my ultimate ability to control, as it does with all humans except for the most vicious totalitarian dictators. My unlimited power allows me to accept evil into creation (although not directly into the divine nature as such) without fear of losing the ability to control, not always at any one time, of course. But I may or may not choose to exercise divine control ultimately. Such a belief that I will is your option.

(3) "In the recent centuries, of course, many people wanted to link unlimited divine power to moral improvement, such as the Enlightenment or Progress theories about the development of human nature. And modern technology seemed to support this, granted all the advances that came from modern science. However, the moral decay so evident in all appraisals of the twentieth century seems to indicate that our natural course may not lead to any real improvement in human nature, much as Hegel projected it and Marx required it in order to predict that their new worlds would come out of natural scientific progress.

(4) "Rather, it now looks as if only massive transforming power from outside nature's process could produce any recognizable change for the better in your human drama, so little able are you to accomplish your own improvement, except in extraordinary individuals from time to time. But of course, massive change in the natural structure of human nature, which would rid it of sin and degradation and power madness, is not anything one can predict just from studying history to date. So I find it amazing that the history of many religions, and most theologies too, are filled with apologies on my behalf for the evil and terror so evident in the evolutionary course. I set nature and human nature on this course from a variety of options open to me. They seem to forget that I make no apologies for my decision, not even to Job. Rather, I still retain the right to perform a massive intervention of divine power to produce basic change, at a time and place of divine choosing, even though it is not at present visible."

(5) The divine response to *Encountering Evil?*

A: "Stop apologizing for my powerful decision in setting evolutionary creation on its course. To me 'omnipotence' means that I'm strong enough to do what I elect, whereas humans cannot, or should not, say that I'm not?"

B: "Leave the deterministic God behind with the twentieth century. Let me accept uncertainty into my nature, and also my responsibility for creating a world so far from necessary and perfect in its basic nature."

C: "Suffering can cause you to grow; yes, sometimes. But we know it can also destroy, leaving no evidence of any redeeming features. Why argue any longer that 'omnipotence' means that my choice in creation was determined? It does not mean that any facet of natural order, or human nature, is not possible to be otherwise. Rather, it means that I retain the power to institute future change absolutely unhindered."

D: "Project, then, what you want, based on what any religious doctrine or sacred scripture's claims. But remember that I did not found any one religion or authorize any one authoritative scripture, but rather many. This uncertainty was placed in all the many religions as well as in the natural world. Surely omnipotence could have allowed any divinity so endowed to speak authoritatively and definitively and in a single voice, had He or She wanted to."

E: "Just remember that your faith still remains as a 'belief in things unseen,' however many clues may have been left in creation, as these have been explored and expounded by many religious seers."

Notes

Introduction

1. David Hume, *Dialogues Concerning Natural Religion*, Second Edition, edited by Norman Kemp Smith (London, Edinburgh, Paris, Melbourne, Toronto, and New York: Thomas Nelson and Sons, 1947).

Chapter 1

1. Albert Camus, *The Rebel*, trans. Anthony Bower (New York: Vintage Books, 1956), 3.
2. See, for example, R. J. Rummel, *Death by Government* (New Brunswick, N.J.: Transaction Publishers, 1997), 31–43.
3. Ibid., 31.
4. Ibid., 13.
5. Raphael Lemkin, *Axis Rule in Occupied Europe* (Washington, DC: Carnegie Endowment for International Peace, 1944), 79.
6. Marilyn McCord Adams, *Horrendous Evils and the Goodness of God* (Ithaca, N.Y.: Cornell University Press, 1999), 3, 193. The italics are Adams's.
7. Ibid., 183.
8. Ibid., 208.
9. These quotations, and those that follow from Blumenthal's book, are from David R. Blumenthal, *Facing the Abusing God: A Theology of Protest* (Louisville, Ky.: Westminster/John Knox Press, 1993), 267.
10. Zachary Braiterman, *(God) After Auschwitz: Tradition and Change in Post-Holocaust Jewish Thought* (Princeton, N.J.: Princeton University Press, 1998), 4.
11. Ibid., 4 n. 3.
12. This quest has included my writing with and about Rubenstein. For example, see Richard L. Rubenstein and John K. Roth, *Approaches to Auschwitz: The Holocaust and Its Legacy* (Atlanta: John Knox Press, 1987), and Stephen R. Haynes and John K. Roth, eds., *The Death of God Movement and the Holocaust: Radical Theology Encounters the Shoah* (Westport, Conn.: Greenwood Press, 1999).
13. See, for example, Frederick Sontag and John K. Roth, *The American Religious Experience* (New York: Harper & Row, 1972), and also our jointly authored sequel, *God and America's Future* (Wilmington, N.C.: Consortium Books, 1977). Related themes are discussed in my *American Dreams: Meditations on Life in the United States* (San Francisco: Chandler & Sharp, 1976), and in my article "William James and

Contemporary Religious Thought: The Problem of Evil," in Walter Robert Corti, ed., *The Philosophy of William James* (Hamburg: Felix Meiner Verlag, 1976).

14. The impact of Elie Wiesel on my religious thought is traced best in my book, *A Consuming Fire: Encounters with Elie Wiesel and the Holocaust* (Atlanta: John Knox Press, 1979).

15. G. W. F. Hegel, *Reason in History*, trans. Robert S. Hartman (Indianapolis: Bobbs-Merrill, 1953), 27.

16. I am indebted to my colleague Stephen T. Davis, the editor of this book, for suggesting this concept of "cost-effectiveness" in relation to God.

17. Camus, *The Rebel*, 297.

18. Richard L. Rubenstein, *The Cunning of History* (New York: Harper Colophon Books, 1978), 67.

19. William Styron, *Sophie's Choice* (New York: Random House, 1979), 392.

20. See, for example, Lawrence L. Langer, "The Dilemma of Choice in the Death-camps," in John K. Roth and Michael Berenbaum, eds., *Holocaust: Religious and Philosophical Implications* (St. Paul: Paragon House, 1989), 221–32.

21. Styron, *Sophie's Choice*, 483.

22. Ben J. Wattenberg, *The Real America* (Garden City, N.J.: Doubleday, 1974), 9.

23. Rubenstein, *The Cunning of History*, 91. The italics are Rubenstein's.

24. John Hick, *Evil and the God of Love*, rev. ed. (New York: Harper & Row, 1977), 386.

25. Adams, *Horrendous Evils and the Goodness of God*, 205.

26. Over the years, my views on God's power and God's relation to evil have been strongly influenced by the work of Frederick Sontag. See especially his books *The God of Evil* (New York: Harper & Row, 1970); *God, Why Did You Do That?* (Philadelphia: Westminster Press, 1970); and *What Can God Do?* (Nashville: Abingdon, 1979).

27. Elie Wiesel, *The Trial of God*, trans. Marion Wiesel (New York: Random House, 1979), 133.

28. Elie Wiesel, *Messengers of God*, trans. Marion Wiesel (New York: Random House, 1976), 235.

29. C. G. Jung, *Answer to Job*, trans. R. F. C. Hull (Princeton, N.J.: Princeton University Press, 1973), 99.

30. Elie Wiesel, *The Oath*, trans. Marion Wiesel (New York: Random House, 1973), 78.

31. Wiesel, *Messengers of God*, 235.

32. See also Psalm 22:1.

33. The sentences quoted in this paragraph can be found in *The Varieties of Religious Experience* (Garden City, N.J.: Doubleday Image Books, 1978), 470.

34. Annie Dillard, *Holy the Firm* (New York: Bantam Books, 1979), 58–59.

35. Annie Dillard, *For the Time Being* (New York: Alfred A. Knopf, 1999), 85–86.

36. In selecting these phrases, I have drawn from the Revised Standard Version, the Jerusalem Bible, and Today's English Version.

37. Elie Wiesel, *A Jew Today*, trans. Marion Wiesel (New York: Random House, 1978), 136.

38. With some liberties of interpretation, I quote from Wiesel, *Messengers of God*, 36.

39. I have done so in *Death and Eternal Life* (Louisville, Ky.: Westminster/John Knox, 1994, and London: Macmillan, 1985).

40. See Greenberg's essay as published in John K. Roth and Michael Berenbaum, eds., *Holocaust: Religious and Philosophical Implications* (St. Paul: Paragon House, 1989), 315.

41. Quoted from Jankiel Wiernik, "One Year in Treblinka," in Alexander Donat, ed., *The Death Camp Treblinka* (New York: Holocaust Library, 1979), 149.

42. Ibid., 148.
43. Elie Wiesel, *One Generation After*, trans. Lily Edelman and the author (1971; reprint, New York: Avon Books, 1972), 214.
44. Elie Wiesel, *Night*, trans. Stella Rodway (1960; reprint, New York: Avon Books, 1969), 14.

Chapter 2

1. R. Held and A. Heim, "Movement-produced stimulation in the development of visually guided behaviour," *Journal of Comparative and Physiological Psychology*, vol. 56 (1963), 872–876.
2. Eugene d'Aquili and Andrew Newberg, *The Mystical Mind: Probing the Biology of Mystical Experience* (Minneapolis: Fortress Press, 1999), 56–57.
3. Fyodor Dostoyevsky, *The Brothers Karamazov*, trans. Constance Garnett (New York: Modern Library, n.d.), bk. V, chap. 4, 254.
4. Eric Fromm, "Values, Psychology, and Human Existence," in *New Knowledge of Human Values*, ed. A. H. Maslow (New York: Harper, 1959), 156.
5. At this point I strongly agree with Marilyn Adams's insistence on the eschatological dimension of Christian theodicy when she argues that "the good of beatific, face-to-face intimacy with God is simply incommensurable with any merely non-transcendent goods or ills a person might experience. Thus, the good of face-to-face intimacy with God would *engulf* . . . even the horrendous evils humans experience in this present life here below." ("Horrendous Evils and the Goodness of God" in Marilyn and Robert Adams, eds., *The Problem of Evil* [Oxford University Press, 1990], 218). I cannot, however, see her contention (in "Redemptive Suffering: A Christian Solution to the Problem of Evil" in Robert Audi and William Wainwright, eds., *Rationality, Religious Belief & Moral Commitment*, [Ithaca, N.Y., and London: Cornell University Press, 1986]) that God is effectively dealing with the problem of evil in the crucifixion of Jesus, by revealing God's love in becoming incarnate to suffer with us, as more than a valid insight within Christian pastoral theology. For those who accept her Christian premises, her vision can indeed be supportive, consoling, and potentially redemptive, and may be used with good effect in the pastoral work of the church. But if God is the God of the whole human race, and not only of its Christian minority, and indeed of those members of this minority who are wholeheartedly committed to the traditional belief-system, then God has not done enough to reconcile his human children to himself among the present realities of pain and suffering. For only that minority regard Jesus as God incarnate, and only for them can his martyrdom have the significance which Adams depicts. However, it is worth adding, that there could be a much broader, global, use of her insight into the redemptive power of a nonviolence which is willing to suffer, that does not require her exclusively Christian presuppositions.
6. John Hick, *Death and Eternal Life* (New York: Harper & Row, and London: Collins, 1976)
7. *The Confessions of St. Augustine*, trans. F. J. Sheed (New York: Sheed and Ward, 1942), bk. I, chap. 1, 3.
8. Hick, *Death and Eternal Life*, chap. 13.
9. *An Interpretation of Religion: Human Responses to the Transcendent* (London: Macmillan, and New Haven: Yale University Press, 1989), 246.
10. Ibid., 239, 246.
11. Ibid., 359.
12. *Philosophy of Religion* (Englewood Cliffs, N.J.: Prentice-Hall, 1963), 40.

13. *Evil and the God of Love* (New York: Harper & Row, 1966), 170–71.
14. *Philosophy of Religion*, 3rd ed. (Englewood Cliffs, N.J.: Prentice-Hall, 1983), 41.
15. *An Interpretation of Religion*, 208, 206.
16. Ibid., 206.
17. *An Interpretation of Religion*, 348.
18. *Summa Theologica*, II/II, Q. 1, art. 2.

Chapter 3

1. Sadly, there is no space here for me to explain why I do not say "*the* normative guide."
2. See, for example, J. L. Mackie, "Evil and Omnipotence," *God and Evil*, ed. Nelson Pike (Englewood Cliffs, N.J.: Prentice-Hall, 1964), 47.
3. Augustine used this argument in many of his writings. See, for example, *The Enchiridion on Faith, Hope, and Love* (Chicago: Henry Regnery, 1961), XXIII.
4. Thus Richard Swinburne, *Providence and the Problem of Evil* (Oxford: Clarendon Press, 1998), 86.
5. Some free-will defenders argue that free will in itself is such a great moral good that it will outweigh any possible bad consequences that might follow from it. But this claim seems both false and unnecessary to the FWD. What if in the end *no* free moral agent chooses to love and obey God? I hardly think God's policy could fairly be called wise if this were to occur, even if free will, as claimed, is in itself a great moral good.
6. Alvin Plantinga has so argued. See *God, Freedom, and Evil* (New York: Harper and Row, 1966), 61.
7. *God, Freedom, and Evil*, 25.
8. Swinburne makes this point cogently. See *Providence and the Problem of Evil*, 139–140, 165.
9. Thus J.L Mackie, "Evil and Omnipotence," 56.
10. See Plantinga, *God, Freedom, and Evil*, 34–44 on this.
11. John Hick has argued along these lines. See *Evil and the God of Love* (New York: Harper and Row, 1966), 68–69.
12. Since I am departing at this point from the Augustinian line that I followed in 1981 on natural evil (the devil as a moral agent is possibly responsible for natural evil), I had best point out that I still believe exactly as I did in 1981, viz., that the devil exists and is possibly responsible for natural evil. For the apologetic purposes of theodicy, however, I now present a quite different argument about natural evil.
13. Swinburne, *Providence and the Problem of Evil*, 167.
14. Eleonore Stump, "The Problem of Evil," *Faith and Philosophy* 2, no. 4 (October 1985): 409.
15. I am indebted to John Roth for making remarks, years ago, that led me to see that the EPE is distinct from the LPE.
16. For a much more rigorous demonstration of this and other related points, see Alvin Plantinga, "The Probabilistic Problem of Evil," *Philosophical Studies* 35, no. 2 (1979).
17. I should point out that a "universe" is not the same thing as a Leibnizian "possible world," and so my claim that there is only one universe is not falsified by our ability to imagine various possible worlds. There is only one actual universe, and all possible worlds are conceived of and talked about in it. The universe is the way the world is (and was and will be); possible worlds are ways the world might be (or might have been). Inductive arguments can only be based on past actual states of affairs, not possible ones.

18. P. T. Geach, *Providence and Evil* (Cambridge: Cambridge University Press, 1977), 58.
19. Please do not think that I am trivializing the pain of, say, people who suffered and/or died in the Holocaust by comparing it to my pain in the episode just described. I am not suggesting that the pain endured by a probably self-centered little brat who one day was made to wear an unfashionable article of clothing was anything like their pain. Their suffering is so much more morally serious than mine as to be on a different moral and theological level. But I am saying that their horrendous pain will be overcome in the eschaton.
20. *God, Freedom, and Evil*, 48–53.
21. For further argumentation on this point, see my *Risen Indeed: Making Sense of the Resurrection* (Grand Rapids: Wm. B. Eerdmans Publishing Co., 1993), 147–67.
22. In a point I owe to Darin Jewell, I could raise similar areas of ignorance in the theodicies of the other 1981 contributors, but for lack of space I won't.

Chapter 4

1. Jon D. Levenson, *Creation and the Persistence of Evil: The Jewish Drama of Divine Omnipotence* (San Francisco: Harper & Row, 1988), 5, 121, 157 n. 12.
2. Plato, *The Timaeus*, 30A.
3. Millard J. Erickson, *Christian Theology* (Grand Rapids: Baker Book House, 1985), 374.
4. Ibid., 277.
5. Richard L. Rubenstein, *After Auschwitz: Radical Theology and Contemporary Judaism* (Indianapolis: Bobbs-Merrill, 1966), 46, 64–65, 153. For an analogous argument, see William R. Jones, *Is God a White Racist? A Preamble to Black Theology* (Garden City, N.Y.: Anchor Press, 1973).
6. Gerhard May, *Creatio Ex Nihilo: The Doctrine of "Creation out of Nothing" in Early Christian Thought*, trans. A. S. Worrall (Edinburgh: T. & T. Clark, 1994). For Levenson's book, see note 1.
7. Levenson, *Creation and the Persistence of Evil*, 121.
8. Ibid., 5, 121.
9. Ibid., 121, 157 n. 12.
10. Ibid., 4, 123.
11. Ibid., xiii, 49, 50.
12. Ibid., 12, 26, 122–23.
13. May's book was originally published in German in 1978.
14. May, *Creatio Ex Nihilo*, xi–xii, 7.
15. Ibid., 7–8, 11, 16.
16. Ibid., 21.
17. Ibid., xi.
18. Ibid., 27.
19. Ibid., viii, xii, 25–26, 77, 161, 174.
20. Ibid., 3–4.
21. Ibid., 150.
22. Ibid., 77.
23. Ibid., 6, 12.
24. Ibid., 25.
25. Ibid., 12, 25.
26. Ibid., 25.
27. Ibid., xiii, 61, 74.
28. Ibid., 122.

29. Ibid., 4.
30. Ibid., xiii, 24.
31. Ibid., 40, 56.
32. Ibid., 43.
33. Ibid., 61.
34. Ibid., 56n., 152.
35. Ibid., 151. It is also important to note that, when the doctrine of *creatio ex nihilo* was affirmed by the Fourth Lateran Council in 1215, it was directed against Catharism, which held Manichean doctrines of matter and creation similar to those of Marcion. See Jeffrey Burton Russell, *Lucifer: The Devil in the Middle Ages* (Ithaca, N.Y.: Cornell University Press, 1984), 189.
36. Ibid., 146.
37. Ibid., 140, 145.
38. Ibid., 142.
39. Ibid., 141.
40. Ibid., 144.
41. Ibid., 142.
42. Ibid., 141.
43. Ibid., 140.
44. Ibid., 146.
45. Ibid., 147.
46. Ibid., 147.
47. Ibid., 159, 178.
48. Ibid., 178.
49. Ibid., 161.
50. Ibid., 167–68, 174.
51. Ibid., 174, 177.
52. David Ray Griffin, *God, Power, and Evil: A Process Theodicy* (Philadelphia: Westminster Press, 1976; reprinted with a new preface, Lanham, Md.: University Press of America, 1991), chaps. 6–7, 9–12.
53. Ibid., chap. 11.
54. David Ray Griffin, *Reenchantment without Supernaturalism: A Process Philosophy of Religion* (Ithaca, N.Y.: Cornell University Press, 2001), chap. 6.
55. *God, Power, and Evil*, chaps. 12 and 15.
56. Ibid., chap. 13; David Ray Griffin, *Evil Revisited: Responses and Reconsiderations* (Albany, N.Y.: State University of New York Press, 1991), 14–22.
57. Alvin Plantinga, "Reply to the Basingers on Divine Omnipotence." *Process Studies* 11, no. 1 (spring 1981): 25–29, at 28.
58. Ibid., 26–27.
59. Griffin, *Evil Revisited*, chap. 2.
60. Ibid., chap. 5.
61. For a summary of the core doctrines of process philosophy, see my introduction to *Reenchantment without Supernaturalism*.
62. See *Evil Revisited*. For a briefer account, see *God, Power, and Evil*, chaps. 17–18, or *Reenchantment without Supernaturalism*, chaps. 3–7.
63. May, *Creation Ex Nihilo*, 141.
64. Charles Hartshorne, *Man's Vision of God and the Logic of Theism* (New York: Harper & Row, 1941), 174–87; *Omnipotence and Other Theological Mistakes* (Albany, N.Y.: State University of New York Press, 1984), 56–62.
65. I have argued this point in *Reenchantment without Supernaturalism*, chaps. 4 and 5.
66. May, *Creation Ex Nihilo*, 137.

67. May himself suggests that Christianity's Easter faith was one reason that Christian theologians adopted the doctrine of *creatio ex nihilo* more quickly than did Jewish thinkers (ibid., 25, 129, 137).

68. On the possibility of life after death within process thought, with supporting empirical evidence, see David Ray Griffin, *Parapsychology, Philosophy, and Spirituality: A Postmodern Exploration* (Albany, N.Y.: State University of New York Press, 1997). For a briefer discussion, see *Reenchantment without Supernaturalism*, chap. 6.

69. David Hume, *Dialogues Concerning Natural Religion*, pt. V.

70. J. S. Mill, *Three Essays on Religion* (London: Longmans, Green, Reader & Dyer, 1875), 176–77.

71. E. S. Brightman, *A Philosophy of Religion* (New York: Prentice-Hall, Inc., 1940), 314.

72. John Hick, *Evil and the God of Love*, 2nd ed. (San Francisco: Harper & Row, 1978, and London: Macmillan, 1977).

73. For such further development, see *Evil and the God of Love*, pt. IV.

74. Some philosophers opt for a wider definition of the term *event*, e.g., as *any instantiation of a property in a substance at a time*. And on that view (which process philosophers can always opt for), you cannot have things without events anymore than you can have events without things. True enough. But I reject the suggested definition as too broad and generous. What about the property *being prime?* Notice that it would be true to say that it is instantiated in the number three on March 20, 2000,. But primeness being instantiated in the number three on March 20, 2000 is hardly an event. This is because the number three is prime no matter what time we pick. There are no everlasting events. Accordingly, there still can be things without events, but not events without things.

75. *Philosophy of Religion* (Englewood Cliffs, N.J.: Prentice-Hall, 1963), 40. For a "sub-Christian" view of deity, see *Evil and the God of Love* (New York: Harper & Row, 1966), 170–71.

76. Levenson, *Creation and the Persistence of Evil*, 4–9, 11, 53–54, 122–23.

77. *Evil Revisited*, 199.

78. *God, Power, and Evil*, 298, 300.

79. *Process and Reality* (New York: Free Press, 1978), 79.

Chapter 5

1. "Introduction" to *The Problem of Evil*, eds. Marilyn McCord Adams and Robert Merrihew Adams (Oxford: Oxford University Press 1990), 3.

2. John Hick, "Remarks" as chair of a Swinburne-Phillips symposium on "The Problem of Evil" in *Reason and Religion*, ed. Stuart C Brown (Ithaca, N.Y. and London: Cornell University Press 1977), 122.

3. Richard Swinburne, "The Problem of Evil", ibid, 129.

4. Hick, "Remarks", ibid, 122.

5. J. L. Mackie, "Evil and Omnipotence," *The Problem of Evil* (originally published in *Mind* [1955]).

6. Kenneth Surin, *Theology and the Problem of Evil*, Oxford: Blackwell 1986, 4. Surin gives evidence of a growing concern about these assumptions among contemporary theologians. He also argues that it is misleading to read the preoccupations governed by these assumptions into the work of Augustine, Irenaeus, and Aquinas.

7. David Hume, *Dialogues Concerning Natural Religion*, edited by Norman Kemp Smith, Second Edition, London, Edinburgh, Paris, Melbourne, Toronto and New

York: Thomas Nelson and Sons 1947, Part X, 198. All quotations from the *Dialogues* are from this edition.

8. Part XI, 203.
9. Part X, 198.
10. Part XI, 212.
11. Part XI, 211.
12. Part XI, 204.
13. Simone Weil, *First and Last Notebooks*, trans. Richard Rees (Oxford: Oxford University Press 1970), 146–48.
14. For example, in the Swinburne-Phillips symposium Swinburne says, "Now a morally sensitive antitheodicist might well in principle accept some of the above arguments", op. cit., 100. I retorted: "This conclusion is a somewhat embarrassing one since it is evident from my comments that one of the strongest criticisms available to the antitheodicist would be the moral insensitivity of the theodicist's case," ibid, 118.
15. Ludwig Wittgenstein, *Culture and Value* (1937; reprint Oxford: Blackwell 1980), 29e. I have quoted Wittgenstein's remarks out of sequence, in this section, for my purpose.
16. I say *some* of the bee stings, since I cannot discuss them all here. For my other discussions of these see not only the Swinburne-Phillips symposium already cited, but also *The Concept of Prayer*, Oxford: Blackwell 1981 (London: Routledge 1965); chap. 5, "On Not Understanding God" in *Wittgenstein and Religion*, London: Macmillan 1993, "Displaced Persons (Edith Wharton)", "Beyond the Call of Duty (Elie Wiesel)", "Revealing the Hidden (R. S. Thomas)" in *From Fantasy to Faith*, (London: Macmillan 1991).
17. Somerset Maugham, *The Summing Up*, collected edition (London 1948, 259).
18. Brian Davies, *An Introduction to the Philosophy of Religion* (Oxford, New York: Oxford University Press, New Edition, 1993), 38.
19. I wish my question were rhetorical, but I know a mother who was spoken to like this at the birth of her severely deformed son.
20. Maugham, op. cit., 62.
21. Rush Rhees, "Suffering" in Rush Rhees, *On Religion and Philosophy*, ed. D. Z. Phillips assisted by Mario von der Ruhr (Cambridge: Cambridge University Press, 1997), 304.
22. Ibid.
23. Swinburne, "Postscript", op. cit., 132.
24. Rhees, "Difficulties of belief", op. cit., 149.
25. Rhees, "Suffering", ibid, 304.
26. Swinburne, "The Problem of Evil", op. cit., 92.
27. Alvin Plantinga, "Epistemic Probability and Evil", *Teodicia Oggi?*, *Archivio Di Filosofia* (1988) 562.
28. Ibid, 558.
29. Swinburne, "Postscript", op. cit., 130–31.
30. A move attempted by Brian Davies. See Davies op. cit.
31. Swinburne, "Postscript", op. cit., 130.
32. H. Tennessen, "A Masterpiece of Existential Blasphemy: the book of Job," *The Human World* 13 (1973): 5.
33. Ibid, 8.
34. Part X, 199–200.
35. Swinburne, "The Problem of Evil", op. cit., 89.
36. Phillips, "The Problem of Evil" in the Swinburne-Phillips symposium, op. cit., 104–9.

37. Hick, "Remarks", ibid, 122–23.
38. Richard Swinburne, *The Existence of God* (Oxford: The Clarendon Press, 1979).
39. Ludwig Wittgenstein, *Philosophical Investigations* (Oxford: Blackwell, 1958), 223e.
40. Hick, "Remarks", op. cit., 122.
41. Charles Hartshorne, "A New Look at the Problem of Evil" in *Religion in Philosophical and Cultural Perspective*, ed. F. C. Dommeyer (Ill.: Charles C. Thomas 1966), 202.
42. John Hick, "Transcendence and Truth" in *Religion without Transcendence?*, eds. D. Z. Phillips and Timothy Tessin (London: Macmillan 1997), 56.
43. See my *Faith after Foundationalism* (London: Routledge, 1988; Boulder, San Francisco, Oxford: Westview Press, 1995), chap. 20.
44. *Yogava'sistha*, I:28; in ibid, 56.
45. Thomas Aquinas, *Summa Contra Gentiles* I (Rome: Leonine Commission, 1934), 25.
46. See Peter Winch, "What Can Philosophy Say To Religion?", ed. D. Z. Phillips, *Faith and Philosophy* (2001).
47. Ludwig Feuerbach, *The Essence of Christianity* (New York: Harper 1952), 57.
48. Richard Swinburne, "The Free Will Defence" in *Teodicea Oggi?*, op. cit., 586.
49. Readers will recognize my indebtedness to Simone Weil's illumination of a Christian conception of creation in works such as *Waiting on God* and *Gravity and Grace*. I am also indebted to Winch's "What Can Philosophy Say To Religion?" for showing me connections between Weil's discussion and the problem of evil.
50. Rhees, "Gratitude and ingratitude for existence", op. cit., 164.
51. Simone Weil, *Waiting On God* (London: Fontana Books 1959), 104.
52. Hick, "Transcendence and Truth", op. cit., 45.
53. J. Greenberg, "Cloud of Smoke, Pillar of Fire: Judaism, Christianity and Modernity after the Holocaust" in *Auschwitz: Beginning of a New Era?*, ed. E Fleischner (New York: KTAV 1977), 23.
54. It is interesting that in *The Problem of Evil*, the editors (Adams and Adams) tell us that they are not going to "discuss theodicies based on the most radical revisions of the conceptions of God's power and the nature of divine action in the world—for instance, those that ascribe to God an extensive power to 'persuade' but no power at all to compel." They acknowledge: "Such theodicies have been much discussed by theologians, but have been comparatively neglected, thus far, in the contemporary debate to which we offer here an introduction" (op. cit., 3). To call the view that God's only omnipotence is the omnipotence of love a *revision* is to neglect that it is as old in Christianity as anything they talk of. This is but another example of that unfortunate strategy of calling "traditional" what is often a seventeenth- and eighteenth-century empiricist gloss on religion. Contemporary theodicies are a major product of that gloss.
55. Johan Vanhoutte gives an encouraging theological survey in this respect. See his "God as Companion and Fellow Sufferer" in *Teodicea Oggi?*, op. cit.
56. M. Wiles, *God's Action in the World* (London: S. C. M. Press 1986), 80.
57. Charles Hartshorne, *The Divine Reality: A Social Conception of God* (New Haven, Conn.: Yale University Press, 1949), 138.
58. See Rhees, "The sinner and the sin", op. cit.
59. Rhees, "Gratitude and Ingratitude for Existence", op. cit., 162.
60. Rhees, "Death and Immortality", ibid, 236–37.
61. Richard Swinburne, *Providence and the Problem of Evil* (Oxford: Clarendon Press, 1998).
62. Ibid., 218.

63. Book review in the *International Journal for Philosophy of Religion* 47, no. 1 (February 2000): 57–61.
64. Ibid., 61.
65. D. Z. Phillips, "Does God Exist?" in *Religion without Explanation* (Oxford: Blackwell, 1976), 165.
66. John Hick, "Transcendence and Truth" in *Religion without Transcendence?*
67. D. Z. Phillips, *Wittgenstein and Religion* (Basingstoke: Macmillan; and New York: St. Martin's Press, 1993), 47.
68. *Philosophy's Cool Place* (Ithaca: Cornell University Press, 1999), 166.
69. D. Z. Phillips, *Wittgenstein and Religion*, 52.
70. *Philosophy's Cool Place*, 63.
71. I owe this point to Sally Bruyneel Padgett.
72. Theo Richmond, *Konin: A Quest* (New York: Vintage Books, 1996), 480.
73. Rush Rhees, *On Religion and Philosophy*.

Afterword

1. Roderick Chisholm, "The Defeat of Good and Evil," in *The Problem of Evil*, ed. Marilyn McCord Adams and Robert Merrihew Adams (Oxford: Oxford University Press, 1990), 53–68.
2. Strictly speaking, he would not *have* to go in that direction, if it were conceivable that an evil be defeated within the context of an individual's life and not within the world as a whole.
3. Not that I think that God is morally obliged to be good to created persons. I join the great medieval theologians in holding that the metaphysical size-gap between God and creatures keeps God from being a moral agent in the sense of having obligations to others than Godself. Even if God is not morally obliged to be good to created persons, encounters with evil force us to reconsider what it would take for God to count as good to us. That is what I am doing here.